The PARROT HEAD COMPANION

The PARROT HEAD COMPANION

An Insider's Guide to JIMMY BUFFETT

Thomas Ryan

A CITADEL PRESS BOOK
Published by Carol Publishing Group

A Citadel Press Book
Published by Carol Publishing Group
Citadel Press is a registered trademark of Carol Communications, Inc.

Editorial, sales and distribution, rights and permissions inquiries should be addressed to Carol Publishing Group, 120 Enterprise Avenue, Secaucus, N.J. 07094.

In Canada: Canadian Manda Group, One Atlantic Avenue, Suite 105, Toronto, Ontario M6K 3E7.

Carol Publishing books may be purchased in bulk at special discounts for sales promotion, fund-raising, or educational purposes. Special editions can be created to specifications. For details, contact Special Sales Department, 120 Enterprise Avenue, Secaucus, N.J. 07094.

Manufactured in the United States of America
10 9 8 7 6 5 4 3 2 1

Library of Congress Cataloging-in-Publication Data

Ryan, Thomas, 1958–
The parrot head companion : an insider's guide to Jimmy Buffett / Thomas Ryan.
p. cm.
"A Citadel Press book."
ISBN 0-8065-2015-9 (pb)
1. Buffett, Jimmy. 2. Country musicians—United States—Biography. 3. Rock musicians—United States—Biography.
ML420.B874R93 1998
782.42164'092—dc21
[B]

98-27639
CIP
MN

This book is dedicated to
Jimmy Buffett, Kathy Shedd, and all those who
consider themselves Parrot Heads.

Contents

Acknowledgments

Special thanks to:

My young sons Dare and Kyle, for their begrudged patience (I can still hear them begging me "Daddy, *please* no more Jimmy Buffett"); my wife, Robin, who I'm certain wanted to join in on the kid's chorus but remained patient; the incomparable (and apparently inexhaustable) John Gomez; Laura Tucker, who got me into this mess; Harry and Reva Tucker, who bear no relation whatsoever to Laura; Chris Markferding, Scott Henderson, Tom Liddle, Bill Lack, Scott Nickerson and the other cyber-people who offered their assistance; Nancy Mayall, for her late-night philosophies on the various meanings of Jimmy Buffett's lyrics; Steve Beery and the staff at Mr. Beery's, for not telling me their late-night philosophies; The Metro Parrot Head Club; The Smoky Mountain Parrot Head Club members; The Nashville Parrot Head Club members; The Atlanta Parrot Head Club members; The entire Parrot Heads in Paradise organization; and finally, to Kathy and Sue, for traipsing me all over Tennessee in their never-ending quest for any and all things Buffett-related—I honestly don't know how you guys do it.

Introduction

Parrot Heads.

Is the term a badge of pride, or is it an affliction? Is it a blessing or a curse? The answer lies in whether it is something that you consider yourself to be. You either understand the phenomenon completely, or it puzzles you. Not since the "Deadheads"—the notoriously well-known and well-abused moniker applied to fans of the Grateful Dead—have there been more consistently loyal fans than Jimmy Buffett's "Parrot Heads."

Since the early seventies, when Jimmy Buffett first appeared on the national music scene, his increase in popularity has been as steady as it has been unpredictable, and it has occurred in enormous proportions. In the midst of constantly changing styles and the fickle whimsy of fashion, Jimmy Buffett has managed to expand his popularity with little or no regard to (con)temporary tastes. As a result, he has built a fan base that is broad and diverse, from beach bums to lawyers, from surf punks to physicians, from fans of calypso to fans of country-and-western music.

Jimmy Buffett's methods are simple. By focusing his music on the laid-back and sunny nature of his tropical lifestyle and using his optimistic demeanor to convey his lyrics, he has made himself attractive to music lovers of all genres and generations. He has eked out a niche in popular culture that was overlooked by most pop singers, and Mr. Buffett now stands as a figurehead for a population that yearns for escapism and a lighthearted approach to music-making.

When Jimmy Buffett's music starts to play, the cares of the workday melt away. An inordinate number of Parrot Heads are professionals—lawyers, doctors, brokers—who envision Buffett as a representation of their own dreams and desires for escape. A few are society dropouts, but most are ordinary people who yearn for excitement. Buffett offers them the opportunity to drift away from the monotony of their workaday lives and, at least temporarily, to dream of a different life.

Put on "Margaritaville" and the broker who has just spent an emotionally grueling afternoon juggling finances for frazzled clients is suddenly transported to a tropical beach, toes in the sand, sipping an exotic frozen concoction complete with a paper umbrella floating on top. Play "Changes in Latitudes, Changes in Attitudes" at happy hour and the middle-aged, gray-suited midwestern real-estate lawyer who has been trying unsuccessfully to close a complex transaction can imagine himself wearing a Hawaiian shirt and beach shorts, surrounded by sexy model-types as he relaxes at the helm of a sailboat with the sun drifting lazily westward. Play "Mañana" and the doctor from Buffalo, New York, who just spent two hours digging her BMW out of a snowdrift can imagine herself with white sun-cream on her nose, sipping rum and pineapple juice from a coconut shell.

For everyone who toils in the pursuit of their goals, Jimmy Buffett stands as evidence that there has got to be a better way. Add to this base the people from sunnier climates who can relate directly to Buffett's easygoing tales of sea and sand, and you will better understand how Jimmy Buffett holds his audience and why they love him for it.

Parrot Heads are dedicated to their mentor as the embodiment of the free spirit that exists in all of us. When our wild side becomes sublimated, when our uninhibited nature rarely gets the chance to expose itself, we yearn to rebel and break free. With Jimmy Buffett around, life becomes less complicated than that. Responsibilities may force us to toil like worker bees, but that doesn't mean we cannot imagine ourselves soaring with eagles (or at least gliding with parrots). It is this ability to artfully capture the fun-loving nature in all of us that has caused Jimmy Buffett to become one of the most popular and successful live acts in the past twenty years, and it explains why so many people simply cannot get enough of this guy.

What can be said about Jimmy Buffett that hasn't already been said? Well, quite a bit. While he manages to remain one of the most consistently successful live performers of our age, he has also developed into a bestselling author whose works have topped the *New York Times* bestseller list and a recording artist whose albums regularly debut in the

Top Ten. Despite this massive success, very little has been written about this man's creative output. His fans, the Parrot Heads, are among the most uniquely dedicated and faithful of any artist, yet little has been written about them, either. Although the media blindly ignore Buffett or dismiss him as a one-hit wonder from days gone by, his popularity increases in proportions that most musicians could barely imagine.

In the nineties, Jimmy Buffett and his Parrot Head following have become the decade's best kept secret. What fans need is a fun, insightful, and informative source of information that accurately captures the irreverent spirit of Buffett's music. Nonbelievers need to understand what the fuss is all about.

The Parrot Head Companion is a critical analysis of Jimmy Buffett's career, not only as it relates to his already convinced fan base but also its relationship to contemporary music in general. By encapsulating the events of his life and reflecting on his creative output, it places Buffett's entire career in perspective, presenting its relevance and its relationship both to his fans and to contemporary trends. In *The Parrot Head Companion,* these corresponding facets are combined to capture a fully realized portrait of the man, his music, and the fans they inspire.

Because Buffett is averse to people probing his personal business, I deliberately avoid extraneous information unless it plays an integral role in his professional persona or his music. I have absolutely no desire to play the role of Kitty Kelly here, or Steve Eng (Buffett's unauthorized biographer), for that matter. Throughout the book, I consider Buffett's personal life to be irrelevant unless it concerns the work he was creating at that time. This is not strictly a biography, although it does contain a condensed compilation of historical information. Nor is it simply a collection of Parrot Head–related phenomena. *The Parrot Head Companion* is a companion to the songs that are responsible for his legacy. It is the music that inspired this phenomenon in the first place, so it is the music that remains the book's ultimate focal point.

Each chapter provides historical details and album critiques with a detailed analysis of the music. In addition, the book closes with a personal account of the author's attempt to discover and define the spirit that stimulates Parrot Heads to such phenomenal levels of devotion.

With each review, I did everything I could to digest the music properly and understand Buffett's artistic intentions. An open mind is the key to understanding, so I took every precaution to remain even-handed and honest in my analysis. Still, though, there are times when I couldn't help but be provocative—after all, I'm not a Parrot Head. My comments are simply my own (not-so) humble opinions. If, then, as you read this book, you come across an opinion or two (or three, or . . .) that ruffles you, don't sweat it. Record reviews should never be written in blood. It's more as though they should be written in sand, because honest persons will admit that their opinions shift as they become more familiar with the subject at hand. For a sublimely blatant example of this, read my review of *Coconut Telegraph.* From the first sentence to the last, I produce something that resembles a complete U-turn.

All reviews try to convey the feeling of hearing the album for the first time, at the time of its release. I have good reasons for doing this. A song that means nothing to me today might take on a level of profundity at some other point in my life. Or the exact opposite can happen. This can't be helped, but it can botch things up if you consider everything from a modern perspective. That is why I vowed to play each album in the order of its release, moving on to the next record only after I fully absorbed the album that preceded it and wrote whatever I had to say. This gives each review a contemporary feel, but it can sometimes contradict the way an album is perceived at a later date. For example, if you look back from today's perspective, *Havaña Daydreamin'* is considered to be an important album in Buffett's career. When it was new, though, it seemed to me that he was slumming. For the purpose of this book, it is important to realize that *Havaña Daydreamin'* was only his fourth album (ABC Records). This means that the only other albums that you could compare it to were *White Sport Coat, Living and Dying in 3/4 Time,* and *A1A.* Compared with these landmarks, *Havaña Daydreamin'* sounded like an artist who was not paying close enough attention to his work. That is why my review of *Havaña Daydreamin'* is harsher than it would otherwise be were I to review it in light of his entire body of work. As for the more recent stuff (post-1980), it was easy for me to view each album as his "new" release, because I was discovering them for the first time, anyway.

Have you ever wondered what a particular song lyric meant? Are you curious about what may have inspired Buffett to write some of your favorite songs? With so many records to choose from, how can you tell the classics from the clunkers? Keep reading and you'll find out soon enough.

If you're a serious Jimmy Buffett fan (don't be *too* serious), then the first thing you should do after buying this book is declare a short holiday for yourself. Break out all of your old albums, stack up the CDs, and start playing some music. Call your boss and tell him that your car wouldn't start. Then, dive into that pile of music in front of you, especially those that you've been neglecting. If you're an old fan, then you probably have plenty of vinyl. If it's still functioning, plop the records onto your old turntable and reacquaint yourself with the scratchy discs that accompanied you through some earlier stage of your life. Once you are comfortably settled, pop a beer or pour a margarita and relax. Listen to the records and keep tabs on how often we have a meeting of the minds. Whatever you do, though, don't get your dander up. I'm not trying to ruffle anyone's feathers here, I'm only trying to convey what I felt while doing the same thing that I'm telling you to do. If you disagree with my observations, well, that's what makes you a Parrot Head, right? It's all about having fun, so view this project in that light and all will be fine.

As a final statement and with all due respect, I would like to say that even when I completely fail to understand the artistic validity of a certain recording, I have nothing but respect for the artist who applied himself to creating it in the first place. I also realize that any overly serious analysis of the music runs counter to the root philosophy of Parrot Heads (i.e., that nothing should be taken too seriously). Sometimes, you just have to laugh at life for it to make any sense.

A quick note on the reviews: Each of the album reviews contained herein employ what I have been referring to as "The Buffett Curve." Since it makes no sense whatsoever in a book such as this to compare Buffett's music with that of other artists, and since it would be ultimately worthless to unabashedly praise (or criticize) his entire catalog, I decided it best to compare Buffett with himself. To do this properly, I tried to define the artist's own "artistic midpoint" and worked from there. As a result, the reviews are more or less evenly split between the critical and the complimentary.

Part One

The Life and Music of a Son of a Son of a Sailor

1

A Brief and Encapsulated History of Jimmy Buffett's Early Years

Little did we know at the time, but on Christmas Day in 1946, an event took place that would have resounding implications on our collective state of mind. James William Buffett was born in the Jackson County Memorial Hospital near Pascagoula, Mississippi, to James D. Buffett Jr. and his wife, Mary Loraine "Peets" (both her maiden name and her nickname) Buffett. Shortly thereafter, the family moved about forty miles northeast, from the Gulf town of Pascagoula to Mobile, Alabama, a city that lies on the western bank of Mobile Bay, which opens onto the Gulf of Mexico. There, "J.D." Buffett found work at the Alabama Dry Docks and Shipyard (ADDSCO), and the family settled down to begin the life of a fairly typical southern Gulf Coast family.

The Buffett family was Roman Catholic so Jimmy and his sisters, Loraine Marie (Laurie) and Lucy Ann, became products of the parochial education that the local Catholic church had to offer. For Jimmy, Saint Ignatius grade school led to the all-boys McGill Institute. While this might have meant that young Jimmy would be raised with a strong sense of practical morality, it also meant that he would sometimes feel trapped or stifled by the strict doctrine of the Church. As a result, Jimmy became a dreamer, and the fuel for his vivid imagination was supplied in large part by his paternal grandfather, James Buffett Sr.

Capt. James Buffett was born and raised in Nova Scotia, where he began his lifelong career as a seaman. In 1904, at the age of fifteen, he left Nova Scotia for Pascagoula, Mississippi, a trip that was similar to that taken by thousands of other Canadian French (the Acadians, who after settling in America came to be known as the Cajuns) a couple hundred years earlier. Here, he met and married his wife, Hilda, and settled down to start a family, at least inasmuch as a sea captain can ever "settle down." Naturally, his line of work took him away from Pascagoula and brought him to some extraordinarily exotic places, particularly in the eyes of a community that rarely had the chance to leave their own hometown. He traveled around the globe, from as far north as the Arctic Ocean down to the southern tip of South America and the Antarctic. During World War II he served as a navy commander and was stationed in the Pacific Ocean.

His lifetime of experience and travel made for wonderfully adventurous tales and he had charged his grandson's imagination unlike anything else possibly could. Few things are as romantic as exotic tales told by your own grandfather, and before he even knew what was happening, Jimmy Buffett was hooked. He became determined to emulate the old man whom he loved so much, and spent most of his time dreaming of exotic ports of call in faraway places. With water playing such a vital role in the culture of his family and with Mobile Bay being so accessible, fishing and sailing were the natural things for a boy to do, and his time on the water fueled his fantasies of escape and adventure even more.

Music was only a peripheral factor in the Buffett household, and young Jimmy's likes and dislikes were shaped mostly by what he saw on television. For the most part, he lived the life of a shy and withdrawn altar boy and he became increasingly confused by the incompatibility of his dreams with the rules and regulations that were presented by small-town southern life and the Catholic church. The late fifties were hardly the time for rampant bacchanalia, and the conservatism and xenophobia that defined the zeitgeist of our nation in those years, particularly in the South, must have frustrated Buffett something fierce. For a child filled with dreams and aspirations of escapism and adventure, the cold war years could not have offered a very promising future.

Buffett responded to the contradictory nature of his rather ordinary reality versus his extraordinary aspirations by often allowing his fantasy side to win, but this trait affected his social life. Buffet spent so much of his time dreaming of alternatives to his lusterless existence that he became uncomfortable with his presumed lot in life. He found it difficult to make friends or even to talk to girls. His main influences remained familial, with his grandfather keeping his hopes alive and providing the impetus for his vivid imagination while his father's brother, Billy, provided a real-life example of how much fun you can have if you refuse to settle down and let the system beat you.

Billy, a merchant marine, was Captain Buffett's youngest son, and he followed in the footsteps of his father's globe-trotting lifestyle, only without any of the discipline. Billy would sometimes disappear for years at a clip, but when he came back home to Pascagoula, he would befriend Jimmy and hint conspiratorially at some of the wilder things he had done while he was away. With these two role models to influence his own ambitions, Jimmy knew that there was only one way for him to go when he was old enough, and he silently hoped that his introverted nature would not prevent him from acting on his deeply rooted impulse to explore his dreams.

In the early sixties American culture started to loosen up, which in turn improved the odds of making Jimmy's goals more accessible. With McCarthyism all but vanquished (Senator McCarthy died in 1957), Americans could finally indulge in their newfound taste for exotica without fear of reprisal. One positive offshoot of World War II was the way it made Americans aware of parts of the globe that they previously didn't even know existed. Besides newspaper accounts of battles from places as far away as Guam or the Philippines, there were friends, relatives, and neighbors who returned home after the war with tales of Southeast Asia and most notably, the South Pacific. While the Allied victory stimulated our national sense of heroism and pride in our hard-earned victory, these accounts also stimulated a subliminal desire for Americans to live in a post-war paradise. The process did not occur overnight (particularly since, for almost a full decade, McCarthyism instilled fear for anything that wasn't red, white, and blue all over), but American culture was eventually awash in exotica. Harry Belafonte (the Caribbean), Martin Denny (Hawaii and the Asian Pacific), and Stan Getz (Brazil) are only a few of the artists who created aural landscapes of faraway places, and they had tremendous success. Each of them represented cultures far different from the stereotypical American culture, but instead of reacting against them, America embraced them. This set the scene for the next major developmental change.

While the postwar anti-Communist paranoia caused the Cold War to reach a feverish pitch during the Bay of Pigs, its outcome caused Americans to heave one huge collective sigh of relief, grateful that the confrontation between the United States and the Soviet Union did not escalate to an atomic war. For a while, the grass looked a little bit greener and flowers smelled just a little bit nicer, as Americans reflected on the fragile nature of their existence. This was a major factor in explaining why introspective folk music would be able to flourish and how an artist as eclectic as Bob Dylan could become so influential. And there was a new president in the White House, the youngest in the nation's history, talking about civil rights and equity for the poor. In a way, President John F. Kennedy brought a youthfulness back to the American spirit, and all of a sudden, the entire country felt as though it was embarking on some adventurous and futuristic quest. Collectively, the nation felt as if it was going somewhere new, and individually, Americans sensed the freedom to choose their own destinies. For the first time in years, Americans saw a vista of possibilities before them, and the overwhelmingly heady sense of potential was so strong that not even the bullet that ended J.F.K.'s life could stop it. Perhaps our optimism was shattered, but our movement toward freedom and individuality had too much momentum for it to suddenly halt. It was this chain of events that eventually brought Jimmy Buffett's traveling jones to the surface and it was also what allowed him to freely pursue his destiny. Heading out was not an act of rebellion, it was simply the right thing to do.

Jimmy graduated from McGill Institute in 1964 and began his college tenure, but his heart wasn't in it. He moved from Auburn University to Pearl River Junior College, and then transferred to the University of Southern Mississippi (USM). By his own admission, he didn't apply himself and for a while he had even considered quitting school entirely and perhaps enrolling himself in the merchant marine (as noted in the lyrics to *A1A*'s "Migration"), a move inspired by his Uncle Billy. In retrospect, the most important thing that he learned in these years was how to play the guitar. After watching his roommate attract girls with his playing, Buffett recognized the instrument's potential as a social tool, so he asked his roommate to teach him a few chords. His playing was functional at best, but it served the purpose of breaking down barriers, and Jimmy quickly became something of an asset at parties. He discovered that he had a natural affinity for performing, and soon enough, he began searching for opportunities to play for money. Music had presented Buffett with an entirely new vista of possibilities, the most enticing of which was becoming a professional musician. He found work in nearby Biloxi and in the vicinity of Hattiesburg, by the USM campus. Soon afterward, he was taking weekend jaunts to New Orleans.

As anybody who has ever immersed himself in the culture of New Orleans could tell you, the city is unlike any other place on earth. It has a self-sustaining cultural identity that is as thick as molasses and the city's indigenous music was, and still is, a primary source of that identity. USM was in reasonably close proximity to New Orleans, so Jimmy would take off for the French Quarter as often as possible, where he eventually got work as a guitar-playing singer in a rock-and-roll cover band called the Upstairs Alliance. Jimmy drank in his surroundings (sometimes literally) while he honed his craft, then returned to USM for his weekday classes. School didn't stand a chance next to the education that was offered by the streets of New Orleans, and the allure of the city kept his hopes alive for a career in music. There were, however, some classes that did inspire him and Jimmy did benefit from the literature and poetry courses that the school offered. Poetry in particular held a certain attraction, and Jimmy immersed himself in the structure of verse and rhyme schemes, applying them to his own creative ideas.

After struggling through the various hallways of higher education for the better part of five years, Jimmy finally graduated in 1969, earning a degree in journalism and history from USM. Finally, he was prepared to begin his life's adventure, but the outset turned out to be much rockier than Jimmy had originally hoped. For starters, he rather hastily decided to marry his girlfriend, Margie Washichek (interestingly enough, they were married in the same church where Jimmy had served as an altar boy a scant ten years earlier), and this changed his immediate priorities significantly.

Out of necessity, money became the first matter of business, so upon returning home and with advice from his naval-architect father, he got an entry level position in the Mobile shipyards. Music, however, remained his passion. For extra cash, and to satisfy his budding artistic desires, he would also moonlight as a weekend musician around Mobile.

Owing to his New Orleans experience, Jimmy's performances were becoming more polished and professional, so he soon earned himself a local reputation, and a small fan base began to sprout. A few professional offers arose, including one from California's Johnny Rivers's Soul City organization, but the move to Los Angeles seemed too far away for a newly married man with no expense account. A radio deejay and sometime recording engineer and musician named Travis Turk had introduced Jimmy to a few of his Nashville connections, including a producer named James "Buzz" Cason, who helped them cut a few casual (i.e., unreleasable) recordings. Nevertheless, Nashville suddenly began to look a lot more appealing, particularly when Cason indicated that he was impressed enough to make an offer. Jimmy and his wife packed up and headed to Tennessee in search of his big break. Nashville, however, showed no signs of being interested in the long-haired outsider without connections of his own. At that point his journalism degree came in handy and Jimmy found work at the Nashville branch of *Billboard* magazine, the music industry trade paper, where he stayed for almost two years. He enjoyed his work at *Billboard* and received enthusiastic support from his boss, Bill Williams. Years later, Jimmy would dedicate an album to him after he received word that Williams had passed away. Almost everything else about his Nashville experience, though, was miserable. Before he would leave town, his marriage would begin falling apart, his beloved grandfather would pass away, and his potential big break would dissipate into thin air, leaving negative impressions of the city that would be hard for him to shake.

With Buzz Cason producing, Buffett began recording demos at Spar Recording Studios in Nashville, and they eventually found their way to the offices of Barnaby Records. Finally, a label was impressed enough to express interest, and after some minor negotiations, a contract was signed. Once *Billboard* started reporting the deal, though, Jimmy had to leave his editorial post to avoid any suggestion of there being a conflict of interest. All that this managed to do, unfortunately, was disrupt the little bit of financial stability that he enjoyed. To coin a phrase, he had to go for broke, and that's pretty much exactly what happened. Barnaby rush-released one of his demo recordings called "The Christian?" while

Jimmy finished work on the remainder of material that was to become his first album, entitled *Down to Earth.* In retrospect, it is easy to understand why the polemical lyrics of "The Christian?" might cause it to fail as a single, particularly in a city as rigid in its Christian identity as Nashville. With a chorus of "You've been acting like Jesus owes you a favor, but he's a little smart for you to fool," Buffett risked insulting the very audience he was attempting to woo. The sales results indicated he shot himself in the foot just as he was stepping out of the gate. Predictably, the album did not fare any better.

Down to Earth (1970)

Barnaby Records Z30093 (out of print)
Most of the songs from this album are available on *Before the Beach*
Margaritaville Records MCAD-10823 (1993)

Copies of *Down To Earth* are as rare as hair on a baby's butt. Unfortunately, the album's also about as dated as a pair of worn-out Earth Shoes, so it might not be worth everyone's while to spend the exorbitant amount of cash that a rare or used record store would probably ask in exchange for a copy. It's been reported that the original release only sold 374 copies, so I wouldn't hold my breath while searching for an original, either. To help his most serious fans get a glimpse of his early work, though, Buffett authorized a combined rerelease of his first two albums on his Margaritaville label, called *Before the Beach,* and it is on this compilation that all but two songs from the original *Down to Earth* appear. It was a low-budget affair all the way, and it sounds it. The record suffers from naive production techniques, most notably the cheesy drum sound and the gratuitous sound effects that are littered throughout (the flanger meant to simulate an airplane on "Turnabout," or the echo loop applied to the vocal track on "Truckstop Salvation"), but if you take into consideration the modesty of Buffett's ambitions and his lack of recording experience at this point, these faults can easily be forgiven.

The album's lead-off track and single was "The Christian?," a twelve-string, hard-strumming tune with a rhythmic feel not unlike the Monkees' "A Little Bit Me, a Little Bit You." When considering the album's next song, maybe John Lennon could keep a straight face when he denied all speculation that "Lucy in the Sky With Diamonds" was about lysergic acid, but I don't think that Jimmy Buffett would be quite as convincing. "Ellis Dee" is the name of the song, and it's hard not to wince when he sings, "Ellis Dee ain't free like you and me."

Another curiosity is the album's closer, "Truckstop Salvation," a poor cousin to Charlie Daniels's far superior track "Uneasy Rider." Both songs relate the tale of what happens when a hippie-type traveler pulls into a small-town gas station and manages to disrupt the lives of nearly every closed-minded person who lives there, but only Charlie Daniels's version does so with panache and humor. Luckily, Jimmy Buffett's writing on future albums would eventually move more toward the sublime and further away from anything else quite this ridiculous. Much better is his ode to his grandfather, called the "Captain and the Kid." Here he does a beautifully touching job of capturing the feeling of awe that his grandfather's tales inspired, as well as painting a loving tribute to a man who had meant so much to him in his formative years. But, because it was later rerecorded and included on a number of albums, including the live *You Had to Be There* and the box collection *Boats, Beaches, Bars and Ballads,* this one song doesn't justify the cost of *Down to Earth,* even if you're a real Parrot Head.

The song that might do the trick is "Turnabout," a thoughtfully touching (and overly romanticized) tale of an encounter with an ex-girlfriend. Otherwise, we have a silly ode to a comic-book hero ("Captain America") and a song that naively questions the moral priorities of the Western world ("The Missionary"). As for "There's Nothing Soft About Hard Times," the embarrassingly obvious title speaks for itself. Perhaps *Down to Earth* didn't deserve to sell much better than it had, but from today's perspective, I'll bet those 374 people are pretty happy to be owning this collector's item, regardless of its merit.

Whatever hopes Buffett might have harbored that the record industry would supply him with a steady income quickly dispersed once the sales figures for *Down to Earth* unearthed themselves. To put it kindly, Jimmy's debut album turned out to be one heck of a tax writeoff for Barnaby Records. Meanwhile, what little money he did have was spent on the road trying to support the album. Within a couple of months, he was broke. The circumstances didn't help his marriage any either, and it was around this time that the couple decided to dissolve their partnership.

Jimmy began work on his second album in late 1970. This time, Jimmy and producer Buzz Cason abandoned Spar Studios for the newly built Creative Workshop in Berry Hill, Tennessee. Here, they recorded a much more salable album, but changes were taking place at Barnaby that would not bode well for the record's future. Mike Shepherd, the man who signed Buffett to Barnaby, had left the label, leaving him with no real ally. Fearing another commercial boondoggle, Barnaby was less than receptive to Buffett's most recent work. As a result all efforts to record a viable follow-up record were for naught. *High Cumberland Jubilee,* as it was called, would go unreleased for six years.

In a matter of a few short months, Buffett came to realize that his identity was due for an overhaul. By his own count, he was rejected by twenty-six record labels during his Nashville tenure. It was time for a new beginning. The chance came in the person of a rebellious hellion of a country singer named Jerry Jeff Walker, whom Buffett had come to know well from time they spent together in Nashville and New Orleans.

Walker, best known as the author of the song "Mr. Bojangles," which he composed during an overnight prison stay, met with Buffett in Nashville and despised the town perhaps even more than Jimmy did. Walker had a place in Coconut Grove, Florida, and he convinced Buffet to head south for a while. Jimmy had made arrangements to appear at a Miami folk club called "The Flip," so he headed south only to find that his gig had been canceled. With nothing much else to do, Buffett moved into Walker's Coconut Grove quarters.

The time was late 1971, and, after a few months of sitting around Miami scuffling for gigs, the pair decided it was time to move on. The question was, Which way should they go? Heading back up north meant returning to civilization and all of the old problems that caused them to go to Florida in the first place. Heading south . . . well, there wasn't much farther south they could go, except maybe for the Florida Keys.

Dangling westward from the southern tip of the state like beads falling away from a broken chain, the Keys jut headlong into the heart of the Gulf of Mexico, as if they are trying to escape from the state that claims them. This string of islands extends southwest one hundred and fifty miles until they end up pretty much in the middle of nowhere.

For a hellacious pair of escapists with nothing better to do, the middle of nowhere didn't sound so bad, so Jimmy and Jerry Jeff decided to keep running until they ran out of road. They packed up Walker's old Packard and took off for new beginnings. Key West was where the road (and the land) stopped. They never could have known it at the time, but Jimmy's career was about to change drastically, and Florida's Key West would never again be seen in the same light.

High Cumberland Jubilee (recorded 1971; released 1976)

Barnaby Records BR6014 (out of print)
Songs from this album are also available on *Before the Beach*
Margaritaville Records MCAD-10823 (1993)

Completed in 1971 as the intended follow-up to his first album, Jimmy Buffett's record label "lost the master tapes," preventing its release until well after Jimmy became a star. Once he did become famous, the tapes were miraculously "discovered," allowing Barnaby Records to capitalize on a career that they had previously decided to abandon. Despite these indignities *High Cumberland Jubilee* isn't such a bad album. OK, it's not such a great album, either.

As with "The Captain and the Kid" from *Down to Earth*, the best songs on *High Cumberland Jubilee* were extracted and rereleased on later albums ("In the Shelter" crops up on *Changes in Latitudes, Changes in Attitudes* and "Livingston's Gone to Texas" reappears on *Living and Dying in 3/4 Time*), so this album is seen by most Parrot Heads as little more than a curiosity. In actuality, the album has more than that to recommend it. Perhaps owing to the mastering process (mastering takes place as the final step in the recording process, just before the record is pressed, and seems to have been neglected on Buffett's first release), *High Cumberland Jubilee* represents a significant improvement in the aural quality when compared with *Down to Earth*. Also, the songs are thoughtfully arranged into a sequence that thematically links them, showing a careful attention to detail. For example, "Ace" is a sympathetic view of a poor derelict that segues into a song about a rich kid who wants to rebel and live on the street ("Rockefeller Square"). Later, the excellent "Livingston's Gone to Texas," a song about a friend who took off and its repercussions on a loved one, is followed by "England," a song about a girlfriend who took off in the opposite direction—sort of a "Livingston" in reverse.

The rest of the album has more than its share of bright spots. "Death

Valley Lives" suggests the harmony arrangements of Crosby, Stills and Nash and even briefly quotes their melody of "Helplessly Hoping." "In the Shelter" and "Livingston's Gone to Texas" are both fine examples of ambitious songwriting, and the arrangements (a string section) are strong enough to recommend these versions to fans who are probably already smitten with the better known later recordings. "Travelin' Clean" is vintage Buffett, an on-the-road love song that humorously rhymes "Fargo" with "Chi-cargo," and "God Don't Own a Car" is really a lot better than the title suggests. The biggest surprise here, however, is the title tune, "High Cumberland Jubilee." With its slightly psychedelic overtones, this song is different enough from the balance of the Buffett catalog to justify the entire package to his fans. As an added bonus, the *Before the Beach* collection adds a relevant postscript entitled "Cumberland High Dilemma," a song that manages to round out and solidify an album that it wasn't originally a part of.

2

The Early Seventies

From the moment he arrived in Key West, Jimmy Buffett felt as though he was home. For one thing, the ocean played a large role in the culture of his seafaring family and in Key West, there was plenty of water. While looking for bars that would let him play a set or two at night, he could supplement his income by getting work as a mate on the local charter fishing boats. There was a support group of friendly locals who quickly came to know the laid-back entertainer through his appearances at the local watering holes, and they almost instantaneously welcomed Jimmy into their clique. All in all, the environment was infinitely more accommodating to his tastes than Nashville ever could have been, so when Jerry Jeff Walker eventually decided to move on, Jimmy opted to stay put and make Key West his home.

Jimmy succumbed rather quickly to the laid-back party atmosphere of the place, and all that alcohol was combined with a marijuana haze, affecting everyone's ability to recount the sundry details of day-to-day living. This was the early seventies. Who remembers what they were doing in the early seventies?

What is known for sure (mostly because much of it is documented on Buffett's albums) is that there was an inner circle of serious party revelers who were more than happy to have an easygoing, good-timey singer-songwriter around to entertain them, and Jimmy was happy to oblige.

The Key West crew that Jimmy hooked up with was mainly made up of mellow, heavy-drinking sun worshipers with a highly refined sense of humor. Each person was unique, but they also had quite a lot in common. Their personalities often combined aspects of the renegade pirate with the romantic slacker expatriate who would have felt out of place, or even marooned, back on the mainland. Many of them would later put this experience to good use. Besides Jerry Jeff and Jimmy, there was a wealth of writers, artists, and photographers, such as Tom McGuane (he went on to marry Jimmy's sister, Laurie), Tom Corcoran, and Jim Harrison.

Curiously, there were comparably few musicians. There was also a sizable number of other notably colorful characters such as shrimper-fisherman Phil Clark, a now-legendary smuggler-bartender who would be immortalized by Buffett in "A Pirate Looks at Forty." Clark operated a local bar and restaurant called the Chart Room with Vic Latham (an old friend Buffett knew from his New Orleans days); their establishment quickly became the control center from which this group of freelance hedonists organized their daily activities. Whether it was Ballast Key Weekend, the Tequila Regatta, a Key West Boogie (their term for a party) or any number of other excuses for a liquor-drenched gathering, the Chart Room was the place to go if you needed to know the details.

Or the Old Anchor Inn. Or, maybe they'd meet at the Full Moon Saloon. Then again, maybe it was Louie's Backyard, a restaurant–bar and grill built by Latham that was located on the Atlantic Ocean right next door to Buffett's apartment. With this arrangement, Buffett could eat, sleep, and go to work (at Louie's) without ever having to put on a pair of shoes.

Inspiration was everywhere, and Buffett simply did his best to catalog in song the motley characters that regularly crossed his path and the myriad events that happened. He had come to a place that he knew little about and while there, he came into his own. Buffett was unequivocally lauded as the town troubadour, and once again it was time for him to see if the world was ready for the likes of him. All along, he had his feelers out, hoping (with some reservation) to reconnect with the music establishment. In 1973, opportunity once again knocked. Once again, the place doing the knocking was Nashville.

ABC Records was a reasonably powerful label that was looking to update its image with contemporary acts, and it sought to do this with new signings and through mergers with other labels. Dunhill Records was a West Coast–based label that made enough money off of the California superstars they recorded (the Mamas and the Papas and Three Dog Night, for example) to make them an appealing target. ABC Records had acquired Dunhill into their corporate family, and it was Nashville's branch of ABC/Dunhill that considered Buffett to be a potential country-rock crossover artist. Or, more accurately, it was a producer named Don Gant who wanted to sign him.

Despite the feeling that Buffett was a commercial pariah, Gant had a stubborn streak, and he fought hard for Buffett's acquisition. After a considerable amount of hemming and hawing, ABC finally asked Buffett to pack up his songs and come back to Tennessee. Because he felt much more prepared than before, Jimmy Buffett heeded the call.

Nashville's musicians are notorious for their workmanlike habits. As a rule, they show up punctually, play admirably (or at least adequately), then part amicably. This time around, Buffett's sessions were nothing at all like that. If there was anything that he learned during his time in Key West, it was to relax and take it easy. Gant was sympathetic to Buffett's work habits and went out of his way to find similar-minded musicians.

Buffett's lyrically playful tendencies came off more as a parody of country music than respectful admiration, but the phenomenally talented musicians he worked with kept things grounded. Greg "Fingers" Taylor was a harmonica player and an old college friend of Jimmy's who also occasionally played a few shows with him. Mike Utley, who with Taylor would go on to become an integral member of Jimmy's Coral Reefer Band, was a well-rounded musician who played with a session group known as the Dixie Flyers, and he added piano. Sammy Creason played drums. Reggie Young was (and still is) one of country music's most in-demand session guitarists, and for good reason. For those who care about rock and roll's historical roots, Young was a vintage player from the original Bill Black Combo. He also played that brilliant electric guitar solo in B.J. Thomas's "Hooked on a Feeling" and the unique sitar-guitar of the Box Tops' "Cry Like a Baby." Vassar Clements's reputation as a fiddle player preceded him as well (he was a member of Bill Monroe's classic western-swing group, the Blue Grass Boys, and went on to become a featured instrumentalist in a David Grisman/Jerry

Garcia project called "Old and in the Way"). Other credited musicians include Steve Goodman (acoustic lead guitar), Doyle Gresham (pedal steel guitar), Ed "Lump" Williams (bass), Phil Royster (congas), Shane Keester (Moog synthesizer), Ferrell Morris (percussion), and Marvin Gardens (maracas and beer cans).

With a cast as diverse and talented as this, the sessions were predestined to work out well. The music sparkled and the humor of the material remained intact; the result was a wholesome, satisfying piece of work. The album was called *A White Sport Coat and a Pink Crustacean,* and this time Buffett made a record that could not be ignored.

A White Sport Coat and a Pink Crustacean (1973)

ABC/Dunhill Records DSX 50150

A White Sport Coat and a Pink Crustacean represents such a significant change in style, purpose, and quality from his earlier work that, for all intents and purposes, fans usually consider it to be Jimmy Buffett's first album. His rebirth not only meant a whole new beginning, but it also signified a new approach to his music-making ideas. Witty, irreverent, wistful, and touching, it manages to effortlessly please his target audience by avoiding any bitter, angry, frustrated, or depressed sentiments while remaining heartfelt and sincere.

A White Sport Coat and a Pink Crustacean is full of autobiographical references about his contemporary life in Key West, but the album kicks off with a purely fictional narrative called "The Great Filling Station Hold Up." Being arrested for armed robbery is not typical subject matter for an amusing, good-time song, but Buffett pulls it off easily. On a similar note, "Peanut Butter Conspiracy" documents a more petty crime (petty theft, to be exact) while playfully depicting Buffett's newfound ability to make light of hard times. Compare it to "There's Nothing Soft About Hard Times" from his *real* first album, and it provides a perfect example of how much more timeless, fun, and commercially viable his latest sound is. Here was a true-life song, written before his "salad days," about not having enough money to buy food, yet it amuses fans enough to make them wonder if, now that he's rich, he ever did manage to "pay the mini-mart back" (he didn't, though he claims that he once intended to, but only made it as far as the parking lot).

The country feel of the album is anchored in the album's second song. Cowritten with Jerry Jeff Walker, "Railroad Lady" is musically cliche ridden but the loopy lyrics and Buffett's low-key, lazy delivery animate the song beyond the predictably wizened sound of your typical country crooner. Another song on the record is also a thoroughly typical country tune—in every way but one, that is. "Why Don't We Get Drunk (and Screw)" has, um, a *directness,* that is fairly unusual for the genre. The result is a perfectly rendered composite—just loopy enough to be a left-field jukebox hit, and just bawdy enough for the rowdy contingent to scream along with at concerts.

"Grapefruit–Juicy Fruit" is another silly feel-good song that succeeds, mostly owing to Buffett's laconic delivery and his amazing ability to convey a pleasantly burned-out morning on the beach. This song makes no mention of sun, sand, or sea, yet the aural landscape is miraculously vivid and undeniably appealing. There's a serious side to the album, too. On "He Went to Paris" and "Death of an Unpopular Poet," Buffett tries to convey nothing less than his own philosophy on the meaning of life, and damn near succeeds. To round out the package, there are two love songs; "I Have Found Me a Home" unabashedly embraces the Key West culture that he came to adore, while "My Lovely Lady" playfully introduces us to Jimmy's then-girlfriend and future wife, Jane Slogsvol.

As for the album's title and cover photo (the lobster claw that sticks from the outer breast pocket of Buffett's white sport coat is certainly more red than it is pink), it signaled the start of a trend to use puns as album titles. Whether or not it was ridiculously silly isn't the point; Buffett came prepared to use everything in his arsenal, and he certainly wasn't going to let a perfectly good pun go to waste. Full of entertaining ideas and creative notions, *Sport Coat* is one of his most definitive and wholly satisfying works ever.

This satisfaction stems directly from Buffett's infectiously pleasant and mellow attitude. Never before has a popular artist sounded so completely at ease with his circumstances, and *White Sport Coat and a Pink Crustacean* overflows with a sense of satisfaction that is derived from simple, uncomplicated pleasures ("I Have Found Me a Home," "Grapefruit–Juicy Fruit," My Lovely Lady"). Heck, according to Buffett, he's "feeling quite at ease" even when he's out robbing gas stations ("Great Filling Station Hold Up")! All in all, the album is a masterpiece in that it conveys exactly what the artist intended. In the hands of Buffett, his simple, relaxed, and undemanding perspective becomes a personal philosophy as much as a style, one that his lifelong fans would adopt with a passion. As naturally comfortable as your favorite pair of jeans, *A White Sport Coat and a Pink Crustacean* proves that escaping anxiety is as simple as a song.

A White Sport Coat and a Pink Crustacean didn't fly off the shelves (at least not initially), but it did do well enough to warrant a second album. Critical reaction ran from the passively indifferent to the genuinely ecstatic, but almost every review recognized Buffett as a voice to be dealt with. The groundwork was laid. Now it was up to Jimmy to prove that he was prepared for the impending limelight. ABC was intelligent enough to perceive the long view anyway, so little time would be wasted before work began on a second album. Meanwhile, Buffett played the club circuit to support his record, touring with Fingers Taylor on mouth harp and a friend from Key West named Vaughn Cochran on percussion (he played the washboard). His career was still decidedly low-key, but things were definitely looking up, making his unflinchingly optimistic demeanor seem to be something akin to clairvoyance. Buffett was becoming living proof that the power of positive thinking actually worked.

In 1973, Jim Croce was another ABC artist whose career was on the rise. Like Buffett, Croce's early career was hampered by a poor-selling album on an indifferent label, but his affiliation with ABC was working miracles. In the summer before Buffett recorded *A White Sport Coat,* Croce was enjoying his first hit. "You Don't Mess Around With Jim" cracked the Top Forty and rose all the way to number eight, kick-starting a string of impressive hits that included "Operator (That's Not the Way It Feels)," "One Less Set of Footsteps," and "Bad, Bad, Leroy Brown," which became a number-one hit for two weeks in the spring of 1973. Croce and Buffett also shared a similar down-to-earth perspective in their music, so naturally they became friends.

Then fate intervened. On September 20, 1973, a plane carrying Jim Croce and some of his band members crashed after takeoff, killing everyone on board. The tragedy struck Buffett profoundly; he not only felt the sudden absence of his friend, but was forced to acknowledge the sometimes cruel nature of happenstance. At the time, Jimmy was residing in Livingston, Montana, as a guest of Tom McGuane and his wife. While there, he continued to write songs in anticipation of his next album.

ABC, meanwhile, needed to react to the sudden loss of its biggest prospect. The first order of business was to release a posthumous single, and "I Got a Name" became a moving and appropriately tasteful Top Ten hit. "Time in a Bottle" followed very soon afterward and became Croce's second number-one hit. The second order of business was to review its catalog of artists for prospects who might best be able to fill the void left behind by Croce, and it didn't take long to realize that Jimmy Buffett would be the best candidate. ABC went into promotional overdrive, spending money in the belief that the world would accept Buffett in the same way that it had embraced Jim Croce. With the full backing of his record label, work promptly began on Buffett's second ABC release. It was barely four months after his debut.

Living and Dying in 3/4 Time (1974)

ABC/Dunhill Records DSD-50132

Called upon by his record label to supply them with additional product, Buffet hastily assembled whatever material he had accrued and immediately set to work. Since much of the material was written while hanging around in Montana, this record takes a noticeable step away from the briny salt spray and sun of his last work and instead dwells on the dusty land-locked terrain of the rural Northwest ("Brahma Fear," "Ringling Ringling," the bridge of "Come Monday"). This change of locale helps make this Buffett's most "countryfied album," but there is also a casually slapdash quality that betrays the label's impatience. As a

result, *Living and Dying in 3/4 Time* lacks the insight and forethought of its predecessor, while retaining much of its inspirational luster. Buffett's career was steadily gaining momentum, and his second album for ABC Records holds the pace nicely by sidestepping the curse that is often associated with sophomore efforts—which is not to say that it is a perfect album.

Some of the lyrics on his second ABC release seem scattered, lacking a thematic base to bind together ideas that sometimes appear to be half-baked. For example, "Ringling Ringling" paints a narrow portrait of a dying town, but never develops a point of view to provide the listener with a sense of perspective. All we can gather is that Buffett passed through a small town, thought it sucked, and then left. "Saxophones" does little else but complain about his lack of airplay in Mobile, presumably due to the lack of a New Orleans–style brass section. In Buffett's hands, this could easily have been humorous, but instead it only sounds like disguised anger. "Brahma Fear" and "The Wino and I Know" both veer about so unpredictably that it is difficult to discern what the hell is lyrically going on in either one of them. "Brahma Fear" moves from bulls to alcohol to planes to boats with no typifier to bind them, while "The Wino and I Know" pointlessly bounces us all over New Orleans like a pinball. This is unusual, since the narrative quality of Buffett's most representative work always contains a sharp eye for detail and a considerable attention to nuance. Without that, it's the music that counts, and each of the above-mentioned songs have melodies that are as comfortable as old flannel. "Ringling Ringling" is so pleasant sounding that it can almost make you feel good about this one-horse town. The same can be said for "The Wino and I Know," which musically compensates for its lack of lyrical perspective by providing a musical landscape instead.

Elsewhere, Buffett's sense of lyricism is intact, painting precise portraits, particularly on "Pencil Thin Mustache." Writing in a style that is reminiscent of his good friend Steve Goodman, this track mischievously captures the likably playful persona and lyrical focus that endears Buffett to his fans. "Brand New Country Star" has a similar appeal, with its tongue-in-cheek portrayal of an ambitious but naive red-necked rookie on the rise.

Not too surprisingly, it is the sensitive material that binds this album together and provides it with a unified identity. "Come Monday" was singled out to be the album's representative pop hit, and it deserves every bit of recognition that it received. Written during a lonely stay in California when he was scheduled for a few showcase performances, "Come Monday" perfectly captures the hollow emptiness that haunts anybody who is forced to travel without the companionship of loved ones. "Livingston's Gone to Texas" makes its debut appearance here as well (it was originally recorded for the *High Cumberland Jubilee* album, which would remain shelved for a few more years) and it stands out as one of Buffett's most sensitive and moving recordings to date. "West Nashville Grand Ballroom Gown" also does a praiseworthy job, with its frankly sympathetic portrayal of the claustrophobic loneliness inherent in upper-class southern social circles.

The two cover songs that close the album best convey the conflicting nature of the record. On the positive side, "Ballad of Spider John" is a thoughtful gem of a song (written by W. A. Ramsey) with lyrics that suit Buffett to a tee and a melody that beautifully captures the sense of loss contained in the words. On the negative side, "God's Own Drunk" (credited to Lord Buckley) can best be described as a "preamble ramble to a rumble" (it is rumored to have been recorded in a drunken studio session prior to Buffett's embarrassing encounter with Sheriff Buford Pusser). More silly than it is funny, this recording would have been put to better use had it been relegated solely to the B-side of the "Come Monday" single.

Ultimately, *Living and Dying in 3/4 Time* is a very good but flawed album, disappointing only because it falls short of expectations brought on by *White Sport Coat*'s fluid consistency. Perhaps if he had more time, this album would have become equal in caliber to its predecessor. Despite its few faults, *Living and Dying in 3/4 Time* is still a better than adequate representation of Buffett's myriad talents.

As a result of the momentum that comes from releasing back-to-back albums that are both intriguing and appealing, *Living and Dying in 3/4 Time* became Jimmy Buffett's first album to chart, climbing to number 176 on Billboard's list of pop albums in March 1974. The chart position may not have been spectacular, but at least Buffett was now getting some national recognition.

An interesting phenomenon of Buffett's early popularity was the way that it defied any standard type of regional appeal. His popularity sprouted at various locations throughout the United States, usually in seaport cities with sizable college populations. In the South, there was Charleston in South Carolina, and Savannah in Georgia. In the Northeast, Boston was the first city to relate to Buffett's music, and on the West Coast, San Diego did the same.

In a short-sighted attempt to find an upbeat, jaunty single for the album, "Saxophones" was released, backed with "Ringling Ringling." Neither song was appropriate for the pop singles market, though, and the 45 was neglected. A follow-up was quickly needed and "Come Monday" was chosen as a stopgap release, with surprisingly excellent results. The sudden rise of "Come Monday" to number 30 on the pop charts and, more remarkably, to number 4 on the easy listening charts, indicated that America was more prepared for Jimmy Buffett than ABC's executives would have predicted.

For Jimmy, the sudden recognition was a mixed blessing that caused him to have some reservations about stardom. For example, he was never particularly fond of the promotion side of the record industry and often made disparaging remarks about the ineptitude of music business professionals, yet here he was with a national hit. Maybe the "suits" were a different breed of animal than Buffett was used to dealing with, but he at least had to admit that they were helping to get the promotion job done.

Another more blatant problem was the sudden influx of new fans. Now that fame had found him, he was wary of the new, leisure-suited audience who came out hoping to hear him play an entire set of tearjerkers like "Come Monday." To offset this, he consciously decided to maintain his profile at a reasonable distance from the limelight. In many ways it might have even helped to promote the image he wanted to convey—that of an independently stubborn iconoclast who stuck with what he believed in. Nevertheless, the song presented him with the chance of a lifetime, so while avoiding excessive press and promotional appearances, Jimmy launched into a grueling schedule of one-nighters.

Somewhere in the middle of this whirlwind, or perhaps just before things really kicked into gear, "The Incident" occurred. Now, I'm not one for dragging up compromising moments from someone else's past (God knows I myself could be made extraordinarily red-faced by segments of my own history), but I would be remiss not mentioning Buffett's encounter with Buford Pusser. The problem, though, is that the story has been told so often and in so many ways (often by Jimmy himself) that, in the final analysis, it's hard to tell the actual event from the embellishments. Like a game of telephone, what started out as a simple recounting of a drunken confrontation has become a tale of legendary proportions. Perhaps the facts are cloudy because the involved parties were themselves feeling a bit "cloudy" at the time, but as any good storyteller knows, the only thing that matters more than the truth is whether or not the story is entertaining. After rummaging through nearly a dozen versions of the story and realizing that none of them seemed completely accurate, I decided—in the tradition of a good storyteller—to throw caution to the wind and assemble the following composite.

After a long day in Nashville recording "God's Own Drunk" and drinking, or playing golf and drinking, or maybe all three, Jimmy found himself in the lounge of Roger Miller's King of the Road Hotel, where he had a room for the night. He spent a few hours there drinking tequila and at some point realized that he hadn't eaten for a while. Despite his condition, he wanted to go to a restaurant for a decent meal. Drummer Sammy Creason was hungry as well, so they retired to the parking lot in search of Jimmy's rented Gremlin. Now, tequila doesn't usually do much in the way of improving short-term memory, but it certainly can do a lot to dissolve common sense. For the life of him, Jimmy couldn't remember where he had parked his rent-a-car, so he decided to elevate himself to get a better view. The Cadillac parked directly in front of them seemed handy enough, so he climbed up on the hood to take a look around. Though it seems unbelievable, a few versions of the story even claim that Buffett was wearing golf spikes at the time. Unfortunately for the drunken pair, the owner of this car happened to witness the thoughtless behavior, staring in disbelief. Even more unfortunately for them, said owner happened to be one Buford Pusser.

Pusser was a southern sheriff with a notorious reputation for his unusually stringent methods of law enforcement, which often entailed removing his gun from its holster and using it, along with his six-foot-six-inch frame, to "help" perpetrators face up to their evil deeds. His legendary status was increased when a series of movies were made portraying his life (*Walking Tall,* parts 1, 2 and 3), with increasingly less autobiographical content.

Though Jimmy didn't know any of this at the time of the incident, what he did know was that a huge man was bearing down on him and Creason, and that the man appeared to be hell-bent on teaching them a lesson in manners and civility, southern style. Being "God's own drunk and a fearless man," Buffett didn't immediately recognize the potential for disaster, and according to one version of the tale, even had the audacity to mouth off to Pusser. Needless to say, Pusser went into attack overdrive, and Buffett and Creason decided that they might be safer in the confines of their own automobile (you see, they apparently happened to spot it from the vantage point of Pusser's hood). They took off like greased lightning, with Pusser in hot pursuit, for the rental car and jumped in, but they couldn't get the car started because early 1970s models of the AMC Gremlin had a safety mechanism that prevented the ignition from engaging until the seat belts were fastened. Pusser took advantage of the delay by jumping up and down on the hood of *their* car while they fumbled with their safety belts. Creason, meanwhile, had his window open, which made it all too easy for Pusser to reach in and pop him in the nose, then reach over to grab a chunk of Buffett's hair. Creason grabbed a Bic pen and started to stab wildly at Pusser's hand in an attempt to make him withdraw his arm (other accounts say Buffett himself was the one who discovered the new practical use for a Bic). When Pusser's arm did finally exit the Gremlin window, a sizable percentage of Buffett's mane was still clenched in his fist. Before round two could begin, the hapless duo managed to buckle up and burn rubber out of the parking lot. Luckily, they never got nabbed for driving while battered, bruised, bleeding, and intoxicated, either.

After dinner (I wonder what the topic of conversation was during the meal?), the much-abused pair returned to the King of the Road. Fearing that he once again may be confronted by his adversary, Jimmy grabbed a tire iron from the car trunk and shoved it into his pants. As they entered the lobby, there he was, as big as life. Maybe even bigger. One version of the story states that Pusser actually managed to get a hold of the tire iron but luckily for all parties, cooler heads prevailed and Buffett and Creason were shuffled away from the lobby. It was not until then that Buffett and Creason learned the identity (and reputation) of their sparring partner.

It may have been an embarrassing moment for them and one hell of a hangover to boot, but it is also something that neither of them will ever forget—that is, if only they could remember. If you check the musicians' credits on *Living and Dying in 3/4 Time,* you'll notice that Sammy Creason is referred to as "bodyguard and drummer." Now you know why.

Jimmy's incident with Pusser was an aberration, albeit a very colorful one. In actuality, he was much too busy to maintain any regular degree of self-destructive behavior. For a guy with an image as a lazy ne'er-do-well, Buffett worked his butt off between albums, touring and performing at hundreds of gigs through the course of the year. Somehow, he also found time to take a trip to Europe. In France, he was hired to work on a soundtrack for a documentary film about fly fishing in Florida. It was an obscure project, but it provided the necessary cash to fund his European "working vacation." Another project that Buffett miraculously found the time for was a feature film called *Rancho Deluxe.* Asked to write a soundtrack, Buffett also found himself in a cameo role, playing himself.

Rancho Deluxe (1975)

A United Artists Film Original Motion Picture Soundtrack UA-LA466G

In the summer of 1974, Buffett was back in Livingston, Montana, working on appropriate soundtrack music for a movie that was scripted by his friend Tom McGuane. From his previous visits to McGuane's ranch, Jimmy was already familiar with the Livingston locale, so indigenous western styles came to him quite naturally. Despite the fact that he was working on a soundtrack for a fictional movie, his familiarity with the area meant that he could retain an autobiographical edge to his writing while remaining relevant to the movie's intent. Songs about cowboys, cows, outlaws, and dust clouds littered the soundtrack, all with an authenticity that helped to make *Rancho Deluxe* an artistic success among most critics. Jimmy even appeared in the film, playing himself as a barroom entertainer lip-synching to a recording of "Livingston Saturday Night." The soundtrack version is substantially raunchier than the version that would later appear on *Son of a Son of a Sailor,* but in a movie that featured cows being hacked up by chainsaws and a handful of gratuitous sex scenes, it fit perfectly.

Being a soundtrack, a full half of the songs are instrumental mood pieces that seem slight and only moderately entertaining when removed from the context of the movie. "A Little Gothic Ranch Action" resembles an instrumental version of Stevie Wonder's "A Place in the Sun," and most of the other nonvocal tracks are generic country-rock or acoustic folk. The title track, which both opens and closes the movie (in alternate takes and with revised lyrics), is the most realized piece of music. The balance of the soundtrack material might appeal to Buffett's most ardent fans but is only peripherally interesting to most everyone else. Ultimately, the *Rancho Deluxe* soundtrack is successful in the context of the movie for which it was intended, but less captivating once it is separated from the film.

While the movie went into postproduction, Buffett began work on his next album. At this point in his career, anyone who was following the recordings of Jimmy Buffett would have been very likely to consider him a renegade country-western artist. The sound that critics described as Gulf-Western was intact, with the emphasis, at this point, being on the "Western." With the exception of *A White Sport Coat and a Pink Crustacean,* beaches, sun, and surf didn't yet figure prominently in his material. With his next release, this would change. In August 1974, he put the finishing touches on what was to become his third ABC/Dunhill release. The stage was set for a breakthrough album, and *A1A* would turn out to be exactly that.

A1A (1975)

ABC/Dunhill Records DSD-50183

If there was any such thing as a letter-perfect example of a "desert island disc," this would be it. Rarely has there been a record that is more suited to the ambience of a desert island, and just as rarely has there been a record that could withstand an entire lifetime of "captive" listenings. In short, *A1A* is the stuff that legends are made of. Both a landmark record and the cornerstone album on which he would build his career, this album is pure and vintage Buffett. As can be judged by the cover photo shot of Jimmy relaxing at the beach with a beer by his side, or the back photo of a highway sign with an expanse of ocean as a backdrop, all of the visual clues are perfectly in place. Even more telling is the artwork that is spread over the inner jacket. Underneath a few small photos of Buffett in the sunny environs of Key West lies a sailing chart of the Florida Keys, complete with depth soundings. Seeing these images together, you quickly realize that this album is going to take you for a trip to someplace that is both very warm and very welcoming.

Just as on *A White Sport Coat and a Pink Crustacean,* Buffett creates music with autobiographical musings about the Key West lifestyle, only this time he is even more convincing. What makes this all the more remarkable is that he achieves this even while covering somebody else's material. There are four cover tunes on *A1A,* but if you didn't look at the credits, you probably would never have guessed that Buffett himself wasn't the songwriter on each and every one of them. This is partially owing to a judicious awareness of what songs suit him well, but more important is the manner in which he conveys the songwriter's intent from a deeply personal perspective. *A1A* proves that Buffett is not only a clever songwriter, but that he can also be a very talented interpretive artist.

From start to finish, *A1A* is chock-full of personal references and the entire album warrants attention. All of the cover songs are on side one, starting with the leadoff track, written by Alex Harvey (a Scotsman best known for fronting the Sensational Alex Harvey Band). "Makin' Music for Money" is an ideal opener, with a rocking guitar riff that kicks in harder than anything else Buffett has yet recorded. The song's lyrics are simple enough, stating that you've got to please yourself before you please the crowd, but in Buffett's hands it comes off as nothing less than a personal creed. Next up is "Door Number Three," a song that was cowritten with Steve Goodman (he wrote "City of New Orleans"). It's a comedic farce of the "Let's Make a Deal" television game show, complete with a plug of the show's host, Monty Hall, the announcer, Jay, and even the "floor model," Carol Merrill. How they manage to turn this game-show spoof into a love song is anybody's guess, but somehow it works. Song number three is yet another cover tune. "Dallas" was written by Roger Bartlett (Bartlett is Jimmy's guitarist on this album and was also the lone Coral Reefer for many of his acoustic performances) and although it might come up a bit short on its autobiographical tie-ins, Buffett's familiarity with the Lone Star State makes it an easy choice for him. The song's instrumental arrangement is the focal point, and Jimmy's third composite of the Coral Reefer Band in as many albums proves here that his latest group is also his best.

Not until the fourth track do we get to hear how Jimmy's solo writing efforts have developed. "Presents to Send You" is so full of unique perspectives and personal information that it would be almost impossible for anyone other than him to sing it convincingly. Mostly, it's a love song to his soon-to-be wife, Jane Slogsvol. However, he does manage to squeeze in a reference to the Buford Pusser incident ("I had my hair pulled out by a man who really wasn't my friend") and his own slacker mentality ("My plans took a skid when I smoked the whole lid"). Just as we are getting warmed up to his own writing, Buffett slips back to another cover song; this time it's John (late of the Lovin' Spoonful) Sebastian's "Stories We Could Tell." "Life Is Just a Tire Swing" closes the side with Buffett reminiscing about his childhood, experiencing a rude awakening or two, then combining these memories into a realization that life is not something to be fretted about. As a composite, it is vintage Buffett, combining autobiography with blunt and simple philosophy. Jimmy told a story once or twice about how he was inspired to write this song after noticing a tire swing in someone's yard while driving to a show. On the return trip, he had fallen asleep at the wheel, but "was quickly wakened up by a Ma Bell telephone pole and a bunch of Grant Wood faces screamin' 'Is he still alive?' " As he tells it, one of the first things he saw when he regained his senses was the very same tire swing, so you could say that his inspiration may have been both serendipitous and fairly drastic.

Side two grants us our first steady look at Buffett's own material. In sharp contrast to side one, the entire second side is self-penned, and each song is better than the last. Also, virtually every song mentions the sun or the water, so it is obvious that this side captures Buffett's spirit as well as it does. The song that leads it off is "A Pirate Looks at Forty," which has been adopted by many Parrot Heads as their spiritual anthem. The lyrics are a moving character study of his Key West friend Phil Clark, and although it glamorizes drug smuggling, excessive drinking, and despondency, it does so in such a sympathetic (and sentimental) fashion that it is almost impossible to remain unmoved. Before it ends, you'll swear that there is nothing more romantic and moving than a renegade pirate facing obsolescence. In 1974 (unlike now), there was an enviable cachet attached to smuggling. Times most certainly have changed, but running drugs was practically a politically correct endeavor in the '70s. Back then, Buffett himself cautiously claimed to have dabbled in smuggling, at least until his music career made the risk both foolish and unnecessary. With "A Pirate Looks at Forty," his moving portrait of Phil Clark's midlife crisis conveys legendary status on a friend whose alternative lifestyle was something that Jimmy truly respected.

"Migration" is probably the most honestly autobiographical tune Buffett ever wrote. While the chorus neatly encapsulates his worldview and summarizes his influences ("a Caribbean soul I can barely control and some Texas hidden here in my heart"), the verses portray his mental assimilation of the mellow ways of Key West. "Trying to Reason with Hurricane Season" contains still more personal anecdotes. While watching a squall from his backyard beach on a Sunday afternoon, Buffett reflects on the painful state of his hangover and reviews his immediate state of mind (including his anticipation for the impending trip to France), all with a languid sense of self-satisfaction and acceptance. "Nautical Wheelers" is yet another romanticized view of Key West contentedness—a melodic waltz that focuses on his relationships and the sea that somehow binds them together. "Tin Cup Chalice" ends this fabulous album, and it artfully summarizes all that comes before it. Sun, sea, salt air, and wine represent freedom to do as you please, with the tin cup being a symbol for the simple satisfactions that can be derived from living a blessed life.

With this album, Buffett paints such an idealized portrait of his surroundings that it's a wonder half of the inhabitants of the continental United States don't pack up their gear and head to Key West. If you aren't a Jimmy Buffett fan, I suppose it is possible that you could miss the relevance of this album, but once you're indoctrinated, you'll realize that *A1A* is not only an album title, but a metaphor for the life-altering journey that it signifies.

3

The Late Seventies

As befits an album so jam-packed with classic material, *A1A* eclipsed Jimmy Buffett's previous album sales. It debuted on Billboard's pop album charts in February 1975 and in just a few weeks soared to number 25. "A Pirate Looks at Forty," along with "Door Number Three," was excerpted for single release, but neither reached Billboard's Top 100 singles chart. The B-side barely scraped its way to number eighty-eight on the country charts. Considering the outright failure of virtually every one of his singles to date (with the exception of "Come Monday"), Buffett's status as an album artist with an unusual niche was becoming more and more apparent. Perhaps he remained a bit shy of outright stardom, but the pace of his career was showing all the classic signs of growth.

Common pitfalls for new artists include the "sophomore slump" and the "compressed life span." The sophomore slump is when an artist releases a second album that completely fails to capture the public's imagination (remember The Knack?). Back in 1970, Barnaby Records solved that problem rather handily for Jimmy when they refused to even release his second effort. A compressed life span is when an artist becomes too popular too quickly, usually resulting in a backlash due to overexposure. (You could ask Men at Work about this one.)

Jimmy's growth was steady almost to the point of being predictable, making it easier for him to get a handle on his current state of affairs before upping the ante. His career escalated in controllable steps, as opposed to leaps and bounds, so he didn't have to worry about the delirious insanity that instant stardom usually brought with it.

Regarding both his popularity and his apparently laid back state of mind, another beneficial factor that aided Jimmy's career was his tendency to avoid venturing overly deep into profundity. While fans were noticing his ability to analyze circumstances from the bright side of the road, he kept things just superficial enough to remain lighthearted. James Taylor, Nick Drake, Paul Simon, or Gordon Lightfoot he most definitely was not.

In the summer of 1975, Jimmy once again hit the road, only this time he took an honest-to-goodness, full-fledged band with him. In his earlier days, when he was unable (or unwilling) to afford backing musicians, Buffett invented an imaginary coterie that he playfully introduced as the Coral Reefer Band. Now, Al Vacado, Marvin Gardens, Kitty Litter and the rest of the imaginary crew were demoted from stage figments to obsolete ghosts, being replaced by real, live human beings. Roger Bartlett was often the entire band before this arrangement, backing Jimmy's acoustic strumming with his own lead acoustic picking, and he retained that post in the first live incarnation of the Coral Reefer Band. Greg "Fingers" Taylor was another faithful regular, playing harmonica as he always did, as well as keyboards; Austin musicians Harry Dailey and Phillip Fajardo rounded out the rhythm section, on bass and drums respectively.

While this group toured the United States through two seasons of live shows, including a stint opening up for the Eagles, there was plenty going on in Key West during Jimmy's absence. Tom McGuane had been a dedicated observer during the filming of *Rancho Deluxe,* and thought that next time around, he could probably handle the director's role himself. McGuane's first project, *92 in the Shade,* was a movie version of his own novel. The story took place in Key West, so cast and crew all descended on the island for some on-location shooting. McGuane's first attempt to direct a movie would also turn out to be his last.

Jimmy Buffett was solicited to provide music for the film but he opted to decline the offer. Touring obligations played a major role in his decision, but he was also less than pleased with the fallout that took place after *Rancho Deluxe* (particularly between himself and that movie's producer). McGuane was not one for manipulating his acting charges, and usually allowed them quite a bit of freedom in their interpretations of the characters they were hired to portray. The resultant movie is a study in casual strangeness, and is now a cult favorite among fans of offbeat films. Offscreen, the ongoing events were even stranger. If McGuane were to make a film about what went on while making this film (à la Fellini's *8 ½*), it would have been even more interesting than the film itself. The combination of professional lunatics (Harry Dean Stanton, Peter Fonda, Elizabeth Ashley, and Margot Kidder, along with the other cast members) descending onto a scene that was already borderline crazy resulted in a pressure-cooker of combustible relationships. Dennis Hopper was hanging around as well, so you can be sure that it was next to impossible for things to ever get anywhere close to "normal."

Another character who was new to Key West and was liable to add to the instability of the locale was Dr. Hunter S. Thompson. Thompson wasn't a doctor at all—that was only an affectation that he used as an occasional means of empowerment—but a writer of legendary magnitude, known mostly for his development of Gonzo Journalism. This unique style of journalism entailed personal involvement in whatever story he was covering, while blurring distinctions between what is real and what is grossly imagined, often with the help of hallucinogens and alcohol. When this is properly realized, paranoia becomes a character unto itself. In lesser hands, this could be a mess, but Thompson was a master. During one of his visits to Colorado, Buffett met and befriended Thompson, seeing in him a kindred spirit with a similar tendency to avoid traditional, socially acceptable boundaries. The pair struck a deal to exchange living quarters for the season, with Jimmy handing over the keys to his Key West apartment while he temporarily used Hunter's home in Aspen.

Thompson settled in and made himself comfortable. He set up quarters at Jimmy's apartment and while there he supposedly managed to run up a $7,000 phone bill. It didn't take too long for Thompson to get into a grudge match with Louie's, the restaurant-bar next door, either. He allegedly won this battle by aiming his stereo speakers toward the restaurant, then repeatedly blasting sexually explicit tapes during the restaurant's dinner hour. Thompson's connection with Buffett fans may be tenuous, but since their paths have crossed, many Parrot Heads now see him as part of the legendary mystique that surrounds their hero. This then provides me with a perfect opportunity to elaborate about his influence on a whole generation of college-age kids, myself in particular, and also his profound impact on contemporary literature.

From my teens and on into my midtwenties, Thompson was a figure that loomed larger than life. His twisting and turning stories convey an attitude of extreme—yet somehow controlled and deliberate—lunacy, but they were always tightly focused and even more important, they were always entertaining. His prose is not for the meek or the timid. Hysterically funny, it can also be emotionally challenging, or even threatening, and sometimes enigmatic. Despite this awesome talent, his writing is easy to digest and as comprehensible as the most commercial pop novelist. For an excellent example of his work, you should check out *Fear and Loathing in Las Vegas,* or the collection of articles entitled *The Great Shark Hunt.* It so happens that Margaritaville Records has released an audio version of *Fear and Loathing in Las Vegas,* narrated by a first-class cast of actors—Harry Dean Stanton handles the bulk of the narration—so if you'd prefer to *hear* the book instead of read it, Jimmy Buffett's label now offers you that option. Yet another option is the screen adaptation, starring Johnny Depp.

No doubt about it, Key West was living up to its legend as a refuge for society's fringe. Meanwhile, Jimmy Buffett had other things to do. The band toured through the summer and fall, honing their ability to play as a unit. When the time came to record the next album, this same group of musicians followed Buffett into the studio. For the first time in his career, he had a Coral Reefer Band that was something other than a temporary agglomeration. That November, tracks were laid down for Buffett's fourth ABC release, *Havaña Daydreamin'.*

Havaña Daydreamin' (1976)

ABC Records ABCD-914

What happened? *Havaña Daydreamin'* isn't a bad album per se, but it just doesn't pay off after the intuitive brilliance of his previous efforts. After the colorful imagery and imaginative melodies of *A1A,* I expected better than this, and the more I listen to this record, the more its shortcomings begin to annoy me. Unlike his previous efforts, this album isn't

laid-back, it's just plain lazy. Without a doubt, *Havaña Daydreamin'* would have benefited from a lot more attention. It has its share of bright spots, but muddy production and unfocused performances are too often exacerbated by poorly considered wordplay.

It takes only the album's first track, "Woman Goin' Crazy on Caroline Street," to realize that there is something amiss with this record's approach. Over sluggish production and a slothful rhythm section, Buffett sings a lyric that conveys little sympathy for the subject of its title, making the song nothing more than an exercise in superficial judgmentalism. Buffett wrote the song with Steve Goodman (a pretty regular cohort of his around this time period), and they strain themselves trying to find humor in a pathetic situation where there isn't very much that's funny. It's simply a glib portrait of a desperate, aging, drink-ravaged barfly. Buffett's detractors often point to an aloof callousness in his songwriting and these lyrics provide the anti-Buffett contingent with plenty of adequate ammunition.

"My Head Hurts, My Feet Stink, and I Don't Love Jesus" is next up, and thank goodness, it at least manages to rise above the sacrilegious impudence of its title. It's a sing-along tune about a nasty hangover, and it aptly describes the discomfort and crabbiness that can result from having much too good of a time. If, however, you happen to be suffering from a hangover like the one described here, you wouldn't want to listen to this song, much less sing along. Just take the lyric's advice—pop a painkiller, drink some orange juice and maybe a pint of chocolate milk, then turn down the stereo and get back into bed.

"Big Rig" is one of the more problematic songs on *Havaña Daydreamin'*, wherein Fingers Taylor proves beyond a shadow of a doubt that he's a much better instrumentalist than songwriter. Most fans deride the song's musical approach, but it's the lyrics that baffle me. What on earth is Buffett singing about? I know it's some sort of a fidelity-on-the-road thing, but when he tries to connote the image of a "big rig" as something sexy, I get awfully confused. For example, he sees "a good-lookin' woman with a bottle of scotch," and sings that "she's lookin' like a big rig." Say what?

Which reminds me of a few other lyrical oddities on this record. Like, how do you "slowly guzzle" something ("Woman Goin' Crazy . . .")? Or, does your skin crawl like mine does when Jimmy offhandedly rhymes "moon" and "June" ("Clichés")? Is it a deliberate play on the song title? I can't say for sure, but in a song that is otherwise full of clever wordplay ("She's got a ballpark figure" is classic), this lame couplet stands out like a Parrot Head at a Kiss concert. "Losin' any more hope of scorin' any more coke" ain't exactly the Queen's English, either. The song that uses this line can *really* drive me crazy. Bluntly put, "Kick It in Second Wind" is another artless whiner, à la "Saxophones" from *Living and Dying in 3/4 Time,* wherein Buffett gets to complain about the trappings of being a working musician. Jimmy, your fans don't feel sorry for you, they envy you, and that's something that you ought to know better than anybody.

The artfulness of the album's best tracks only serve to highlight the lack of attention that was paid to the balance. "The Captain and the Kid" dates back to 1969 and it is touching enough to salvage almost any collection of songs. "Defying Gravity" was written by Jesse Winchester, and it contains words that are a concisely simple and a clever reflection on mortality. Buffett's voice is well suited to a song as easily paced as this, and he sings it beautifully and wistfully. "Havaña Daydreamin' " is perhaps the best-written song on the album and it might even qualify as his best song to date, period. With languid rhythms that add depth and mystery to the words, it is difficult to decipher exactly what the central character has at stake, but it sucks us in until we can almost feel the hot breezes from the ceiling fan as it twirls above the bed of the song's main character. It is this penchant for detail and nuance that makes Buffett's work so appealing, and "Havaña Daydreamin' " is so good because it places the listener smack-dab in the middle of the action.

Compared to the artful beauty of these highlights, the balance of the album falls flat. "Something So Feminine About a Mandolin" is drab and uninspiring, and the album's last track, "This Hotel Room" (written by Steve Goodman) is nothing more than a whimsical song about the accoutrements of your typical hotel room. At this point in his career,

Buffett was peaking, meaning he was most certainly capable of producing more than a handful of keepers. The album's last line is "Stick a candle in the window, I'm comin' home," but if the truth be told, *Havaña Daydreamin'* doesn't hold a candle to the albums it is sandwiched between. Next time around, he'd do a lot better.

Havaña Daydreamin' was an equal opportunity album: *Record World* described it as "having something to offend everyone." Whereas each of Buffett's previous albums effortlessly eclipsed its predecessor in sales figures, *Havaña Daydreamin'* was the first album not to outperform all others. It peaked at number 65 in the winter of 1976, forty positions below *A1A*'s peak of number 25.

Buffett usually expressed satisfaction with ABC and their financial arrangement. Royalty checks were coming in fairly regularly and they afforded him the opportunity to splurge a bit. He bought a new home for his parents, then purchased a thirty-three-foot Cheoy Lee ketch, which he named *Euphoria.* For landlubber-types who get confused by sailing jargon and wouldn't know a ketch from a rowboat, a ketch is defined by Webster's as "a ship with fore-and-aft rigging similar to a yawl but with a larger mizzen and the mizzen-mast set closer to the mainsail." I hope that clarifies things.

With sailing in his blood since birth, Buffett now owned a boat that would become the tangible reflection of his aspirations of freedom and adventure. For more mundane pursuits and obligations, he purchased an elaborately decked-out (literally—it was made to resemble a boat's cabin on the inside) tour bus to ease the boredom of relentless traveling.

Buffett feigned indifference to his record sales, stating that he wanted nothing to do with the rat race that comes from excessive stardom, but this didn't prevent him from railing at his record company, accusing it of incompetence and failing to pay proper attention to his career. He blamed the lackluster sales figures of *Havaña Daydreamin'* on the ineptitude of ABC, which he felt was insistently trying to cubbyhole him into being a Nashville-based country artist while overlooking the fact that his music was only marginally related to the style of music that Nashville typically produced. His contract with ABC was soon due for renewal, and his business instincts told him that taking an adversarial stance in the upcoming negotiations would probably benefit his financial standpoint. As it turned out, he was right. ABC grew nervous that Buffett was going to flee the label for Warner Brothers Records, a more rock-oriented label with plenty of marketing power, and their fears were made all the more real when Buffett hired a California-based show business attorney to represent his interests. Rather than lose him, ABC drew up a contract that gave him greater artistic freedom, a better royalty rate, and, perhaps most important, the ability to retain his own publishing rights. If he could sustain his career, he was now in a position to get very, very wealthy.

The year 1976 followed the pattern of previous years. For the fifth straight year, he toured through the summer, took some time off to write, then went into the studio in the fall to record an album that would be released the following winter. Buffett's bicentennial summer tour included a few dates in support of presidential candidate Jimmy Carter along with the usual tour dates that helped him pay the bills. When a window of opportunity presented itself, he and Jane boarded the *Euphoria* and sailed around the Caribbean islands.

When his schedule would permit, Buffett would return to Key West, but the island no longer held the same appeal that it once had. To his eyes, the bloom was off of the rose. Owing to his absence, he could no longer sustain his role as an active member of the elite partying contingent, and his burgeoning career made it difficult for him to blend in with the crowd as easily as he once had. An influx of tourists also played a major role in changing Buffett's perceptions. These outsiders appeared to be taking over, leaving him with an overall feeling of disillusionment about the place. Like a weary traveler who returns home only to find that it has changed irrevocably, Buffett had become disenchanted with his beloved Key West. He could no longer be the aloof insider, so instead, he became the informed observer. Like any good journalist would do, Buffett took note of his observations, and like any good songwriter, his observations became song lyrics. Some of these lines ended up in the verses of what would become "Margaritaville."

"Wastin' Away Again in Margaritaville" was a song that Buffett had lying around since 1973, when a bar in Austin served up a margarita that inspired the words of the song's chorus. He claimed that particular margarita to be alternately "wonderful, one of the best I ever had," or "not even (that) great," but it wasn't the quality of the drink that mattered, but rather the quality of the inspiration. Though it took three years for him to piece the whole thing together, this was one simple idea that would develop well beyond its humble origins.

After he had accumulated enough material, he scheduled his usual November recording dates, only this time the circumstances would be considerably different. Instead of returning to Nashville, Buffett opted to use Miami's Criteria Sound Studios and in place of Don Gant, who produced all of his ABC work to date, he decided to call on the talents of Norbert Putnam.

Changes in Latitudes, Changes in Attitudes (1977)

ABC Records AB-990

Just as I was beginning to suspect that Jimmy's carefree ways were going to start yielding careless music, along came the most well crafted album of his career. My review of his previous album, *Havaña Daydreamin',* was undeniably harsh, but I felt certain that he had it in him to do a lot better. Beyond a shadow of a doubt, *Changes in Latitudes, Changes in Attitudes* goes a long way toward proving Buffett's case. Song for song, it rivals *A1A* in its overall consistency, and in some aspects it may well even surpass that landmark album. For example, Norbert Putnam's production style put a new spin on Buffett's approach, allowing a few of the songs to rock a bit harder, generating a more mainstream sound than the country-oriented production of previous producer Don Gant. Not that the country sound didn't suit Buffett well—it was sometimes brilliant—but a change of pace was overdue and, if he was hoping for a larger audience, necessary.

If you were already a Buffett fan when this album was released, then you can surely remember its impact. Long before it was played to the point of abuse, "Margaritaville" was a very welcome soundtrack to the summer of 1977. The song almost instantly became *the* signature tune of that time and to this day it still conjures pleasant memories of that season over two decades ago (has it really been that long?). Of course, this was before there was any such thing as a Parrot Head, many of whom complain nowadays that the song is worn out from overplay, but imagine how Jimmy must feel! If you had to sing the same song every single night of your performing life, wouldn't you eventually lose interest in it? While that is a rhetorical question, every time he lets loose with another live performance of "Margaritaville," Buffett still manages to sound inspired, so I'm convinced that this can only be due to one (or both) of the following reasons: either Jimmy has superhuman self-motivational skills, or the song is simply good enough to withstand forty-some-odd billion performances. Like a Timex watch, "Margaritaville" just keeps on ticking, and over time Jimmy's well-worn voice complements the lackadasical lyrics more and more.

As anybody who has been to a Jimmy Buffett concert can attest, "Margaritaville" is no longer simply a hit tune from a long time ago, but rather a signature tune for an entire movement. There are many Buffett songs that give Parrot Heads a feeling of warm camaraderie and vocal gusto, but by the sheer power of its melodious and laid-back message, only "Margaritaville" can qualify as the national anthem of the Parrot Head Nation.

Most telling about *Changes in Latitudes, Changes in Attitudes* is that "Margaritaville" doesn't stand out in the pack but blends in with the songs that are collected here. There is a sense of balance and continuity that unifies the otherwise disparate tracks. Although the production is punchier than before, the material itself is often pensive and analytical, resulting in a rather brilliantly wrought contradiction."Wonder Why We Ever Go Home," "Banana Republics," "In the Shelter," "Lovely Cruise," and "Biloxi" are all reflective in their mood, yet none of them drag or sound even the least bit weepy or morose. A valuable characteristic of Buffett's songwriting is his ability to analyze a situation without getting too weighty, and this album is chock-full of pithy observations. On the title song and opening track, he cleverly diffuses a verse that discusses estranged friends when he concludes it by spending the night drinking with one. This tendency to think, but not too much, is exactly what makes Buffett's lyrics such a pleasure to hear.

Even the songs Jimmy didn't write have a similar feel. "Lovely Cruise" (Jonathan Banam), "Banana Republics" (Steve Goodman, Steve Burgh, and Jim Rothermel), and "Biloxi" (Jesse Winchester) are all succinctly rendered mood pieces that Buffett magically transforms into very personal statements. That leaves "Tampico Trauma" and "Landfall" to take the role of straight-ahead rock numbers, and both feature well-rehearsed arrangements with plenty of ear-catching riffs. Besides the excellent guitar work, Fingers Taylor deserves recognition for his tastefully unobtrusive harmonica playing. From beginning to end, virtually everything clicks into place. The band rocks soulfully, the songwriting is alert and focused, and the production is sympathetic throughout. Even the structure is impressive. Just as the album begins with the theme of thinking about life's changes, so does it end, with Jimmy singing, "I'm just trying to make a little sense of it all." If I ever need to convey what the big deal is all about, *Changes in Latitudes, Changes in Attitudes* is the record that I usually recommend to neophytes. More often than not, it hooks them, and that makes more than enough sense to me.

Until recently, the summer of 1977 was probably the closest that Jimmy Buffett ever came to becoming a household name. *Changes in Latitudes, Changes in Attitudes* debuted on February 12 and by the summer had climbed all the way up to number 12. It remained on the album charts straight through to December and was eventually certified platinum. The single "Margaritaville" became Buffett's first (and only) top Ten hit, spending an entire fifteen weeks on the Top Forty while traversing its way up to number 8. As proof of the song's mass appeal, it also reached number 1 on the adult contemporary charts and number 13 on the country charts. The attention to mainstream tastes on *Changes in Latitudes, Changes in Attitudes* was the primary catalyst that thrust him into the limelight where he would remain for the next few years. His unique style of country-Caribbean-rock had finally come into its own. Through talent, good fortune, and hard work, Jimmy Buffett turned a small niche into an entire genre, of which he was the founding father and, if truth be told, the sole participant. Others may have dabbled in styles that were similar, but only Buffett could claim an entire catalog of laid-back, sun-drenched, water-soaked, booze-laden, stone-headed music.

Before recording *Changes in Latitudes, Changes in Attitudes,* Buffett met with a staff writer from *High Times* magazine, to whom he spoke frankly about his use of drugs and alcohol in a manner that would be almost unimaginable in today's political climate. The seventies were a time that is hard to explain to anyone who didn't experience those years firsthand. In many ways, the seventies were little else except the aftermath of the sixties. While the sixties counterculture originally constituted an entire manifesto of revised political and social thinking, it never properly gelled into anything tangible. No truly charismatic and visionary leader emerged to capture the public's imagination, and eventually the movement just died. By the mid-seventies, all that was left was the shell of a dream. Unification gave way to individuality.

The only thing that really survived from the sixties counterculture, besides its legacy, was its drug habits. Drugs were no longer anywhere near as taboo as they once were. Marijuana, cocaine, and practically anything else that was psychoactive were being used (and abused) in abundance. Like long hair (another superficial seventies characteristic that in the sixties was meant to stand for something), drugs became fashionable. The experimentation and idealism that symbolized life in the sixties fell prey to the jaded debauchery and cynical indifference of the seventies.

No wonder "Margaritaville" did so well! It was not intentionally written to be a reflection of the nation's zeitgeist, but that (along with another hit song by his friends, the Eagles) is nevertheless exactly what it was. Welcome to the Hotel California, on the pleasant and sunny island of Margaritaville, where you have no responsibilities and no petty morals to impinge upon your hallucination. Just sit back on the porch. Have a few drinks, eat some shrimp. The world is a bother, so you might as well get wasted. When hedonistic narcissism was the rule, Jimmy Buffett was appointed king.

Buffett's newfound celebrity status had caused some rather interesting rumblings in his old home base of Nashville. Old-fashioned, conservative, and set in its ways, the musical institutions in the country music capital of the world once had little use for a renegade such as Jimmy Buffett, but now they were forced to look down a double barrel that was threatening their very existence. In essence, what Jimmy Buffett had done was to prove that by leaving Nashville, he could greatly increase his popularity among a wider variety of audiences. Waylon Jennings and Willie Nelson had just proven the same thing when they united for a huge hit album that dubbed them (along with Tompall Glaser and Jennings's wife, Jessie Colter) the Outlaws. Suddenly, it was cool to be anti-Nashville even in Nashville, and the "outlaw" image became the driving force in country music.

Buffett must have reveled in this sudden turn of events, in which a town that once shunned him was now itself being humbled. You can imagine the mixed feelings of celebration and vindication that Jimmy Buffett must have felt when he and the Coral Reefer Band were invited to play at country music's recently built mecca (replacing the Ryman Auditorium), the Grand Ole Opry House. Barnaby Records, which had no use whatsoever for Buffett when he was contractually obligated to it, was suddenly finding its way around to seeing some value in his music, and that's not all that it was finding. Buffett's newfound popularity prompted Barnaby's management to try and locate his missing 1970s sessions for their label. In the middle of "Margaritaville" madness, Jimmy's long-lost second album, *High Cumberland Jubilee,* was finally released. The cheesy and outdated packaging did not fool anybody, though, so this blatantly retroactive attempt to cash in on his present reputation never sold enough to touch the album charts.

Before touring, Jimmy spent some time sailing around the Caribbean and then hobnobbing about in Aspen, Colorado. With his royalty payments rolling in, he attended a few boat shows and decided to treat himself to a brand-spanking-new forty-eight-foot Cheoy Lee clipper (a fast sailing ship with long slender lines, an overhanging bow, tall raking masts, and a large sail area), which he named *Euphoria II.* When he returned to dry land and the mountains of Colorado, he met the Eagles' manager, Irving Azoff, who worked out an arrangement for Buffett to get the opening slot on the Eagles' summer tour of stadiums in support of their *Hotel California* album. In his inimitable way, it was only a matter of time before the voracious Azoff, through his company, Front Line Management, had taken complete control of Buffett's management contract. His previous manager, Don Light, had kept a low profile while he steered Jimmy's career toward stardom, but with Azoff all of that would change. Jimmy was freed from his Nashville ties and was now affiliated with an entire family of West Coast–based artists, including the Eagles, Dan Fogelberg, Jackson Browne, and Boz Scaggs.

Buffett's rise to the pinnacle of stardom was complete and the chips were all falling into place, but there was one outstanding matter that still needed to be addressed. That was settled on August 27, 1977, when James Buffett married Jane Slogsvol in Redstone, Colorado. Invitations stated that the celebration would "begin at five in the afternoon and last until it is over. In addition to the usual eating, drinking, dancing, and carrying on, we intend some time during the evening to be married. Please come." Guests included most of Irving Azoff's Front Line clientele, and such luminaries as Emmylou Harris, Bonnie Raitt, and Hunter Thompson. Buffett was already a fixture among Aspen's in-crowd but with their wedding, he and Jane had entered the strata of the West Coast's social elite. Later that same year, their friend Tom McGuane (who had divorced his second wife, Margot Kidder—they had met during the filming of *92 in the Shade*) would exchange vows with Jimmy's sister, Laurie.

A second single was culled from *Changes in Latitudes, Changes in Attitudes* and on September 17, a remixed version of the album's title song scraped to number 37 on the pop charts (number 24 country). Collectors might care to note that this was his only 45 to feature a custom picture sleeve. Soon afterward, it was November, meaning that it was once again time to record a new album. Buffett stated that he had written virtually all of the material for *Son of a Son of a Sailor* while sailing around on the *Euphoria II*. This time, he knew that he could afford to take his time, so a bit more attention was paid to detail and the sessions lingered on a bit longer than usual. Recording was split between Nashville's Quadrophonic Sound and Bay Shore Recording Studios in Coconut Grove, Florida. The lackluster pace delayed his customary February album release until April.

When *Son of a Son of a Sailor* did eventually hit the street, its release coincided closely with that of the film *FM*. Starring Michael Brandon and Martin Mull as hipper-than-thou representatives of the contemporary music scene, *FM* intended to portray events at a rebellious, cutting-edge FM radio station, with strictly AM results. Real life completely usurped the film's authenticity and relevance. While various punk and new wave acts were rapidly pushing their way on to the scene, *FM* attempted to sustain its mock-hip stance with music by Linda Ronstadt, Billy Joel, the Eagles, and Bob Seger. By 1978, these artists had a collective image that was about as cutting-edge hip as a set of dull Ginsu knives. Buffett's presence didn't add much, either. The film shows Buffett and the Coral Reefers performing "Livingston Saturday Night" at a (pretend) "Save the Whales" benefit concert. With so much good material to choose from, why he would appear in a film doing the same song that he already performed in another movie (*Rancho Deluxe*) is beyond me. At least it can be said that Buffett fans will probably enjoy his appearance here more than in *Rancho Deluxe,* because the film only occasionally cuts away from the stage for a few obligatory dialogue shots. The band comes off well also, with a pair of great solos from Fingers Taylor and Tim Krekel (which, unfortunately, are talked over). Jimmy Buffett adds some dialogue at the end of his performance, and it might very well be the most believable scene in this otherwise terrible movie. *FM* was completely out of touch with its intended audience and failed miserably at the box office. The musical artists still had plenty of draw, though, and they launched the corresponding soundtrack album all the way to position number 5. The album's inside cover features two photos, one of Linda Ronstadt and the other of Jimmy Buffett.

Son of a Son of a Sailor (1978)

ABC Records AA1046

As you would expect after the windfall from "Margaritaville" and its album, *Changes in Latitudes, Changes in Attitudes,* no expense was spared on the production of Jimmy Buffett's next release, *Son of a Son of a Sailor.* The elaborately designed packaging included a carefully staged gatefold photo of Buffett, his wife, band members, and their compatriots posing as pirates in the hull of a ship (with a room steward, of course) along with a heavy-gauge cardboard inner sleeve with lyrics, a photo of Buffett in rain gear, and lots of credits. The production was equally elaborate, with background vocals on the choruses, horns, and strings interweaving their way through the pristinely recorded arrangements. Everything about this package screams at you that this is going to be a *big* album. Only the songs themselves are sometimes lacking in their scope.

Son of a Son of a Sailor can be neatly divided into conflicting halves, and Buffett was kind enough to separate the good from the bad when he arranged the album's track sequencing. All of the clinkers appear on side

one; side two is saved for four of his best recordings.

Side one starts off promisingly enough, with the excellent title song that melodiously touches on some of his favorite and oft-used themes. The side then loses focus until it eventually sinks all the way to goofy irrelevance. "Fool Button" serves little purpose except to give the band a chance to extend their instrumental abilities with some phony phunk, and "The Last Line" does nothing at all but take up space. "Livingston Saturday Night" was great as a soundtrack number four years ago, but here (with whitewashed lyrics) it sounds out of place, forced and uninspired.

Next up is my personal choice for a Buffett song to loathe, "Cheeseburger in Paradise." This "novelty" record (as it is classified by *Billboard*) has got to be one of the most annoyingly forced efforts at a hokey musical joke that I have ever laid ears upon. The lyrics in the verse are promising enough, but the chorus is just out of hand. Maybe I would appreciate it more if he would only calm down and not try so hard to emote. It's ground beef he's singing about, right? The way he yells his way through the chorus, you'd think someone just shot his dog. In my opinion, singing about food is like dancing about beer. It just doesn't make any sense to me.

Almost miraculously, the album springs back to life on the second side and maintains a level of excellence that outweighs the shortcomings of the first side. It's here that the pensive songs take hold of the controls and stop the album from crashing. "Son of a Son of a Sailor," "Coast of Marseilles," "Cowboy in the Jungle," and "African Friend" are the album's four best songs and the last three share side two with the rhythmic and entertaining "Mañana" (which in my opinion should have been the first single). "Coast of Marseilles" is one of two songs Buffett didn't write himself on the otherwise all-original album (the other is "The Last Line," both written by Buffett's buddy, Keith Sykes). Love songs are rare in the Buffett repertoire but this sad beauty of a song perfectly captures the heart-wrenching realization that you are still very much attached to somebody whom you might not ever see again. "Cowboy in the Jungle" and "African Friend" are almost as affecting, combining excellent storytelling techniques with fetching melodies.

Throughout this album, the instrumentalist who constantly stands out is Fingers Taylor. He's always had a deft touch that was nothing less than great, but here he outdoes himself and even salvages some of the weaker tracks ("Fool Button," "The Last Line") from utter uselessness. If only the entire album had the same tasteful subtlety, it would have been an absolutely brilliant piece of work. Instead, *Son of a Son of a Sailor* is merely a noble attempt to make something grand from occasionally ordinary material, and it succeeds only half of the time.

By sheer force of will and the momentum that naturally resulted from having the country's most powerful management organization behind him, Buffett earned the highest album chart position of his career with *Son of Son of a Sailor.* Coming on the heels of "Margaritaville" and served up in a well-heeled package, it peaked at number 10 in the spring of 1978. Advance orders alone totaled over 500,000 copies, making it a gold-certified record right out of the gate (it would eventually go platinum).

"Cheeseburger in Paradise" was scraped off of the grill and released as the album's first single. After the tasty wordplay and subtle sophistication of his recent singles, this lowbrow menu selection failed to stir up the attention of the pop audience and it stalled at number 32, despite promotional efforts. It spent only four weeks in the Top Forty. After the failure of the initial single release, most second or third choices don't stand a chance. This is because most fans have already bought the album by then, so they can overlook a product that offers nothing new. Predictably, then, subsequent extracts from the album fared even worse. "Livingston Saturday Night" debuted in August but climbed no higher than number 52, and by the time they finally rolled around to releasing "Mañana" as the package's third single, nobody cared. It didn't help, either, that it was forced to compete against a new live double album that hit the streets one month earlier. It didn't need confirmation, but these results offered three more reasons to reconsider any attempt to market Buffett as competition for ABBA and the Bee Gees. As an album artist Buffett made sense but as a singles artist, he was an anomaly.

While these releases were being plotted by the people who do such things, Buffett was once again concerning himself with his summer tour schedule, only this time with a twist. The series of shows that took place at Atlanta's Fox Theatre and the Gusman Cultural Center in Miami were to be recorded for posterity and assembled into a live album that was to be unleashed on the public in November. Another thing that was twisted for this series of shows was Buffett's right leg, which he broke during a softball game while sliding into second base. Anybody who couldn't go to the shows but still wanted to catch a glimpse of the leg cast could tune in to the season's hottest comedy show, *Saturday Night Live,* where Jimmy guested as the featured musical act. If you missed both the television show and the concert, then at least you could listen to the live album. If you listen closely to his revised lyrics, you'll hear plenty of references both to his cast (and sliding into second base) and the *Saturday Night Live* cast as well.

You Had to Be There (1978)

ABC Records AK1008/2

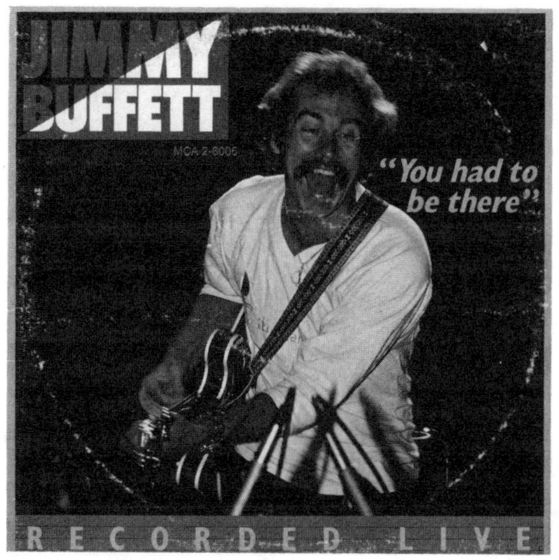

In the wake of artists like Peter Frampton, Aerosmith, the Allman Brothers, Eric Clapton, the Eagles (I could go on!), Jimmy Buffett jumped on the mid-seventies double-live-album bandwagon and released his own.

Now, by their very nature, live albums tend to be boring and mediocre collections of poorly recorded music designed as little more than souvenirs for people who want to believe that the album will somehow make them feel as good as the show did. But, due to the fact that almost every rock-and-roll show is augmented by a stage presentation of visual effects and lights, a live album often fails to reach the same sensory heights as the actual show did and therefore falls flat on its face.

But you know what? *You Had to Be There* is great! By some miracle of God, this album stands head and shoulders above the pack. Maybe it's because the band keeps things focused while Buffett entertains the audience; or maybe it's because things sound so loose and haphazard, as if at any moment almost anything could happen. Another possibility is that the stage patter is left intact—most live albums delete all between-song dialogue, so the artist comes off as mute or incommunicado. Mostly, though, I think *You Had to Be There* is an exception because it is contagious. It sounds like a fun place to be at the time, so it is easy to have fun just listening in.

Some of the songs even manage to beat out their rather excellent studio counterparts. "Pencil Thin Moustache" retains all of the campy originality that can be heard on the studio version, but the Coral Reefers infuse it with a rocking, gospellike energy that was not even hinted at back then. New verses and ad-libs bring new life to familiar material like "Margaritaville" and "Miss You So Badly." "Wonder Why You Ever Go Home" is outright beautiful here, with the band sounding uncannily like Springsteen's E-Street Band. "He Went to Paris" is so simple that it can bring a tear to your eye, especially after Buffett's introduction helps us to visualize the human beings he is singing about. "Dixie Diner" is a new instrumental that features Fingers Taylor and guitarist Tim Krekel, and it boogies so hard it leaves listeners begging for more.

This is a simple collection of songs that spans Buffett's career, caught at a time when he and the band were as lively as they've ever been, and that's something that you ought to hear. The most intelligent things about this record are what it's not; it isn't edited to hell, for instance, or sanitized for public consumption. The occasional bad chord, swearing, extraneous talk, and missed cues only make a show like this more appealing. Sometimes randy and a little bit bawdy (almost trashy), it's as off-the-cuff as you could hope it to be, but Buffett's fan base is not what one would consider prudish. Yeah, the narrative parts can get old real fast, so it's not the kind of record that you can play over and over; it's more the kind that you can return to every few months and smile about all over again. It will make you wish that you were there, but it does such a good job of capturing the show's spirit that you'll realize it isn't at all imperative that *You Had to Be There.*

For a double album, *You Had to Be There* performed well, though not as well as was hoped for. It reached number 72 and clung to the charts for a total of eighteen weeks. While the record brought Buffett's show into people's living rooms, Jimmy went back out on the road to refresh his audience with an updated version. While he toured, new things were developing behind the scenes.

On a personal note, Jane was pregnant and making preparations for the birth of their daughter, Savannah Jane (born June 1, 1979). On a business note, all hell was breaking loose at ABC Records. In a commerce-based society, corporate mergers are a way of life and in the late seventies, few industries had been as besieged with shifting ownerships, relocated personnel, and corporate restructuring as the record industry. In spring 1979, ABC Records found itself behind the eight ball when MCA, a conglomerate with a frugal reputation and a voracious appetite, decided to swallow them up. A lot of dust was kicked up during the ensuing transaction, but when it cleared, ABC's roster of artists was now affiliated with MCA. To Buffett, that meant his contractual obligations for future releases now belonged to MCA, and his catalog also became their property. To his fans, this would eventually mean a series of ludicrously cheap, no-frills reissues. With little regard to aesthetics or the original design intent, MCA would turn Buffett's catalog of recordings into homogenized slabs of plastic with negligible liner notes, no gatefold packaging, and generic inner sleeves. The musical content remained the same, but MCA's monetary tunnel vision and lack of respect for the consumer meant no more lyric sheets and severely crimped artwork. While they took an accountant's-eye view of their catalog and hacked at it with all the subtlety of a slasher, they also attempted to intitialize an across-the-board increase in the list price of all new releases.

Almost laughably, these maneuvers ultimately caused MCA to shoot itself in the foot. By reducing the quality of its album packages to simple cardboard sleeves with vinyl inside, MCA's catalog became a primary target of bootleggers, who could profit in the inexpensive reproduction of such cheapness. Buffett, meanwhile, remained aloof from the politics of the merger, leaving manager Irving Azoff to handle all of the screaming and yelling. As maddening back-and-forth phone calls took place, Buffett peacefully went about the business of preparing his first album for MCA. While sitting on top of the world, Buffett sailed the *Euphoria II* to the volcanic island of Montserrat in the British West Indies, where he wrote most of the songs for his upcoming album at a blissful and leisurely pace. He recorded there as well, using George Martin's newly built AIR Studios.

Back in 1972, a band called Dr. Hook and the Medicine Show (later, they simpified it to just Doctor Hook) had a hit song called "Cover of the Rolling Stone," about the instant hip status that is bestowed upon the benefactor of this privilege. On October 4, 1979, Jimmy Buffett's image as a counterculture hero was apotheosized when his likeness graced the cover of the country's hippest magazine for a feature article written by Chet Flippo. The *Rolling Stone* article chronicles a couple of days on the island of Saint-Barthélemy, an island in the proximity of Montserrat, where Buffett and his bandmates would occasionally sail during a break in the recording sessions. Besides pointing out that, in true rock star fashion, he could sometimes be less than reliable at keeping his appointments, the article portrays Buffett as a full-blown hedonist who is as genuine as the characters in his songs. His time is split between occasional thoughts of actually recording something and unabashedly relaxed abandon. If nothing else, the article leaves the reader with the distinct impression that Jimmy Buffett must be the luckiest man alive, blessed with fame, fortune, and the good sense to enjoy every last bit of both. Not that it required confirmation, but it leaves little doubt that Buffett was leading a fantasy life that was remarkable even by his own standards.

Volcano (1979)

MCA Records MCA-5102

Prerelease statements indicated that Jimmy Buffett figured *Volcano* to be his biggest album in years, if not ever. Judging by the harsh critical reaction and indifferent sales figures it was met by, he must have been disappointed with the net results. Longtime Buffett fans were less than kind to this album also, feeling somewhat betrayed by its stylistic shift. I, however, fail to see what all the complaints were about.

From my vantage point, the album doesn't "blow," it only sputters a bit here and there. It certainly isn't one of his best efforts, but it does at

least contain its share of memorable and well-written songs. As an entity unto itself, it's a fine album, but once you take into consideration Buffett's back catalog, as well as the sudden shift in musical styles that was taking place at this time, it is easy to perceive *Volcano* as being out of touch.

Buffett was always an autobiographical songwriter so the shift in his social status and the arrival of his child were bound to have their effect on his music. In light of this and his own expectations, *Volcano* attempts to be a relatively ambitious collection of material meant to convey a sense of growth and maturity. The only problem is that the resulting album sounds less ambitious than simply pleasant. Russ Kunkel flew in from the West Coast to play drums and James Taylor and a few of his brothers showed up to sing, but none of this had any significant effect on the album's overall sound. Buffett wrote every song on *Volcano* (and only four of them with cowriters), making it one his most personal efforts in some time.

"Fins" is the album's first single and leadoff track, and it rocks admirably with a verve that maintains the energy displayed on the previous live album. The concept that men are land sharks waiting to devour their female prey is perfectly suited to an audience that is more than very familiar with the nature of these carnivorous creatures. The title song, "Volcano," is a mild calypso-based number recorded with a local group known as The Woop Wap Band that steers its audience smack-dab into the heart of Caribbean culture. Never as popular in the United States as that *other* island-based style—reggae—calypso is extremely popular in the Caribbean region, particularly in Trinidad, where it allegedly originated. Buffett's version is almost childlike in its rhythmic simplicity and tame in its lyrical structure when compared with more authentic fare, but an undeniable melody and topical lyrics keep things lively enough, and it makes for an infectiously welcome change of pace.

Speaking of childlike, "Chanson Pour les Petits Enfants" is a complete departure for Buffett. With lyrics and melody that convey a sweet and imaginative bedtime lullaby, it bears absolutely no resemblance to the artist who only recently could be heard singing "God's Own Drunk." It's cute and pretty enough, but requires a good dollop of understanding on the listener's part to grant him the license to sing this ode to his newborn daughter. The foreign title and lyrics were probably inspired partially by the French-speaking inhabitants of Saint-Barthélemy (Saint Barts).

Nondescript songs occupy an inordinate amount of the space here. "Stranded on a Sandbar" gives Buffett the chance to cover his view of life once again, but with no insights that haven't already been covered on his earlier work. "Dreamsicle" updates us on his social and family status, but not much more. Better are the album's love songs, one to his wife and one to the sea. "Lady I Can't Explain" moves along at an easily rocking lope while Buffett shares with us more of his personal relationship than he is usually inclined to, and "Treat Her Like a Lady" nicely captures the sensual allure of the sea. "Survive" (cowritten with Michael Utley) might also qualify as a love song, but the subject of long-distance love veers dangerously close to carbon-copying that of his previous hit single, "Come Monday." In his *Rolling Stone* interview, Buffett stated that he deliberately set out to write this ballad in the style of Billy Joel, so the result should come as no surprise. Manager Irving Azoff would supply "Survive" for the soundtrack of a Robert Blake–Dyan Cannon vehicle called *Coast to Coast,* a thoroughly ridiculous romp that used perhaps ten seconds of the song in the actual movie (I had to sit through it twice before I was able to catch it).

Elsewhere, Buffett moves on to new territory with better results. "Boat Drinks" is an entertaining departure whereby Jimmy takes a refreshingly sympathetic view of a harried northerner being tortured by a harsh winter. Instead of focusing on the northerner's touristy presence, he sings from their perspective and acknowledges their need to escape, probably earning himself a few more fans in the process. It also marks Buffett's first use of the pan (steel drum) on a recording. "Sending the Old Man Home" is not the most musically inspiring piece on the album, but its lyrics are a vivid character portrayal of an ex–naval officer being retired to civilian life. Colorful tales like these hold a large part of Buffett's appeal, and his well-fleshed-out character study makes for an appropriate end to an album that itself signifies an end to one stage of his career and the beginning of another.

4

The Early Eighties

The music scene in the late 1970s and early 1980 was significantly different than it was at the time of Buffett's first experience with stardom. In the mid-seventies, disco was reigning, with the likes of the rejuvenated Bee Gees and Chic controlling the charts, and Jimmy Buffett represented a natural alternative to the commercialized metronomic rhythms of those times. Most rock fans were put off by disco anyway, so artists who maintained a semblance of their roots were in turn championed by the traditionalist Luddites for nothing else so much as being antidisco. Buffett disliked disco as much as anybody, so he didn't mind the attention and even made a reference to it now and then (e.g., "Morris' Nightmare").

By late 1979, though, the music industry took on an aura of plasticized hipness that estranged the more earthy rock-and-roll veterans of the music scene. Artists who once were considered to be perennial favorites were now being shunted aside as ancient dinosaurs. While bands like the Who, the Allman Brothers, and Fleetwood Mac struggled to retain their relevance, new-wavers such as Blondie, Devo, and the Cars tried to hijack the entire industry with high-energy music that refused to acknowledge any debt to its predecessors. Lines were drawn, and Buffett was 100 percent entrenched in the camp of the disavowed.

For a while, record labels appeared prepared to abandon their historic mainstays completely in favor of a reactionary shift to the new. Entire careers teetered in the balance, but the record-industry slump of recent years indicated that a change of some sort was necessary to revitalize its finances. Never mind that most label executives were commanding exorbitant salaries and planning ludicrously elaborate promotional events that would have made Liberace blush; they wanted change, and it was not going to cut into their cocaine budget if they could help it. A rebirth of contemporary music was predicted, and if you weren't in on it, then you were on the way out.

While crystal ball gazers shifted to the new wave, Buffett aligned himself with the old school, and thank God he did. Imagine, for instance, if Buffett added a Farfisa organ to the band and started jumping around the stage wearing skin-tight leopard pants under a black-and-white-checked sport coat (sans crustacean), while singing about sharks and volcanoes. This is one indignity that I am happy to say the world (and Buffett) was spared of. This ignorance of musical trends would eventually work in his favor but in 1980, it simply made him appear to be an anachronism. While Jimmy continued his fascination with Caribbean rhythms, the rest of the world was adjusting its ears to the Clash, the Pretenders, and the Police.

Buffett was so indifferent to (or hostile toward) current trends that he instead decided to do exactly what he felt like doing. If people followed along, fine. If not, then he wasn't going to break his back or make a fool out of himself trying to hold on to a fickle audience. His relaxed demeanor would result in some of his most decidedly noncommercial releases to date. The turning tide was made most apparent when sales results for *Volcano* began to come in. Both Buffett and manager Irving Azoff had extremely high expectations for the album. Buffett thought it was his best work yet, and Azoff predicted Top Five status, but the album petered out at number 14. That in itself was not so bad, but the fate of the singles-oriented material indicated worse. "Fins" and "Volcano" were much more pop-oriented than Buffett's previous singles efforts had been. Nonetheless, their chart record ranged from disappointing to appalling. "Fins" was the first choice and it rose no higher than number 35, peaking in October 1979. It lasted in the Top Forty for three weeks and fell completely off the singles charts eleven weeks after its debut date. It would be the last Top Forty single Jimmy Buffett would ever know. "Volcano" (number 66) and "Survive" (number 77, with three weeks in the Top 100) followed, but they sounded out of synch with the times and fared accordingly.

While the sales figures were being tallied, Buffett had plenty of other things to occupy his time, not the least of which was his new family. The fall of 1979 was the first time since he began recording for ABC Records that he decided to forgo his traditional schedule of summer touring and fall recording sessions, followed by a winter album release. Family deserved to be prioritized, and his professional schedule was now a bit more sporadic than before.

Of course, he did tour, but there were plenty of stops and starts, as opposed to the more lunatic, nonstop continuous pace of previous outings. Because the schedule was broken up into more manageable pieces, the touring lasted longer than in previous years. It extended into the winter months and in some ways the entire procedure was becoming more of an ordeal than a party. Bad weather and bad health (including a broken collarbone for Fingers Taylor, who slipped on some ice while touring through Washington) plagued the band and the crew, almost as if to warn the warm-blooded caravan that venturing northward in midwinter was a perilous proposition.

When the touring finally ended, Buffett tried to normalize things once again by returning to his traditional annual routine. A major factor in formulating this point of view must have been that his favorite part of the schedule was due up. Buffett usually did most of his writing in the spring and summer while vacationing, so by getting things back on track, he could do what needed to be done and also spend some quality time with his family. Earlier, he had decided to unload the unwieldy *Euphoria II* for something a bit more manageable, and a smaller, twenty-six-foot, custom-built, sloop-rigged sailboat was prepared for their use. To maintain the integrity of the boat's original design, there is no engine aboard. The family vacationed on the *Savannah Jane,* named after Buffett's daughter, while Jimmy occasionally searched for his muse and drew a song or two from the well. Because he was now writing in the presence of his family, it was to have a significant effect on his outlook, and you could hear the familial influence in the topics covered on his upcoming album.

While he wrote and sailed with his family, *Urban Cowboy* hit the theaters in June 1980. Starring John Travolta and Debra Winger, the film featured a Jimmy Buffett recording written by Brian Collins and Robby Campbell, and produced by Buffett himself, called "Hello Texas." The movie was a hit through the summer, and the soundtrack did just as well, reaching number 3 on the album charts. "Hello Texas" was the leadoff track on side one of the double soundtrack album, and that makes for a much better way to appreciate the song. Buffett's recording is a credible version of a country-rock dance tune, but the film uses it solely as a backing track for a barroom dance late in the movie. In September, the Coral Reefers were reunited in Sheffield, Alabama, for the next album's recording sessions. Most recording was done at the Muscle Shoals Sound Studio (but without the famed Muscle Shoals session players, as Jimmy brought in his own band), with some additional recording taking place at Quadrophonic Studios in Nashville and Bennett House in Franklin, Tennessee. Once again, the sessions were produced by Norbert Putnam, who also happened to be the owner of Bennett House.

Coconut Telegraph (1981)

MCA Records MCA-5169

If ever there was an album to demonstrate how tastes may change, this is it. *Coconut Telegraph* is another in a never-ending series of albums that makes me realize just how transitory some negative opinions can be. Given enough time, most of us will eventually come to realize some aspect of a work that we previously overlooked, and learn to like, or at least appreciate, music that we initially disdained.

That being said, my first reaction on hearing *Coconut Telegraph* was one of consternation. After playing the album through, I couldn't believe I was listening to a Jimmy Buffett record. I considered running back to the record store to get my money back but decided to keep the album anyway, just in case anybody cared to hear what had become of Jimmy Buffett. Being out of touch with contemporary styles is one thing but here, he sounds outright antiquated. Listening to the record a second time, I thought that maybe I cared more about how it sounded than the artist responsible for making it. In short, I felt ripped off and it made me angry that my trust had been so abused.

It didn't help matters that contemporary styles had conditioned my tastes toward music of a more immediate and gritty nature. In the cover photo, Buffett's lack of stylishness made him appear to be not casual but dorky, and the vinyl inside contained evidence that he was turning into Mel Tormé. Like so many other people in 1980, I preferred to hear music with an energetic edge, and Buffett sounds so laid-back you'd think he has the covers pulled up over his head. Even the gray-toned artwork that decorated the album package left me flat. The custom-designed black-on-white record labels appeared so bland that at first glance I thought I had accidentally obtained a promotional copy. At its worst, it all seemed like a bad joke.

Quite frankly, I was judging the album from a perspective that was completely irrelevant to the intentions of the artist. After all, a mildly pleasant collection of superficially introspective and thoroughly romanticized pop was not exactly your typical fare for early to mideighties culture but it was exactly what Buffett does best. In an honest moment, I would wonder why the record bugged me so much. Over time, I'd return to it and, little by little, I even began to enjoy the damn thing. I could still recognize a number of things that horrified me initially: the crooning, the middle-of-the-road posturing, the elaborate piano intros, the ornate prettiness of it all, the sobering lack of a rebellious perspective . . . all of that, but something else began to creep through. Just as I was no longer a teenager with a teenager's interests, Jimmy was no longer the rebelliously indifferent outsider. It was time for a new perspective. He had a wife and daughter now, and if ever there were circumstances that would modify your behavior and change your outlook, then believe me, having a family is it. As I came to understand that, *Coconut Telegraph* began to sound better and better.

Mostly, I think it was the unabashed romanticism that initially repulsed me but as I began to get over it, I found that I was also getting into it. His take on John Wayne's death in "Incommunicado" (written with backing singer Deborah McColl and percussionist M. L. Benoit), with its geographical references to the mystery character Travis McGee from the work of author John McDonald, splits reality and fantasy and drops you on a line somewhere between the two. Mac McAnally's "It's

My Job" is sweeter than marzipan, but if you don't mind the lack of nutrients and catch it at the right moment, it can make you feel a little bit better about the menial events of an average workday. Worth noting is the reference to "an uncle who owns a bank, he's a self-made millionaire," for although Buffett didn't write the song, the implicit reference to his own (adopted) rich Uncle Warren would eventually be unavoidable. (Warren Buffett is an investment tycoon whom Jimmy had befriended, and because of their shared name, Jimmy refers to him as "Uncle" Warren.)

"Growing Older but Not Up" is the song that I found myself humming continuously despite myself, and I find that I am now in awe of the well-metered phrasing ("My metabolic rate is pleasantly stuck") and a few of the clever lyrical couplets ("Crack went my leg like the shell of an egg, someone call a decent physician"). "The Weather Is Here, Wish You Were Beautiful" was problematic for a while longer, not only because of the implicit sexism but more because of its deliberate cleverness. Starting off with some seemingly irrelevant staged dialogue revolving around the daily headaches of fronting a band, it eventually evolves into a tale of escapism that takes on a glow almost as brilliant as the melody that contains it. The song that I least expected to like but now find to be the album's highlight is "Stars Fell on Alabama." This chestnut dates all the way back to 1934 and though you may suspect that it has no business on a Jimmy Buffett album, his crooning is so convincingly natural that you'd think the song was custom-made for him.

Even the less extraordinary songs now manage to hold their own. "Coconut Telegraph" and "The Good Fight" have both rebounded from my intense scrutiny and prejudgment. "Island" (cowritten with Dave Loggins) has slowly revealed itself to be yet another inspiring chronicle of introspection that Buffett does so well, and "Little Miss Magic" gives me something to relate to since the birth of my own first son, who was also "constantly amazed by the blades of the fan on the ceiling." This last song probably holds the key to my almost schizophrenic about-face regarding this album. My own circumstances had changed, so I was now more capable of relating to this material. Most of it was written while Buffett spent time with his own family, and it shows through the work. Before, this meant nothing to me, but that changed as my own life changed.

It may have taken me a very long time to come to terms with this album, but now I think that I get it. Nowadays, I think of *Coconut Tele-*

graph as Buffett's first "designated driver" album. Whereas on *A1A* he sounded like the type of guy you might have to carry home after the party was over, here he sounds like the guy you'd give the car keys. I can relate to that now. Despite my initial reservations, I now feel that there isn't a bum track on the album. Go figure.

Something else was taking place here as well that at the time was much less apparent. With Buffett chronicling his life as truthfully as he ever had, he lost a few fans who would have preferred for him to remain the same, but more important, he began to accrue a life's work that told the story of a man in a constant state of transition. For fans willing to accept the artist's changes, that is a priceless commodity, because his life and his work become inseparable. No longer a one-trick pony, Jimmy Buffett began to see things from both sides, and he began to develop a catalog of songs that, by the nature of their differing perspectives, contained contradictory points of view. For longtime Buffett fans, *Coconut Telegraph* is where you could determine your level of commitment to the artist. It's just as personal, maybe even more so, than previous outings and his unrelenting perspective seems to be saying, "Take me as I am or don't bother to take me at all. Your call." That's a fairly irresistible attitude and that is why I now think that this album is unintentionally more responsible than any other for the transformation that would eventually turn mere fans into Parrot Heads. If you could follow Jimmy this far, then you could follow him anywhere. It's no longer simply about the music, it's the whole shebang.

You know, it's been a while, maybe I should go back and relisten to *Havaña Daydreamin'*. . . .

Coconut Telegraph debuted in February 1981 and peaked at number 30 during its eighteen-week chart appearance. "It's My Job" was elected to be the corresponding single and appeared simultaneously with the album but stalled at number 57 during a paltry eight-week run on Billboard's Hot 100 singles chart. It would be Jimmy Buffett's last release to qualify as a hit single. MCA's days of attempting to establish him as a singles artist were unofficially over. All of Buffett's ten singles charted on Billboard between 1974 and 1981. Since then, there has never been another. One was in the Top Ten ("Margaritaville," of course), and four more spent some time in the Top Forty. It wasn't exactly a stellar chart record for such a renowned artist, but singles aren't what mattered to Buffett's fans. No hits meant no airplay, but this also didn't affect Buffett as negatively as it would seem. His concerts continued to draw dedicated crowds and this recognition was enough to keep him in the public eye and helped to sell a substantial number of albums.

As time wore on, his fans were becoming more interested in the subject of their affection than his music, anyway. His catalog continued to sell well, but music was merely a fraction of Buffett's long-standing appeal. Now that styles had changed, Buffett was more of a lifestyle artist than ever and as long as he continued to be himself, he would continue to have a loyal fan base. His management still had visions of grandeur, however, and MCA was pushed to manufacture more records than it probably should have. Distributors were given more product then they needed, which only resulted in an abundance of returned product from the retailers. When *Coconut Telegraph* and its follow-up, *Somewhere Over China,* turned out to be only modest sellers, there was a huge quantity of leftover albums that ended up in bargain bins all across the United States.

In early 1981, Buffett began dedicating his own time and effort to help save the manatee. For anybody who might be unfamiliar with this ocean-dwelling mammal, a manatee has the face of a walrus, is almost as huge as a hippopotamus, as peaceful as a deer, as slow as a turtle, and as graceless as a cow. In fact, they are commonly referred to as sea cows. Although their sudden appearance above the surface can be quite startling or even terrifying, they are harmless and usually even friendly. Unfortunately, nature did not prepare the manatee for technology. Before powerboats became as ubiquitous in Florida's waters as oranges are in its groves, the manatee thrived. The introduction of the propeller-driven boat and its subsequent popularity proved dangerous to the very existence of the manatee. Because they are huge and slow and tend to hover just beneath the water's surface, manatees are sitting ducks, so to speak, for any powered vessel that happens to come along. Carcasses mauled by propeller blades have become a fairly predictable sight, and it is rare to find a living manatee that doesn't carry the scars of a previous encounter.

Governor Bob Graham had previously met Buffett (when he presented him with the *A1A* plaque), and he decided to confront him to ask for Buffett's support in helping to publicize the plight of this regional mammal. After one of his Florida shows, the two met and discussed the problem at hand. Because Buffett's sympathy for the manatee had become public knowledge, and because he was also an advocate of wind power with an aversion to powerboats, especially regarding their abuse, he agreed to help. Shortly afterward, Buffett announced his intention to check the senseless slaughter, and set to work organizing a nonprofit committee. Teaming up with the state-run Department of Natural Resources, Jimmy set out to help save the manatee.

"What we're seeing now is an increase in irresponsible boat operators," Buffett told a television interviewer. Numerous public appearances followed while he spoke at length about the manatee and what could be done to save it. Revenues from concerts and T-shirt sales were contributed to the cause. He even bought property in north-central Florida, placing him close to Tallahassee and the natural habitat of the manatee. To add yet another address to his real estate collection, he also bought property on the Caribbean island of Saint Martin. (This, by the way, was in addition to his property in Colorado, Key West, and the French Mediterranean.)

In a few years, political agendas would intervene on the simple purity of trying to do the right thing, particularly when the Audubon Society and the Manatee Committee (which for one reason or another was controlled by the Audubon Society) began to feud. Accusations of misguided intentions also clouded the issue, particularly when rumors arose suggesting that the impetus for Buffett's agreeing to assist Graham was to have Buffett's appalling driving record cleared. Without being pedantic about this, I think it is only fair to note that Buffett's long-term commitment to the cause has been unswerving and that he has gained little or nothing from this commitment.

Summer writing, fall recording, and a winter album release meant only one thing: a spring tour. Besides his Florida shows, which included a benefit gig in Key West for the local Arts Center, Buffett toured the Northeast, including a few shows in New York City. Then it was back to the schedule of summer writing followed by a fall recording session. This time, all recording was done at Norbert Putnam's Bennett House, with Putnam once again producing the sessions as he has for every album since *Changes in Latitudes, Changes in Attitudes.* The band consisted of the predictable but welcome Michael Utley (all keyboards), Greg Fingers Taylor (harmonica), and Harry Dailey (bass), with Barry Chance once again playing guitar along with new member Josh Leo. Matt Betton and M. L. Benoit handled drums and percussion, respectively.

Somewhere Over China (1982)

MCA Records MCA-5285

Well, there's not much sense in beating around the bush on this one. While *Coconut Telegraph* at least offered up the promise of something to believe in, this album seems to be withholding vital information from the listener. I couldn't help but notice that Buffett's recent material was drifting further and further away from topics that would be of interest to his core fan base. On *Somewhere Over China,* he seems to be tackling material that doesn't mean much to him, either. The album is filled with exoticisms that could potentially titillate and engage the listener, but instead they only serve to distract us from the real problem of the record, which is Buffett's sudden unwillingness to be forthright.

With *Somewhere Over China,* it's almost as though Buffett would rather not tell us what was really on his mind, so he decides to serve up a couple of pleasantries and nonsequiturs to distract us from his personal issues. Buffett is certainly inclined to keep his personal life away from the limelight, yet marital difficulty is an unavoidable subtext to this entire album. To avoid the issue, he vainly attempts to distract the listener, but it doesn't work, particularly because the troublesome overtones begin immediately on the album's first two tracks. "Where's the Party" is a moody piece about everybody expecting too much of him.

Although he doesn't deny that he probably would be the right guy to ask the title question, he also makes it plain that there are moments when he'd rather not be bothered with such trivialities. He also cleverly slips in the line "Sometimes I wish the radio would learn another song," and I can't blame him, because he certainly wasn't getting much airplay at the time. "It's Midnight and I'm Not Famous Yet" is next up, and it deepens the sense of foreboding that hovers about the proceedings. Besides its too-late-in-the-game overtures to new wave styles, the minor key menace of the song further alienates listeners and prevents them from enjoying the party. Though you would never guess it by listening, both of these songs were cowritten with Steve Goodman.

"I Heard I Was in Town" attempts to rectify things by reminiscing about the old days of hanging around Key West. Not that I expect Jimmy Buffett to stand in one place for the rest of his life, but at least this song gives us what we had come to expect from him. Still, though, the title could also be interpreted as a slight dig to all the rumor-mongers who plague him with questions concerning his whereabouts. The biggest surprise comes next, when he tries to entertain us with a nonautobiographical story about the Orient. Technically speaking, "Somewhere Over China" is a very well arranged song, but the ploy is too obvious for the listener to miss, so the forced exoticisms of the vibraphone and the Chinese gong sound vapid if not outright annoying. Side two picks up the exotic theme with "When Salome Plays the Drum." Here, we find that he is still avoiding the subject at hand by leaning on instrumental tricks and exotic story lines, hoping to distract us from the all-too-obvious fact that he is no longer reflecting on his own life.

Now, I realize that every artist is entitled to his privacy, and that some things are better kept out of the public eye, but Jimmy Buffett's fans had grown accustomed to expect annual updates on his state of affairs. Of course, we all must realize that his albums contain songs, not pages from a diary, but these circumstances are those that were established by Buffett himself. When an album is loaded with distractions and the songs that do seem to be autobiographical are either moody or dull, you're bound to disappoint those who came in with certain expectations. That is why it is disturbing to hear a song as maliciously derogatory as "Lip Service" or as bland as "If I Could Just Get It on Paper" on a Jimmy Buffett album. The former makes us wonder why he is no longer singing about marital bliss; the latter at least manages to resemble the

> old-style method of giving us a straightforward account on his recent doings. Still, it is a monumentally safe revelation, doing nothing more than expressing his rekindled ambition to write prose.
>
> Like *Living and Dying in 3/4 Time, Somewhere Over China* ends with two songs not penned by Buffett; one reminiscent of better days with overtones of regret and the other absolutely ridiculous. "Steamer" is a gorgeous mood piece that could be about time's effect on true love, and "On a Slow Boat to China" is reason to leave the room before the record ends. Bluntly put, bad lounge music is not something to emulate, and it makes for lousy parody, too. The only justification for its inclusion here is its thematic link to the title song, but even then, it only makes us wonder what might have been going on behind the scenes while we were distracted by this puppet show. Perhaps it is an aberration, but *Somewhere Over China* is a bum trip. Hopefully next time, Buffett will stay a little bit closer to home.

For a less than extraordinary album by a less than cutting-edge artist, *Somewhere Over China* didn't fare all that poorly. In fact, its chart position was fairly identical to its predecessor, reaching number 31 as compared with *Coconut Telegraph's* number 30 position. The tour to support *Somewhere Over China* brought the Coral Reefer Band a bit farther afield than previous perambulations. In addition to stateside shows in typical whistle stops such as Baton Rouge, Nashville, and Colorado, where he played to assist John Denver's antinuclear Windstar organization, the tour wended its way to the mid-Pacific for a few shows in Hawaii. While there, Jimmy took advantage of an offer to visit Tahiti, and he thought enough of the exotic locale to plan an extended vacation. Now, instead of the usual Caribbean ports of call, he had a whole new ocean to explore. While there, he was able to turn down the typical whirlwind pace of his life and return to a more organic style of songwriting; it was at this time that he penned "One Particular Harbour."

When he returned to the real world, a number of projects were waiting for him. Miller Beer had implemented a new advertising campaign and Buffett was recruited to sing a jingle on behalf of its product, prompting him to state, "This is the closest thing I've had to an AM hit in five years." Another Irving Azoff film project was developing as well (the *FM* and *Urban Cowboy* soundtracks were Azoff's work, too), so once again Buffett was asked to contribute a song. Written by *Rolling Stone* journalist Cameron Crowe and directed by Amy Heckerling, *Fast Times at Ridgemont High* hit theaters in 1982. Along with such artists as the Go-Gos and Jackson Browne, the soundtrack featured a Jimmy Buffett/Michael Utley composition called "I Don't Know (Spicoli's Theme)," based on the film's lead character as played by a very young and convincingly burned-out Sean Penn. To be honest, it barely sounds like a Buffett song at all and in the film itself, this new wave–tinged song appears only briefly and in a highly edited form.

Earlier in the year, Jimmy had paid a visit to Elizabeth Ashley, who was working on the set of *All My Children,* and he surprised viewers (perhaps maybe even shocked them, if they were fans) by doing a short walk-on appearance. At about the same time, strange goings-on were taking place down in Buffett's old haunt.

It appears that Key West had been targeted by the Reagan administration for a crackdown in its war on drugs, and all hell was breaking loose. Roadblocks were erected and traffic was snarled for miles while the feds hassled tourists and residents alike with equal disregard to their civil rights. In the tradition of true red-blooded southern Americans, Key West revolted, announcing that it was withdrawing from the union and declaring war on the United States! All hail the newly founded Conch Republic!

On a more grounded note, Buffett took some time in August to attend the William Faulkner Yoknapatawpha Conference, an annual gathering that celebrated the writings of the famed southern novelist. Anybody who has listened to Buffett's lyrics, with so many various literary references, could tell that the man was a well-read songwriter, and now his own ambitions to pen prose were beginning to rise to the surface. Being from Mississippi, Buffett felt a certain geographical kinship with the author. The song "If I Could Just Get It Down on Paper," from *Somewhere Over China,* not only mentions Faulkner but also displays the songwriter's own yearnings to write something of consequence. At the conference, Buffett took the opportunity to announce that he was working on his own short story called "Evening in Margaritaville," which he was proud to have finished while sitting at Faulkner's very own desk—or at least he thought he had finished it.

"Evening in Margaritaville" was intended to be the story of an atypical "day in the life" based on his own Key West experiences. Barry Hannah was an author-friend Buffett met at the Yoknapatawpha Conference who was recruited to help round out the story line. Soon enough, it was also delivered into the hands of humorist and political correspondent P. J. O'Rourke, who worked on a second draft of the script. O'Rourke was a satirist for the *National Lampoon* magazine who went on to work as the right-wing political editor at *Rolling Stone* magazine, a position that flanked none other than the now low-profile Hunter Thompson and resident leftist William Greider. In time, O'Rourke would be publishing his own humorous travelogues and political observations, such as *Holidays in Hell* and *Parliament of Whores* (both make for great reading, by the way).

Plans existed to turn "Evening in Margaritaville" into a major motion picture release, but such ambition meant that an unusual number of people would end up sticking their fingers into the pie. In time, it would be hard to tell whose pie it was, or even what type of pie it was supposed to be. While Buffett was marketing his script for "Margaritaville" (in one of the rewrites, the title was simplified) he also was compiling a collection of short stories and miscellaneous odds and ends under the working title of *My African Friend and Other Stories*. He intended this to be his first book.

In March 1983, Buffett's connection with the Audubon Society (through the Save the Manatee organization) led to his being teamed up with Walt Disney Productions to help save the dusky sparrow. Apparently, Florida's rapid economic expansion had taken its toll on the creature and no female members of the species could be found anywhere. Disney provided funding and scientific assistance to mate the males with a close sparrow-type relative to propagate a near-identical species, while Buffett performed a benefit concert to raise more money for and increase awareness of the efforts being made on behalf of the dwindling breed. Later in the year, he played another interesting gig in Florida, this time at his old friend Vic Latham's newly refurbished Full Moon Saloon. For an evening, it was almost like old times, except now the crowds were overflowing into the street and out beyond the curb, while everybody in town craned their necks trying to get a glimpse of the now famous but not-quite native son.

By mid-1983, there were so many distractions taking place in Jimmy

Buffett's life that he felt compelled to temporarily disband the Coral Reefers. Fingers Taylor in particular felt the need to take some time away from the dangerously high-strung pace of nonstop partying that usually encompasses life on the road. He took his temporary dismissal as a chance to enter a rehabilitation clinic, hoping to get rid of a few vices that had turned into habits. He also poured much of his energy into organizing sessions for his first solo album, a bluesy burner of a record called *Harpoon Man,* released in 1984. With Fingers absent, Jimmy's stage show meanwhile relied on a cardboard replica of his sidekick that was attached to a spring mechanism causing it to pop up whenever a prerecorded Fingers solo would roll around.

For a while, the "classic" lineup of Fingers Taylor, Barry Chance, Mike Utley, Harry Dailey, and Debbie McColl would be waylaid. He took this opportunity to focus on his movie script and the *African Friend* collection while continuing to write songs for his upcoming album. At the same time, lawsuits began to break out on all fronts. Richard F. Buckley, the son of Lord Buckley, decided to sue Jimmy Buffett for defamation of his father's work, because he felt it was inappropriate for Buffett to use swear words while performing a piece of theater based on drinking yourself into oblivion ("God's Own Drunk"). Buffett even wrote a hysterical little ditty about the experience, entitled "The Lawyer and the Asshole" (with a chorus that goes "Kiss my ass, kiss my ass, kiss my ass"). He'd occasionally sing this number in concert, to rapturous applause. The lawsuit was even more ridiculous than the song-story it was based on, and the case was dropped in 1985.

Most notable of the legal tribulations was Irving Azoff's ongoing feud with MCA, which he accused of being so inept that it didn't even constitute a working record label so therefore had welched on its end of the bargain to act in his client's best interests. Jimmy was warned that he should prepare a final release, which had the tentative title of *My Dog Ate My Homework and Other Great Excuses.*

MCA tried desperately to hold on, but the tenacious and unyielding style of Irving Azoff acted like sandpaper on wood, and soon there was little will left on the part of MCA to fight back. Amazingly, by the end of the year, Azoff himself would be named president of the label. For Buffett, this meant the elimination of the middleman, so to speak, and now nothing stood between him and the label responsible for promoting him. Azoff's organization would still handle Buffett, but day-to-day responsibilities would come to be handled by Nina Avrimedes at HK Management. Now that Azoff was overseeing not only the Nashville operation but the whole kit and caboodle, the time had come for Buffett to make peace with the town that once spurned him. His perspective had gradually changed about the town anyway, because Nashville now represented a style of music that was much more closely linked to his own. Nashville never fell victim to the disco, punk, or even the new wave craze, and he felt firmly ensconced in the womb of a town that was now glad to have him around.

His next album for MCA would have an overriding Polynesian theme with a subtle undercurrent of various other styles. The artwork and Polynesian lyrics of the title tune would reflect his time spent in Papeete, Tahiti. In the liner notes, Jimmy would thank his "former manager," Irving Azoff, and an insert would offer rough translations of the title song's chorus, as follows:

Ia ora te natura
E mea arofa teie ao nei
Ia ora te natura
E mea arofa teie ao nei
Ua pau te maitai no te fenua
Te zai noa ra te ora o te mitie

translated as

Nature lives (life to nature)
Have pity for the earth (love the Earth)
Bounty of the land is exhausted
But there's still abundance in the sea

One Particular Harbour (1983)

MCA Records MCA 5447

For those who are not intimately familiar with the vast minutiae within Parrot Head culture, it should be noted that a certain rebellious group exists within the circle that tends to dismiss everything released

after 1979 as subpar, overproduced, or redundant. They call themselves GOPs, for "Grumpy Old Parrot Heads," and revel in the earlier albums such as *A1A* and *Havaña Daydreamin'* while lamenting most of his later work. Well, I have news, because their inflexible predisposition just may be preventing them from appreciating one of Jimmy Buffett's best records ever. *One Particular Harbour* happens to be as classic as Buffett gets and might even qualify as his most musical album to date.

Circumstances surrounding the making of this album would indicate the exact opposite tendency. First of all, it was not made in one marathon session at one particular locale, as earlier albums usually were. Although this procedure could give the earlier albums a sense of cohesiveness, it also meant that things had to be completed within a certain time frame. For *One Particular Harbour,* Buffett recorded as he went along, recording a track here and a track there in a piecemeal fashion until he compiled enough for an album. These sessions took place at a time in his life when distractions were immense, so for the first time in his career, Buffett took the better part of a year to compile this finished product.

Considering the haphazard circumstances, the results are astonishing. Not only is the record cohesive, but the musicianship and production are well above par. This is made all the more remarkable by the fact that the Coral Reefer Band wasn't on hand to assist with the recording, and that Buffet decided to handle the production chores himself, along with keyboardist Mike Utley. Replacing the Coral Reefers are an assorted bunch of studio cats such as Russ Kunkel (drums), Earl Klugh and Josh Leo (guitars), Bob Glaub and Timothy B. Schmit (bass), and Sam Clayton of Little Feat (congas). It might sound crazy, but their work here proves beyond a shadow of a doubt that they can handle the material at least as well as Buffett's regular band (a sacrilegious thing to say to the GOPs, you can be sure), and that sometimes the artist can be his own best producer. Sure, you miss the Coral Reefer Band a little, particularly Fingers Taylor, but the change of pace is refreshing and the overall professionalism and beauty of the results simply cannot be denied.

A Rodney Crowell song called "Stars on the Water" kicks things off, and its limber pace and atmospheric production set the appropriate mood for this excellent record. The second track, however, is the sore thumb cut of the album. Like "Fool Button" was to *Son of a Son of a Sailor,* they both stand out for all the wrong reasons. "I Used to Have Money One Time," disappoints because its inherent silliness overshadows whatever Buffett may have intended by writing a song about losing his financial stability. I can't figure out his inspiration for penning this white lie, but at least it makes me laugh out loud when the backing chorus (which includes Bonnie Bramlett and Rita Coolidge) sings "Bubba used to have money one time." "Living It Up" marks a Buffett first because it is almost completely synthesized, including the incongruous presence of a drum machine, yet the song still manages to sound organic without disrupting the pleasant melody. Speaking of organically pleasant melodies, Steve Goodman's "California Promises" is downright beautiful in its presentation, representing a high-water mark for this wonderful songwriter. Goodman would pass away the following year, succumbing to his longtime battle with leukemia, but "California Promises" stands as a testament to the man who is remembered mostly for writing what is perhaps the best railroad song of all time, "City of New Orleans."

Cover songs on the album include Art Neville's "Why You Wanna Hurt My Heart" and Van Morrison's "Brown Eyed Girl," with varying results. Neville's song sounds about as natural as if Buffett had written it himself, but it is hard to feel the same about "Brown Eyed Girl." Being a lifelong Van Morrison fan, it goes against my grain to praise an alternate version of a recording that was already perfect, but I must admit that Buffett's version remains true to the original recording and that his performance is full of energy and heartfelt vigor.

"One Particular Harbour" is the album's centerpiece, and its scope is anthemic in its reach. Containing Tahitian words in the chorus, this song is a feast for people who can sing along phonetically. With its dreamy lyrics, lilting melody, and rhythmic shifts, it might qualify as the best beach song he's ever written. Another masterpiece here is "12 Volt

Man." The song is one of my all-time favorite Buffett songs, with a Polynesian sound that reminds me of my parents' old "Adventures in Paradise" records which I loved so much as a wee 'un.

"We Are the People Our Parents Warned Us About" is his latest in a series of thoroughly catchy, irreverent, and autobiographical songs, and "Honey Do" takes a humorous and nostalgic look at time spent alone. The implication of the lyrics could even be stretched to include a date with the "hairy palm"—not a subject that Hoagy Carmichael (to whom it is dedicated) would have been very likely to cover, I'm sure. From today's perspective, it is interesting to note how "We Are the People . . ." has changed in its relevance. Now that Jimmy and many of his followers are parents themselves, the axiom has shifted a bit. Now, it's more as though we are the aging parents that we'd never imagined we'd one day become. What goes around usually comes around, so perhaps our kids will sing this to *us* one day.

The album's last track gives us a disarmingly candid look at Buffett's marriage. "Distantly in Love" speaks of the difficulties that can plague a long-distance love relationship and the damage that can be done when too much time is spent apart. With its confessional tone and honest depiction of resignation, it stands as one of the most painfully beautiful things he has written.

So don't be swayed by well-intentioned fans who try to steer you away from Jimmy Buffett's midperiod work. If you want to hear consistently excellent songwriting and recordings that flaunt the spit and polish of some first-class production work, not to mention an adept and limber band that plays as sharp as nails, then *One Particular Harbour* is an excellent place to start.

One Particular Harbour was released in October 1983 and went no higher than number 59, although it did spend a full twenty-four weeks on the album charts. It was his best album in years, but where was the audience? Musical tastes continued to shift in a direction that led away from where Jimmy Buffett was headed, but he was going to stay the course and weather the changes. The mid-eighties crunch that hit the record industry was particularly cruel to MCA, and many artists who had hoped for better instead found that their tenure had come to an end. With Irving Azoff in the president's chair, Buffett was safer than most and had even gained a certain amount of freedom from this turn of events. Because his ex-manager ran the label, Buffett had a bit more leeway to try something different, which would have explained his confident attempt to produce his own record along with his decision to record that album at a relaxed and meticulous pace. He also fared well from an agreement with his old producer, Buzz Cason, whereby his Writer's Group USA would now handle a large piece of Buffett's publishing.

The time that he gained by reducing his workload and disbanding the Coral Reefers was spent working on writing projects. Ex-Monkee Mike Nesmith was soon brought in as a production consultant for the much-abused *Margaritaville* script and finally, it seemed as though things were falling into place and the project would get off the ground. At the time, Nesmith was also working as an executive producer for a truly strange film called *Repo Man.* This connection led to Buffett being offered the tiny role of a slick and shady "blond agent" in a script that called for seven of them. His one speaking line ("Hey happy face, wanna ride?") passes in the blink of an eye, but I couldn't help but be amused to see Buffett in a movie that featured the Circle Jerks, Black Flag, and Iggy Pop on the soundtrack.

Another pairing between Buffett and Nesmith would take place in 1985. *Doctor Duck's Super Secret All-Purpose Sauce* was an often hilarious collection of comedy skits, interspersed with a few music videos. The skits feature the comedic talents of Whoopi Goldberg, Gary Shandling, Jerry Seinfeld, Bobcat Goldthwait, and Jay Leno, and the musical guests include Buffett and Roseanne Cash. Buffett is represented here by "La Vie Dansante," one of his best songs but also one of the stupider videos I have ever seen (this was the mideighties, when almost all videos were pretty stupid).

Every time Buffett made a public announcement regarding a potential release date for *Margaritaville,* something went awry and new setbacks would descend on the project. The gist of the script consisted of a series of loosely connected barroom tales from a mythical island known as "Margaritaville," largely based on Buffett's own experiences during his Key West heyday. The story had gone through too many changes, though, and it became increasingly difficult for him to keep his project focused and on track. After a while, it was hard to tell if it was even *his* project anymore. Terry Southern (*The Blue Movie, The*

Magic Christian) was the next recruit to rewrite the script, "basing" it on Buffett's original ideas. Estimated release dates were no longer discussed. Instead, start-up dates became the issue, particularly because virtually all major Hollywood studios had lost interest in the project. For something to work in Hollywood, it must be fresh and appealing, but the *Margaritaville* script was beginning to resemble a week-old fish carcass. Opinions had congealed into a consensus that Buffett was an icon whose time had come and gone. If Hollywood refused to take the bait, then a whole new tack was necessary. The focus shifted from a major motion picture to a smaller independent film, or perhaps a cable movie with home video potential. The plot was once again restructured to suit the scaled-back ambitions, but enthusiasm began to wane until it vanished almost entirely. Buffett recognized the situation and elected to halt work on the movie, but to this day, the possibility exists that *Margaritaville—The Movie* will once again rear its head.

The shakeup at MCA that brought Irving Azoff to the top of the heap had a few other positive results, at least from Jimmy Buffett's perspective. In the early part of 1984, producer Jimmy Bowen was named head of the label's Nashville branch. Bowen was a hands-on manager who preferred the recording studio to the office. This rather cozy arrangement meant that Buffett would be guaranteed sufficient attention from the Nashville hierarchy; not that it would help much on the pop front, but Buffett was all but prepared to abandon the pop front anyway. The constant and unpredictable demand for newer, better, and faster that defined the pop marketplace caused him to feel estranged from that scene, and more than a little bit too old to remain an active player. It was a race that he knew he would eventually lose, and because things had worked out so swimmingly at MCA Nashville, he decided to play up the country aspect of his music. Besides, country music was gaining in popularity. Here, the target demographic was older, and he could do what he liked to do without looking foolish.

Bowen liked his work (his resumé as producer include a pair of huge but unlikely hits for Frank Sinatra—"Strangers in the Night" and "That's Life," and a hit for Dean Martin—"Everybody Loves Somebody") and hated to waste time, so it was only natural that he, as president of the Nashville operation, would become the producer for Jimmy Buffett's next project, along with Michael Utley and Tony Brown. In June, sessions were scheduled to record a few takes for the upcoming album. With Bowen driving the procedure along, this casual intent quickly resulted in formal album sessions. The entire album was recorded in less than one week. After the off-again, on-again methodology that defined work habits for the previous album, this was remarkable and unexpected, and the efficiency of the process suited Buffett just fine.

Riddles in the Sand (1984)

MCA Records MCA 5512

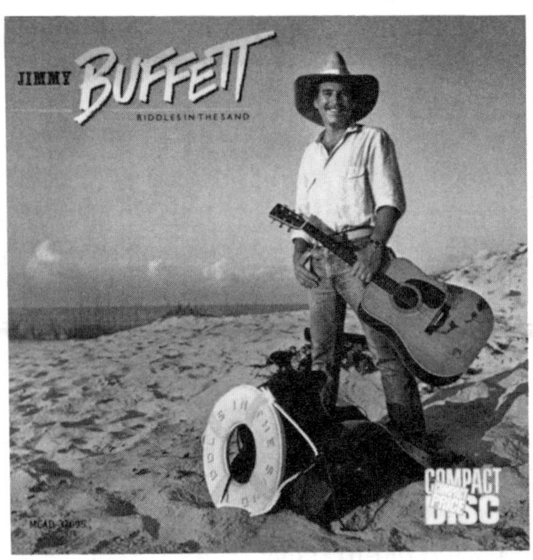

To my taste, nothing is worse than something that is boring. If you hate something, at least it provokes a reaction. It's the boring things that are dangerous because they allow you to let mediocrity slip by with such indifference that it can destroy your passion for whatever it is you once loved.

To use the word *boring* is a harsh assessment for any album, but this record almost qualifies.

The saving grace that prevents this album from falling completely through the cracks is Buffett's inability to give up. He may be exhausted and, as evidenced by the songwriting, he may be distracted by personal complications, but he at least still tries to make a good album out of it. Unfortunately, the blandness overwhelms the effort. Buffett's impending separation from his wife surfaces all over *Riddles in the Sand,* but since he is inclined to avoid relating any direct reference to what is on his mind, the album suffers. Instead, he seems more obsessed with creating an album that will hold its own with the Nashville crowd. The "Gulf-Western" thing is overly conspicuous and consciously played up to a fault—the term surfaces in the liner notes and in song lyrics (the fade-out of "Ragtop Day")—and the playful "cowboy-in-the-sand" photos on the cover make the Nashville flirtation a little bit too obvious.

All of his life Buffett has recorded music with blunted edges and, throughout his career, it has certainly served him well. Since his first album, his songwriting has taken all the prickly aspects of his life and smoothed them out, whittling away the pain and anger until it is safe and palatable. Most of his fans love him for it, but here it only gets in the way. On *Riddles in the Sand,* he's as unthreatening as ever, but his instincts fail him when he tries to convey the pain of a broken heart. It's something of a quandary when circumstances that would normally yield another artist's most compelling work only seem to stifle Buffett from expressing himself honestly and openly, but instead of sharing his circumstances, he becomes guarded. He appears to be less than truthful and once that happens, he has lost an essential ingredient to his continued popularity.

It is an oxymoron that Buffett's need to communicate ended up yielding his most emotionally muted album to date. With a broken heart to sing about, he disguises circumstances by placing them in silly settings or constructing characters who are less than three-dimensional. "Who's the Blonde Stranger" is a perfect case in point. It concocts a couple who unknowingly have simultaneous affairs, but instead of conveying the pain that this situation would normally yield, it treats marital infidelity as though it were a cute aberration. Just as bad is "Love in Decline," a shallow song that playfully relates three tales of spontaneous but empty sexual encounters.

Virtually every song on the record deals with infidelity, breakups, and restless or broken hearts. Even "Ragtop Day," which is mostly a fun and playful ode to a convertible, is ultimately a monologue about hiding his female companion from her husband, who passes in a station wagon loaded with kids. When he does try to look the circumstances head-on, all he can manage are sidelong glances at the truth. "Knees of My Heart" and "Burn That Bridge" both seek acquittal but are so cutesy and roundabout in their wordplay that they become vapid. "Knees of My Heart" is particularly awful, consisting of an inauthentic reggae rhythm that would be better suited for a Coke commercial, and "Burn That Bridge" is no better. These overly sweetened melodies with bummed-out lyrics sound like little more than well-preened confessions. If it's pain, then give me pain, dammit, not some bright-eyed calypso dance rhythms. The album's best song about resolution is "Come to the Moon" because the melody conveys the yearning in his heart. Even here, though, the silly commercialism of the lyrics dissolves his earnestness before it can strike a true chord.

The closest the album ever comes to touching a raw nerve is "When the Wild Life Betrays Me," a stock country weeper that could have sounded emotionally fraught but instead sounds benign. Why is this happening throughout the record? I can only hypothesize, but my bet is that the songs lose their impact because they were written by committee. Eight of the album's ten songs were written by the tag team of Jimmy Buffett, Michael Utley, and Will Jennings (one adds Josh Leo to the mix), and this style of writing can hamper the uniqueness gained from a single perspective. Heartbreak is something that you are destined to experience alone. If you have an idea for a song that is based on this fundamentally singular emotion, then ask others to temper your thoughts, the raw inspiration will become watered-down representations of the truth. If you hide behind a curtain, your frustrated audience will peek around it, and critics will simply tear it away.

It's telling that the most emotionally harrowing song on the album isn't written by Buffett at all but by Mac McAnally. "She's Going Out of My Mind" is very Buffett-esque in its lingual trickery, but that is where the similarity ends, because it conveys more emotion than you would normally expect from Buffett. Actually, it's more than emotional, it's morose. By song's end, the lead character is being driven to the psycho ward, for chrissakes! "Bigger Than the Both of Us" is a much better choice of a cover song (written by Rhonda Coullet). At least here the lyrics work from any point of the relationship spectrum, so long as you maintain faith in the overwhelming power of love. It doesn't contradict Buffett's optimism, so it is one of the most convincing tracks on the album.

The forced balance between country songs and Caribbean rhythms comes to an end on the album's last track, "La Vie Dansante." It also easily qualifies as the best song in the collection. Here, Buffett's lyrics attempt to justify his penchant for skimming the surface, and the anthemic quality of the song marks it as a statement of purpose. In its relevance to the overall package, it makes its point well enough to justify some of the near misses that precede it. *Riddles in the Sand* is an album about heartbreak sung by a man who would rather not be sharing his personal traumas with us. In thirty-five minutes, he shows us little, intimates plenty, and then wraps it all up with a fairly valid excuse.

5

The Late Eighties

Buffett's deliberate attempt to woo Nashville with *Riddles in the Sand* yielded three moderate hit singles for the country music charts ("When the Wild Life Betrays Me," "Bigger Than the Both of Us," and "Who's the Blonde Stranger"). All three were ignored by the pop charts. The album did only slightly better, reaching number 87 and then falling off after only fourteen weeks.

Perhaps this happened partially by design, especially because Buffett appeared to have less and less in common with what constituted a "pop" act and so concentrated his efforts elsewhere, but there was little doubt that these circumstances also caused him to see the handwriting on the wall. Few artists worked as consistently as Buffett did; whereas other artists took years to complete a record, he still managed to continue the breakneck pace of completing an album a year. Music remained his primary focus, but now there was no guarantee that it would be enough. He wasn't necessarily old, but he was no longer young. His choice of material and the topics he chose to write about reflected a mature perspective that was no longer in fashion. In short, things had changed and he needed to align himself in a place that would ensure his well-being. He needed to diversify, if he was to continue living the lifestyle to which he had become accustomed, so he searched for ways to broaden his interests.

Jimmy Buffett's efforts would soon enough bloom into a cash cow of astounding proportions but in the beginning, his intentions were fairly modest. The Margaritaville empire could all be traced back to the simple idea of manufacturing and distributing a few T-shirts.

Steve "Hobbit" Humphrey was a member of Buffett's road crew who is credited as the person responsible for setting the wheels in motion. Humphrey had seen previous T-shirt designs by an artist named Michael LaTona, and he brought them to the attention of his boss. Buffett liked the style and gave Humphrey the go-ahead to commission a few designs. LaTona came up with nearly a dozen, including the now classic "Margaritaville" shirt, as well as the "Honey Do," the "Cheeseburger in Paradise," and "Son of a Son of a Sailor" designs, which were considered by all parties to be adequate, if not tasteful, composites of the songs they represented.

With Buffett's approval and a minimal capital investment, the Caribbean Soul clothing line was launched. As business picked up, Jimmy's wife, Jane, would be recruited, along with designer-artist LaTona, to expand the T-shirt business to a full line of clothing. At first, Humphrey handled day-to-day operations from a garage in his home. Business was brisk, so the next logical step was to find an appropriate location for a retail outlet. Donna "Sunshine" Smith was an old friend of Buffett's from his Key West days. It was only too obvious that Key West would be chosen as the best place for a flagship store. Not only did it hold relevance to Buffett's personal history, but the always expanding tourist trade and the year-round temperate climate promised a better than average chance of success for the fledgling business.

After a short search, a location was established at No. 4 Lands End Village in Key West and the doors were opened in January 1985. Smith managed the "Margaritaville" store, selling Humphrey's T-shirts and rounding out the inventory with various knickknacks (jewelry, beach towels, maps, books, etc.). To draw further attention to Buffett's venture, the opening coincided with a Jimmy Buffett "feature" at the nearby Strand Theatre, as part of the "First Annual Margaritaville Film Festival." At regular intervals, the theater scheduled viewings of Buffett's music videos, promo films, and even the French documentary on Florida fly fishing for which Buffett supplied the original soundtrack music.

From the very beginning, sales at Margaritaville exceeded their most optimistic expectations. Not so much a matter of coincidence as of astute planning, the very first *Coconut Telegraph* newsletters coincided with the opening of the Margaritaville store. The first issues appeared in February 1985 and were distributed to the general public. To reach potential customers who couldn't travel to Key West but still yearned for Buffett-related paraphernalia, a mail-order business was established, based on the grassroots mailing lists from Humphrey's T-shirt sales. The initial mailing went to fewer than 700 recipients. It was a triumph of financial acumen that was unlike anything else that had yet existed in the pop music world. Whereas most fan clubs existed as close-knit circles with the implied purpose of generating interest in the artist and his work, Buffett's retail operation was about generating interest in the products being offered. This was no fan club. Instead, it was a semi-independent retail business that was headed by the artist responsible for establishing an almost mystical desire in his fans to be a part of the universe that he invented through his music. He created this imaginary place called Margaritaville, and the job of the business was to make this fantasy a bit more tangible, and a bit more lucrative.

Coconut Telegraph serves the dual purpose of being a newsletter and a catalog, generating complementary interests from both sides of the spectrum. The music aroused interest in the paraphernalia, and the paraphernalia increased interest in his catalog of songs. While fans read about upcoming albums, tour dates, and various other details of Buffett's career, their curiosity about how much it would cost to buy a colorful hat with a parrot on top would be piqued. In reverse, sales of the various products aroused a renewed interest in Buffett's original "product," his music. Buffett had become the mascot for his own organization. The effect was similar to the way that Walt Disney Productions waltzed out Mickey Mouse to promote its various ventures.

Buffett wasn't the only person who was working overtime for diversification. His song publisher and management continued to actively promote Buffett's material to Hollywood for soundtrack inclusion; their efforts earned him yet another film credit, this time Hal Ashby's adaptation of Neil Simon's *The Slugger's Wife.* From a critical perspective, the film was a hopeless bomb with a soundtrack from hell, mostly consisting of a very young Rebecca DeMornay singing atrocious versions of "Hungry Heart" and "Little Red Corvette," among other songs. These hair-raising performances were almost as amusing as watching a pouty

Michael O'Keefe slug a petulant Loudon Wainwright III (yes, the folk singer took an acting role in this picture) in the jaw. Buffett's "Ragtop Day" is used to accompany this scene in a truckstop diner, but its inclusion is peripheral at best.

In April 1985, the second issue of *Coconut Telegraph* made the first official mention of fans as "Parrot Heads." The story behind the term's genesis stated that it was derived from a bemused conversation between Buffett and the Eagles' bassist Tim Schmit. The band had just taken the stage for an afternoon concert at Cincinnati's King's Island Amphitheatre. Schmit looked out over the audience and couldn't help but comment on the colorful and sometimes bizarre audience attire. At first, he hypothesized that they looked like Deadheads, only more tropical, then perfected his observation, stating, "They're Parrot Heads!" By the end of that summer's *Last Mango in Paris* tour, the catchphrase would be an honest-to-goodness classification.

Last Mango in Paris (1985)

MCA Records MCA 5600

It's titles like this that give puns a bad name, and it's records like this that . . . wait a minute. Earlier, I alluded that any overt criticism is usually the result of simply not understanding the intent of the artist. I honestly believe that to be true, but what if the record at hand really is just plain bad? It reminds me of a story that I once heard told by comedian Bill Cosby. A person he knew justified his use of cocaine by claiming that it exaggerated his personality and made his character traits larger than life. Cosby responded by saying "Okay, but what if you're an asshole?" It's a funny retort and it's relevant to this album. I absolutely do not intend to infer anything about Buffett (as I write this, I see any chance that this book might have had of being sold at Margaritaville flying out the window). I have the impression that he is a genuinely fair-minded and all-round decent guy—only that *Last Mango in Paris* seems to take some of Buffett's worst *musical* traits and exaggerates them beyond the point of my comprehension. Simply put, the record strikes me as being too casually lighthearted and deliberate in its artlessness for serious consideration.

Last Mango in Paris sounds dumb by design. The production, handled once again by the team of Jimmy Bowen, Michael Utley, and Tony Brown, strives for a commercialism that upsets my ability to appreciate the record as anything other than "product." At its worst, *Last Mango in Paris* contains moments that are completely ignorant of music's power to be a soulfully creative and self-expressive force, and yet there are some really good songs on here! So what gives? How do you take valid material and botch it so badly? Why, for instance, do we need to hear Harrison Ford crack his whip à la Indiana Jones for a percussive effect on "Desperation Samba"? Is it because it adds musical value, or is it simply because Buffett knew him well enough to ask, and it struck him as a commercially hip thing to do? On "Gypsies in the Palace," why must we be subjected to a well-rehearsed discussion between Buffett and Glenn Frey, in which they share house-sitting tips? Does it justifiably increase our awareness of the song's lyrical value, or is it only a crass and hokey attempt to shove the premise down our throats? I know the intent was to add a humorous coda, but weren't the lyrics enough? When an album strives to be a success at the expense of valid musical ideas, I lose interest, or maybe I just fail to grasp the whole picture.

On *Last Mango in Paris,* Buffett once again teamed up with Michael Utley and Will Jennings for songwriting, only this time things are further complicated by employing additional writers to add their own two cents into the mix—if this were a poker game, there would be a small fortune in the pot. Marshall Chapman, Glenn Frey, and Timothy B. Schmit are all partially credited with assisting the first-string team.

The album begins and ends with two songs that partially credit Marshall Chapman as the songwriter, but I hear none of her spunky, blues-inflected influence on either of these songs. Instead, "Everybody's on the Run" drifts along aimlessly, telling us nothing except that people are busy these days, and the album's closer, "Beyond the End," should have been named "Over the Top." The production team attempts to salvage this disaster with huge, anthemlike strokes and in the process, they make everybody sound ridiculous. I have friends who swear that Roy Orbison is the best vocalist of all time, so out of kindness to them and to the memory of Orbison, I vow to never again mention the overwrought warbling that constitutes the "climactic" fade here. "The Perfect Partner" is one song written exclusively by Chapman (and the only solo-written song on the entire album), and although it is a better song than the other two, the gender switching and subject matter suit Buffett miserably.

The album's best songs are those that aren't choked to death by too many ideas. "Please Bypass This Heart" and "If the Phone Doesn't Ring, It's Me" don't overreach themselves or try to paint the entire universe in broad strokes (the album's liner notes quote Hemingway, saying "I am trying to make . . . a picture of the whole world"). Consequently, they succeed simply for what they are: well-written, country-influenced microcosms of a relationship on the rocks. Except for the beeping heart monitor at song's end (sigh), "Please Bypass This Heart" is a straightforward tune that candidly discusses cheating and its exhausting effects, and "If the Phone Doesn't Ring, It's Me" is much more serious than the humorous title suggests. Indeed, it may be one of the most hopeless songs in Buffett's entire catalog and is probably the closest that he ever comes to saying goodbye, at least on vinyl.

The song that should have been the album's strongest cut, though, is "Gypsies in the Palace." Typically clever lyrics with a bouncy and fun melody supported by crack musicianship should be more than enough reason to recommend this tune, yet the producers manage to blow it. Instead of letting it remain a *song*, they try to turn it into a "production," and sink it in the process. The opening dialog (Is that Jason Robards? If so, why isn't he credited?) is yet another unnecessary flourish in a song that is chock-full of them. Crowd sounds, ringing telephones, and party noise all jockey for top honors in their ability to distract us from enjoying the damn thing, and by song's end, they succeed. Instead of letting Jimmy Buffett handle the humor in the lyrics himself, the song is dressed up like the aural equivalent of Little Lord Fauntleroy going out on a big date.

The title song, "Last Mango in Paris" is a romanticized tribute to Tony Tarracino, the legendary proprietor of Key West's Captain Tony's Saloon. By some miracle, the song manages to survive the horrendous pun of the chorus and what remains is Buffett's umpteenth depiction of the joy that can be derived from following your dreams. Speaking of dreams, "Jolly

Man Sing" is perfectly successful in its quest to be a juvenile fantasy, so it sounds utterly out of place on an album that I assume is otherwise intended for grown-ups.

I don't *want* to dislike this album, believe me. It would be a lot easier if I were to just pretend that I liked it. That way, the readers would be happy. *Jimmy* might even be happy. Even my *publisher* would be more pleased. So, why don't I just shut up and write some gibberish about how *Last Mango in Paris* is a transitional album, or a good album under certain circumstances? Why don't I just state that it's fun to listen to, with lots of exciting guest stars? I don't know. I just want to tell the truth about my impressions. I've tried like hell to figure out a way to like this record. I've subjected my family to near-torture while I sat through dozens of listening sessions but I just can't seem to find my way around it. Why don't we assume that I was right in the first place when I said that I just don't get it, and then we can all move on? Thank you.

In 1985, Buffett appeared on the *Tonight Show* to discuss his latest business ventures and promote his new album, *Last Mango in Paris*. He also contributed a song called "Turning Around" to a Carl Reiner–produced film starring John Candy called *Summer Rental*. The music may have been his intended agenda, but conversation instead turned to the state of his marriage. Buffett was not one to talk freely with journalists about his personal affairs, yet here he was on national television explaining to Johnny Carson the reason behind the couple's separation and the terms of their relationship. He mentioned that he traveled to New York to meet his wife for a "date." Afterward, he might have regretted discussing details from his private life, but he left his audience with the distinct impression that although their marriage was unconventional there was still a great deal of love between the couple. Jane's involvement in Margaritaville was evidence enough that their marriage was more intricate than any hasty synopsis could adequately represent anyway.

Last Mango in Paris hit the record stores at the peak of summer in 1985. It marked the first time that Buffett had released an album in the midst of his most celebrated season. It climbed as high as number 53 and held on for twenty weeks before letting go. It was Buffett's first album to outperform the previous release since *Son of a Son of a Sailor*.

The downward trend he had been experiencing since *Volcano* started to turn around. Simultaneously, the interest in his back catalog was effectively strengthened. Early copies of *Last Mango in Paris* contained an entry form for a contest called "The Last Mango Cruise." Five winners would be randomly selected from all entries received. These five winners (with one guest each) would be treated to an all-expense-paid trip to Key West, the highlight being an intimate concert held exclusively for the winners. While helping to promote the album, this gesture had the ulterior motive of broadening the mailing list for the *Coconut Telegraph* newsletter. Jimmy's promotional activities were now kicked into overdrive. He decided to parlay his campaign into a few relatively obvious areas, that being a greatest hits collection and a concert video. Only a few months after the release of *Last Mango in Paris*, a greatest hits collection had hit the stores.

Songs You Know by Heart: Jimmy Buffett's Greatest Hit(s) (1985)

MCA Records MCA-5633

What a great title for a greatest hits collection, and because it's *Jimmy Buffett's* greatest hits that we're talking about, the parenthetical *s* is only too perfect. It blithely acknowledges that Buffett only had one song that could accurately be called a hit, but it also claims bragging rights due to his fans' ability to sing every song verbatim. All selected songs were culled exclusively from his first seven (post–Barnaby Records) studio albums (excluding *Havaña Daydreamin'*, which is overlooked entirely here) from 1973 through 1979 (before Buffett's sales slump). For obvious reasons this is the album with which newly recruited Parrot Heads often start.

The songs on this album follow. Reviews can be found earlier in the book in the reviews of the respective albums.

"Cheeseburger in Paradise" (*Son of a Son of a Sailor,* 1978)

"He Went to Paris" (*A White Sport Coat and a Pink Crustacean,* 1973)

"Fins" (*Volcano,* 1979)

"Son of a Son of a Sailor" (*Son of a Son of a Sailor,* 1978)

"A Pirate Looks at Forty" (*A1A,* 1975)
"Margaritaville" (*Changes in Latitudes, Changes in Attitudes,* 1977)
"Come Monday" (*Living and Dying in 3/4 Time,* 1974)
"Changes in Latitudes, Changes in Attitudes" (*Changes in Latitudes, Changes in Attitudes,* 1977)
"Why Don't We Get Drunk and Screw" (*A White Sport Coat and a Pink Crustacean,* 1973)
"Pencil Thin Mustache" (*Living and Dying in 3/4 Time,* 1974)
"Grapefruit–Juicy Fruit" (*A White Sport Coat and a Pink Crustacean,* 1973)
"Boat Drinks" (*Volcano,* 1979)
"Volcano" (*Volcano,* 1979)

Released at a time when CDs were rapidly replacing albums as the format of choice among consumers, *Songs You Know by Heart* may have gotten caught up in the shuffle of numerous rereleases and new products. Initially, the album sold sparsely and peaked at number 100, but over the years, sales would remain steady until it eventually became Buffett's bestselling album, with over two million copies sold. The self-promotional juggernaut continued when he taped a live 1985 appearance in Florida and then made it available for sale. Now Parrot Heads could take the party home with them.

Jimmy Buffett Live by the Bay (1986)

MCA Home Video

In certain critical corners I have heard it said that a Jimmy Buffett concert is not, in the traditional sense, a concert at all. Instead, it is viewed as a roving party, a mobile event (he refers to it as a circus) that provides a more-than-adequate excuse for like-minded revelers to join together in a warm, welcoming atmosphere where they can participate in inebriated singalongs. As for Jimmy himself, his role is considered to be like that of the ringleader at a circus. It's his job to set the right tone and provide the lead-in while the featured act provides the entertainment, only in this case, the audience is viewed as the center of attention. With *Jimmy Buffett Live by the Bay,* Buffett appears anxious to dismiss this cynical observation and prove himself and the Coral Reefers to be one hell of a live act. Before this video documentary ends, you will have to agree that Buffett deserves much more credit than the naysayers provide.

If there is just one thing that can be said unequivocally about Jimmy Buffett, it's that you cannot watch him perform for long without eventually being captivated by the guy. He enjoys himself too much, and the feeling simply becomes contagious. There are few people in the music industry who can handle themselves so naturally in front of a microphone, but he appears as comfortable onstage as most people would be in their own living rooms. No doubt about it, he's a showbiz natural. It's inescapable. Buffett's charm lies in the way he coaxes an entire audience into thinking that it is their job to entertain *him.* We love it when he is amused and nothing makes his audience happier than to see him smile. Even when you think that he's being insincere or just going through the motions, you want to see him laugh. He's just so damn charming, especially when he gets a rascally twinkle in his eye, and that's why I think that this video would be a good place for Parrot Heads to start if they are thinking of initiating someone into the fold.

With a version of the Coral Reefer Band that is deadly in its musical agility, *Live by the Bay* contains good-to-excellent versions of Buffett's best-known material. Accompanied by Fingers Taylor, he starts things off acoustically with a playful version of "Door Number Three." After being joined onstage by Michael Utley, Sam Clayton, and Robert Greenidge, he follows with a near-perfect rendition of "Grapefruit–Juicy Fruit." The only thing that prevents this from being as loose-limbed at it ought to be is Michael Utley, who at first seems to be a bit stiff. Once Tim Schmit, Josh Leo, Matt Betton, and Vince Melamed join in, everybody loosens up and the party is in full swing. The band kicks in hard for the chorus of "We Are the People Our Parents Warned Us About" and doesn't let up until Buffett calls for his midset break.

Josh Leo's energetic performance in particular deserves attention, especially when the band starts rocking. "Stars on the Water," "Coconut Telegraph," and "Ragtop Day" all feature top-notch riffing and tasty solos, so I can only wonder why it is that he's mixed so low. It's a fault that doesn't ruin the tape, but things surely would have benefited from a hotter guitar mix, especially because the playing befits a stronger presence, or at least one that is commensurate with his stage antics. Say what you will about Buffett's overuse of steel drums on his recent recordings, Robert Greenidge is a vital presence here also. He never gets in the way of the arrangements, instead colorizing them with just enough flair to give each song an appropriately exotic flavor. Even Utley eventually loosens up and adds some spice. He's no rocker (nor is Buffett, come to think of it) but his role in the overall sound of the Coral Reefers is probably the most vital of anybody's, excluding Fingers Taylor. Besides playing a mean harmonica (or blues harp, or whatever else you want to call it), Taylor acts as Buffett's onstage foil and lends most songs a healthy dose of credibility.

Production quality is better than you might expect, because it's not all filmed from a pair of handheld cameras at various angles to the stage. We get to see the stage from above, below, and either side, sometimes all within the same shot. It's edited well, too, with audience scenes interspersed at key moments. Some of the most entertaining audience shots occur in the bay itself, where a few dozen boatloads of crazed Parrot Heads float around on inner tubes screaming their support for a show that they probably could not see. Judging from the volume of their revelry, I wonder if they could even hear it.

After the short midshow break, the rhythm section returns to reinvigorate the audience. Greenidge kicks in with a complex contrapuntal melody that will leave you wondering where the "one" is, at least until the syncopated rhythms of Sam Clayton and Matt Betton join in and rock the house. As the band takes the stage, the driving rhythm downshifts into "One Particular Harbour." This song's melody is one of Buffett's best and is perfectly suited for his voice, so it's unfortunate that he gets overexcited toward the end and starts yelling the song's lyrics instead of singing them. "If the Phone Doesn't Ring, It's Me" may have marked a lull in the show's momentum, giving attendees a chance to go out for a drink refill, but on video the thoughtfulness of the songwriting is in full display while the understated performance works to the song's advantage. "Why Don't We Get Drunk," "Cheeseburger in Paradise," and "Fins" all up the ante on audience participation, while the live version of "Last Mango in Paris" that appears here surpasses the overproduced version that appears on the studio album of the same name. "A Pirate Looks at Forty" suffers from the opposite fate. On record, it is a pensive character study that touches on desperation, but this live version disperses that energy by being too corny, with the emphasis in all the wrong places.

It wouldn't be a Jimmy Buffett concert without "Margaritaville," and the Parrot Head national anthem impressively closes out the set, except for the encore of "Son of a Son of a Sailor." With this song playing in the background, Buffett adds to his already burgeoning mythology by telling the story of purchasing his first boat with his very first royalty check. Touching base on all of his classics, *Live by the Bay* is a solid document of Jimmy Buffett's mideighties live show and his post-Margaritaville (the corporation, not the song) persona. Best of all, it works as an ideal means for frustrated Parrot Heads to take the party home with them while waiting for the next tour to come around.

With a greatest hits album and a video package to promote, Buffet's 1989 tour was his most successful to date. It gave new life to his *Songs You Know by Heart* material while providing him with the chance to present new work. However, now that a new breed of fans were familiarizing themselves with his greatest hits, it presented both an opportunity and a problem for Jimmy Buffett. The opportunity, obviously, was the renewed commercial interest in his catalog of work.

The problem was that time stands still for no one: Jimmy Buffett was growing older and distinctly away from his reputation as a full-time party animal. Simultaneously, Margaritaville was growing exponentially, and its success was driven mostly by the well-defined image that Buffett's organization put forth, and it made good business sense for that image to remain consistent.

Buffett didn't shy away from the imagery. In fact, he embraced it, referring to himself as "one of the few living legends that are left." This is only conjecture—I doubt he'd admit it, and I don't want to overanalyze the point—but I'm willing to bet that this is a primary reason for his guarding his privacy so zealously. In essence, it was becoming harder for Jimmy Buffett to remain "Jimmy Buffett."

It's interesting to think that throughout the eighties Buffett's image as an all-night partyer hardly diminished at all, even though his newer material did little to promote this fantasy. Even in his prime, he remained inured to the damaging incidents that waylaid so many others. Despite the fact that he had an image of ill repute in a field where ill repute is the norm, there were no drug overdoses, no outrageous busts, no serious drug-related accidents, no show cancellations due to excessive behavior, no paternity suits, no compromising circumstances involving naked, underaged girls found unconscious in the bedroom. . . . While so many other star types with much cleaner images ran afoul, Buffett walked a straight line, or at least managed to keep any excesses out of the press. No doubt about it, his years of hard-earned experience made him a well-disciplined soul. He had an inborn awareness that to everything there is a season; there are times to party and there are times to stay dry. Now the time had come for him to retain his market share without becoming a parody of himself.

As it turns out, Buffett once again managed to turn a shortcoming into an advantage. His new fans clamored for the *Songs You Know by Heart,* and his older fans preferred the music of that era as well. Buffett was caught up in the typical "catch-22" that eventually confronts every successful artist. Do you repeat yourself or do you change, letting the emotional growth that you inevitably experience influence a new perspective? Most artists who force themselves back into the niche they discovered in younger days find themselves accused of either suffering from a paucity of ideas or lacking in credibility; artists who stray from what made them famous are accused of "selling out" or abandoning their traditional fan base. It's often a no-win situation that causes many artists with long careers to disappear entirely. The only chance of survival is managing to straddle the fence and alienate neither camp. By the turn of the decade, this is exactly what Jimmy Buffett would manage to do. Ultimately, each side sees mostly what it wants to see, so old fans hang on (though sometimes reluctantly) and new fans can still discover an artist with a predefined image that, in all actuality, no longer exists.

Things weren't going so well at MCA Records while Buffett prepared his next record. A lot of unwanted (not necessarily unwarranted) attention befell the label regarding its business practices. It seems that once Irving Azoff became head of MCA, a whole new slew of obligations filled his plate, so his management company was not prioritized in the way that it once had been. Rather than allow this business to slowly disintegrate, a deal was struck whereby ownership was ostensibly sold to MCA. To avoid the obvious conflict of interest that would result from such a maneuver, a new figurehead named Howard Kaufman was put in charge of the management company. The purchase price resulted in a large profit for Azoff. This alone was cause enough to raise eyebrows, but the questionable legality of these circumstances caused some executives to gripe about a record label cutting deals with their artists and representing them at the same time.

Adding to the confusion was the bootleg boondoggle in which MCA became embroiled. It was discovered that a large amount of unsold records that were returned to the label for credit were not licensed for manufacture by MCA. The question was whether MCA might have been something other than a victim. To make matters worse, the entire music industry was under suspicion of maintaining ties to promoters who used payola and other dubious promotion methods. Because it had so many other problems, MCA was singled out and the government called it onto the carpet. Congress organized an investigative committee, led by then Senator Al Gore, but Azoff managed to deflect any suspicion of his involvement. While this turmoil swarmed above his head, Buffett peacefully completed work on what would turn out to be one of his best albums in years.

Floridays (1986)

MCA Records MCA D-5730

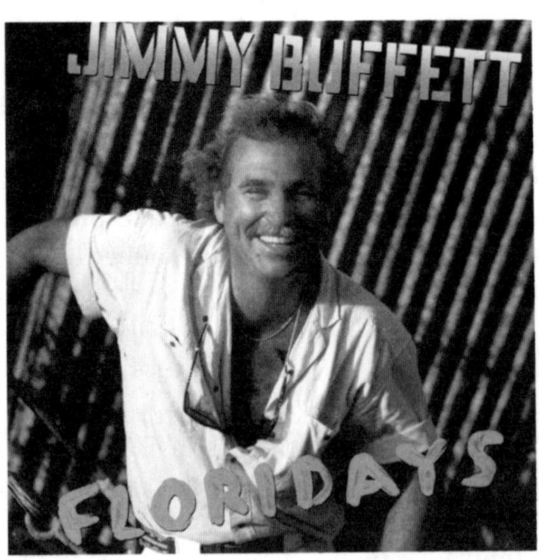

Before I even get into a detailed analysis, I ought to confess that I find myself thoroughly infatuated with this record. Maybe it's because it came at a time when I least expected it. Maybe it's because this album holds a contemporary clue to the whole Parrot Head phenomenon. I'm not exactly sure of the reasons, but I consider *Floridays* to be Jimmy Buffett's best effort in years. Rarely do albums have an aura that so consistently conveys a specific attitude or, in the case of *Floridays*, the lack of one. In recent years, Buffett has sometimes betrayed a subtle tendency to hold himself at arm's length from his audience, as if he would prefer to remain at stage height while we sit below and gaze upward. On *Floridays,* he abandons this stance. He's not being pedantic. Instead, there is a tendency to express himself openly and confide in his audience. He isn't preaching at us so much as he is sharing his thoughts. It is the unguarded moments that I find appealing and this album is overflowing with them.

Simplicity is the key to strength and that is what makes this such a great album. When they are done right, simple songs can convey subtle sentiments, and when that happens, they resound. I'll give you two shining examples. Superficially, "No Plane on Sunday" is solely about getting stuck somewhere and having to make the best of it, kind of like a miniaturized "Gilligan's Island." Listen deeply, though, and you'll hear a haunting song that paints reality into a fantasy vision. In three minutes, it conveys an emotional depth that is almost magical in its spirituality. I easily fell under its spell, and that is why this is one of my all-time favorite Buffett songs. Another work of beauty is "Floridays." On the surface, "Floridays" is no more than a simple reflection on escapism. Listen, though, and it's also about being lost or misdirected. It's about being unable to find the answer to your problems so readily. Mostly, though, it's about the lengths we'll go to to escape the acknowledgment of our predicament. Listen as the song fades away to Buffett's crooning of the title and you're sure to realize that this is no ordinary sentiment.

Maybe I find myself so infatuated because the production is continually astounding. It's ironic that I would single out the production as being the single most destructive force on his previous album (*Last Mango in Paris*) only to have Buffett counter with the most flawlessly produced record of his career. Michael Utley is the sole producer and he handles the controls with a deft and understated brilliance. Both figuratively and literally, *Floridays* is a great example of the axiom "less is more"—figuratively, because Utley's production avoids the tendency to layer too much information, and literally, because this album would have benefited immensely from losing one track (more about that later).

In many ways, this is a very unusual Buffett album. Instead of being another "lifestyle" album, *Floridays* captures an ethereal mood and holds on to it up until the album's last track. Over everything else, the production creates a wholesomely consistent atmosphere, which makes for a captivating change of pace. "Creola" is not what many would consider to be a "classic" Buffett song—it sounds more like a classic Boz Scaggs recording—but it would be wrong to dismiss this song so lightly. It's not easy to make this blend of instruments sound so lush, languid, and lilting but if you try hard enough, you'll smell the damp heat of the bayous and see the steamed mudbugs on the kitchen table. To my ears, the only flaw lies in the "parroting" harmonies, which could have been pulled back into the mix—way back.

Yet another example of shining production work is "First Look." With its brilliant balance of exotic chordal piano and Portuguese (Brazilian) lyrics, it captures the mood of the place as accurately as a Pulitzer Prize–winning photograph. "Meet Me in Memphis" does the same, though perhaps a bit too literally. In this song, the lyrics read like a film-noir character study and the music accurately mimics the classic Stax-Volt sound (did you catch the "Dock of the Bay" whistle on the fade-out tag?). "Nobody Speaks to the Captain No More" is another rich character study, but here it tends to get a bit too rich. The lyrics are a moving but morose suicide tale of an aging veteran who can't equate his heroic past with an insecure and neglected present. Perhaps, though, it is the jarring vulnerability of this song that manages to make the others resonate so deeply.

Production alone is not enough reason to recommend an album, but *Floridays* has plenty more to recommend it. For example, "If It All Falls Down" struck me at first as a cartoonish autobiography, but then I saw the writing credits. Buffett's drummer wrote this? I need to shake that man's hand, because these are some of the most convincing Buffett-esque lyrics I've ever heard. Using Buffett's own lyrical style, Matt Betton goes to the trouble of painting a stunningly creative portrait of his boss. The words are as clever as those written by the man he emulates, and the melody sticks to your brain like glue. "I Love the Now" may not be a masterpiece, but its live-for-the-moment sentiment is at least as convincing as others he has written on this topic. Besides, it has a catchy melody that resembles Leon Russell's "Back to the Island" (one of those songs that might suit Buffett as a cover tune) and, surprisingly, it was written with Carrie Fisher.

"When the Coast Is Clear" is an emotional tale of rediscovery and rejuvenation that ought to have been the album's last track—which brings me to the one recording that should have been lost, or better yet, should have never been written. Credited to the entire band, "You'll

> Never Work in Dis Bidness Again" is so miserably conceived and wrong-headed that it stands as its own testament to close-minded ignorance. Remove just this one song and *Floridays* would have been an effective statement of purpose. It's a shame that such a masterful album is stained with a song as pitifully dumb as this. So, take my advice and ignore it, because less this song, *Floridays* qualifies as Jimmy Buffett's most relaxed, least commercial, most provocative, and least contrived album since *A1A*.

Whether the record was good, bad, or indifferent didn't amount to a hill of beans, at least as far as sales figures and radio airplay went. *Floridays* may have been one of his most original albums and an artistic triumph, but it climbed no higher than number 66 and disappeared from the charts after sixteen weeks. The reason behind this is not too hard to figure. Buffett's traditionally dedicated fan base, those who would buy virtually anything the man records, remained constant, and new fans were just as likely to delve into his back catalog as they were to buy new product. Buffett's catalog became invaluable, whereas new releases did little more than keep him current and provide new material for fans to compare against the beloved older material, which was gaining steadily in stature.

Perhaps because of the insanity taking place at MCA, the country-influenced input of Jimmy Bowen was markedly absent from *Floridays*. Although it had no debilitating effect on the album's artistry, *Floridays* was Buffett's first album in some time to yield no country-based hit singles. Buffett's days as a "country" artist were effectively over. Pop radio also continued to ostracize him. Judging from the audience that came out to see him, though, the effect of their ignorance was negligible. Buffett's "A Parrot Looks at Forty" tour was even more successful than the last. With the help of Margaritaville and the *Coconut Telegraph*, his empire was growing and his audience grew with it.

Plenty of other things were happening to occupy Buffett's time and distract him from the plebeian pursuit of a contemporary hit record. He had recently taken up flying as a hobby and purchased a single-engine seaplane named *Lady of the Waters*. With his tendency to change locations on a whim and his property (and family) distributed all over the map, flying was not only a fun and challenging new venture, but a practical one (albeit expensive) as well.

He also quietly maintained an active interest in environmental concerns. He had donated $35,000 to the state of Florida for the purpose of protecting the manatee, and as a result, signs now existed to warn boaters when they were in areas where manatees are known to live. In 1987, he appeared before the Senate Environmental Protection Committee to speak on behalf of the manatee. Legislation that would affect the budget for the Endangered Species Act was being debated and Buffett did what he could to convey the need for continued funding. "If we as humans want to assume the role of landlord then we have to take care of all the tenants. We are the reason that endangered species exist. . . ." Around this time he also formed the "Friends of Florida," a committee dedicated to preserving land and wildlife that otherwise would be threatened by expansion. He funneled his energy toward fighting condominium developers who were planning construction in an undeveloped and wildlife-rich area in Key West known as the Salt Ponds. Buffett wouldn't win outright, but his efforts at least curtailed the expansive intent of the condominium project by saving the lion's share of land from any future development.

In January 1987, Buffett headed off to Australia for the America's Cup. Besides enjoying the race, he performed at a black-tie affair that also featured Lionel Richie and Elton John. While there, he debuted a song that was written specifically for the American cause, called "Take It Back." Some of the people whom Buffett met while Down Under would become essential allies later in the year, when the city of Pascagoula would name him the honorary captain of a 110-year-old schooner called the *Governor Stone.* The ship was built in Pascagoula in 1877 and its owner decided to gift it back to the city that was responsible for its creation. Because his father was readying himself for retirement, Jimmy Buffett named J. D. Buffett as port captain and general manager.

It wasn't long before the T-shirt shop called Margaritaville had expanded with the addition of a luncheon grill. Soon enough, the ramshackle but pleasant storefront had outgrown its location entirely. In 1987, the operation was relocated to Key West's main drag (500 Duval

Street), and the T-shirt shop was relegated to an appendage of the new business, which had grown to include a full-blown restaurant-nightclub-bar called the Margaritaville Cafe. The *Coconut Telegraph* was now reaching over ten thousand subscribers (its list would eventually expand to over fifty thousand). Between these two outlets, the T-shirts were becoming as popular as the songs for which they were named.

It was corny and tacky, and Buffett himself admitted that he wouldn't want to wear some of the merchandise his stores were selling, but it was *fun,* and the popularity of the items could not be denied. If Buffett himself no longer cared to maintain his glorified image as a full-time tropical party animal, then his products would do it for him. As they grew in popularity, faithful and gullible fans were left with the impression that Buffett was frozen in a time warp of beach parties and margaritas.

Yet another project that continued to occupy Buffett's time was his writing. He continued pushing the Margaritaville script, only to see it continually pushed right back. In his spare time, he would formulate other short stories and autobiographical accounts of his life, much as though he were writing songs, but with the stricter discipline that writing demands. Over time, these bits and pieces would coalesce into *Tales From Margaritaville,* but for now they were still a hodgepodge of unrelated segments.

A less burdensome project was the children's book he was writing with his daughter, Savannah Jane, called *The Jolly Mon.* As Buffett recounts on the book's jacket, he once came upon his eight-year-old daughter sitting at the typewriter and writing a story from her imagination. Aware that it would be a wonderful (though occasionally difficult) bonding experience, he and Savannah Jane decided to set a children's story to paper. For their subject, they settled on the retelling of a Caribbean folk tale that Buffett had used in the song "Jolly Mon Sing" (from *Last Mango in Paris*). The song itself was a jumbled attempt to condense too much information into too little space, but a children's book was ideal for the subject and the result, with illustrations by Lambert Davis, was absolutely charming. Meanwhile, another album was being pieced together between his other projects. Like his previous few albums, it hit stores in the middle of summer.

Hot Water (1988)

MCA Records MCA-42093

Hot water, indeed. With so much going on in his personal and business life, it was becoming increasingly difficult for Buffett to concentrate on his music, and it shows on this album. It had been two full years since his last effort, yet this record sounds as though it is held together with sticky tape and glue. *Hot Water* was mostly recorded in Key West at Shrimpboat Sound, a "state of the art" studio that was purchased and outfitted by Buffett. It was a convenience that didn't help as much as it could have, though. Probably owing to the fact that it *was* so convenient, sessions weren't formalized in the normal sense. Recording took place sporadically and the resulting album reflects it, resembling a haphazard collection of songs more than an album per se. It features five (count 'em!) different bass players and before it was finished, used a total of nine different recording studios spread out over eleven songs. It's enough to make you miss the good ol' days when the Coral Reefer Band was a viable entity and all of his material was laid down in Nashville.

Hot Water is a thematic mess that never seems to gel into anything cohesive. Even the individual songs seem to stray all over the map. For example, on "Homemade Music," Buffett attempts to equate moving to the suburbs with Sony's purchase of CBS Records. Hey, if you can figure out the correlation, please clue me in, because I'm confused. The lyrics pose the question "Where did all the good songs go?" and by album's end I found myself wondering the same thing. "Prince of Tides" is another song that manages to confuse me thoroughly. Who's Judy? Or Goodman? Is he talking about *Steve* Goodman? Or Giovinno? And what does John MacDonald have to do with this? It sounds like a nice song, but these references are confusing as all hell. Besides, look at the structure. It starts off like a formal reading from a novel, builds up to a head-crunching guitar solo, drifts off (pardon the pun) into a verse of "Save the Last Dance for Me," and then sinks back into more narration. I'll have to read three novels and two biographies just to figure out what is going on with this song.

All of the overindulgent tendencies that I was so happy to see evaporate on *Floridays* have returned in full force. The most annoying trait here is Buffett's tendency to litter the album with spoken dialogue. It's distracting enough to use narration when it serves the specific purpose of making a thematic connection, like it would in an opera or a soundtrack from a Broadway musical, but what is the point when the songs themselves have absolutely no connection to one another? With few exceptions, a song that requires narration to make its point must mean that there's something wrong with the song. Besides intimating that the audience cannot think for themselves, it destroys the very song that it attempts to support by forcing us to ruminate on the literal intentions of the narrator. Narration also limits the song's shelf life. Like a bad video, it dampens our imaginations. Once you do that, you deprive your audience of music's fundamental strength as an interpretive artform.

Ask a GOP's opinion, and you'll get the impression that this album is the product of the Antichrist, but the truth is that it's not that bad, although some songs do come awfully close. Not to sound sacrilegious, but even the Saviour himself couldn't salvage a song like "Pre-You." The very concept for this song should have been thrown into the dustbin before it was developed, placed on a garbage scow and buried at sea, but now it's too late for that. Like radiation, once it escapes, the damage is already done. Let Wayne Newton have this one for his Vegas shows, or give it to the cruise ship lounge lizards, but please, please, don't resurrect it on purpose.

"King of Somewhere Hot" is another dog, though at least it's a noble failure. The playing is stupendous but the melody never takes hold and the steel drums simply don't supply enough muscle to support such a weak and tedious song. By the last verse, Buffett's vocal line seems lost in space while everyone else is holding on for dear life just to make it to the finish line. As for "My Barracuda," the way I figure it is, if Steve Cropper, Duck Dunn, Stevie Winwood, and the Neville Brothers can't save it, then it's unsalvageable. The instrumental tracks work, the melody works, the arrangement works, and the harmony vocals are strong, so why does this song suck? Could it be the songwriting? Is that guy who understands "Prince of Tides" still around to figure this mystery out, too?

On a more pleasant note—how about "Baby's Gone Shopping?" It at least has a cool Memphis feel to it, but it sounds like nothing more than Buffett taking a cocky turn at attracting his wife's attention in a bid to get her to listen to the album's next track. I know it's a mistake to take these things too literally, but if "Bring Back the Magic" isn't an autobiographical song about reconciliation, then I don't know what is. It's also the second best song on this album. Despite the gratuitous narration and the unbelievably painful Mark Twain pun, "That's What Livin' Is to Me" qualifies for this honor. "L'Air de la Louisianne" is quite nice, too, but it's sung entirely in French, which will probably kill it for the majority of Buffett's audience. It's beautiful, though, and touching, especially in the context of what surrounds it.

Hey, it may not be original, but Johnny Clegg's "Great Heart" isn't so bad either. This Americanization of South African turf was adequately covered by Paul Simon, but Buffett and band comport themselves well enough (although Aaron Neville does sound like he might break into a yodel at any minute). With an album like this, you have to steal small "moments" instead of entire "pieces." It's nice to hear James Taylor and Tim Schmit harmonize beneath Buffett. It's also nice when the snippet of "Save the Last Dance for Me" rolls around. Grover Washington Jr.'s horn playing on "That's What Livin' Is to Me" is nice, too.

The small pieces are all that you have to grab on to here because as a package, *Hot Water* is a mess. In the words of One-Eyed Rosie the pirate, "That's quite enough, Mr. Jolly Mon." If you recall the book, the pirates then pushed the Jolly Mon into the sea. An interesting concept, especially if you consider the album title and cover photo—just imagine that the water is considerably deeper and instead of jumping up, he's plunging downward. I suppose it wouldn't be right to have Buffett walk the plank on account of this album, but as a fantasy it sure is a tempting proposition.

While Buffett sang warily in "Homemade Music" about Japanese conglomerates buying up American businesses, his own label, MCA, along with all of its affiliates, was sold to Matsushita Electric Industrial for over six and a half *billion* dollars. Things like this were going on all over the music industry. Even the country's two oldest and most prestigious labels had fallen prey to international conglomerates; Germany's BMG (Bertelsmann Group) Music purchased RCA and Sony scooped up CBS/Columbia.

Speaking of "Homemade Music," whose idea was it to release this as *Hot Water*'s first single? Whoever it was is probably back to licking stamps for the mail-order department, because this record never even showed up on the charts. "Bring Back the Magic" was the second choice (and infinitely more appropriate than the first) and though it was ignored by pop radio, it became a moderate hit in the adult contemporary market.

For all of my griping about the album itself, *Hot Water* obtained Buffett's highest chart position since *Somewhere Over China* (1982). Debuting on July 9, 1988, it reached position number 46 and lingered for fourteen weeks before dropping out of sight.

Concert audiences continued to grow, as did the venues that would sell out with little or no advertising. "Mainstream" music fans continued to ignore Buffett, but what do you call somebody who consistently sells out 16,000-seat arenas? Alternative? I don't think so. Once the "alternative" bands such as Nirvana and Soundgarden had become too popular for their moniker to make any sense, they simply changed places with what was once considered to be mainstream. While traditionally popular acts were shunted aside to make room for this new breed, Buffett remained unaffected by the shift.

Now that *The Jolly Mon* was completed and selling well, it was time to finish work on one of his "mature" writing projects. He had dallied long enough. His publisher loved Buffett's idea of a book that would correspond with a similarly themed album, so songwriter-author J. Buffett set out to write songs *and* corresponding stories. As he readied his compilation of "fictional facts and factual fictions," Buffett went into promotional overdrive by granting numerous interviews, most effectively on Larry King's televised interview program and the widely syndicated National Public Radio. By the time it was completed, *My African Friend and Other Short Stories* had been transmogrified into *Tales From Margaritaville.* The movie project was going nowhere, so at least the book could benefit from its titular association with his most well known song. When it was completed, Buffett would go on a tour promoting his book at bookstores throughout the country, interspersing these appearances with a few shows backed only by acoustic guitar. The corresponding album, *Off to See the Lizard,* was readied for a near-simultaneous release. It would be Buffett's last collection of songs available on vinyl.

Off to See the Lizard (1989)

MCA Records MCA-6314

This record is so slick that you could ice-skate on its grooves. That's not necessarily a bad thing, though. After *Hot Water,* I had fully expected *Off to See the Lizard* to be awful, but the truth is that it is actually quite good. Most surprisingly welcome is the absence of narrative bits to disrupt the flow of the songs. Five of the album's twelve songs share titles with short stories that appear in *Tales From Margaritaville,* but despite the literary connection, Buffett never feels compelled to read his words. The stories are stories and the songs are songs, helping the album to stand on its own two feet away from the corresponding book.

Off to See the Lizard is a very musical album, with carefully structured lyrics that remain well focused and literate throughout. It is also quite different from Buffett's previous style of work. Originally, the production struck me as a tad too pristine for my taste, but the record's consistency eventually won out over any preconceived notions of what a Buffett album ought to sound like. Despite my lowered expectations and my initially negative reaction to the polished sound, I soon found myself enjoying the many-faceted pleasures of *Off to See the Lizard.*

For all of the hubbub regarding the presumed superiority of Buffett's earlier songwriting, the truth of the matter is that although entertaining, his lyrical focus often strayed far and wide from his intended target. Here, his thinking is much more linear and deliberately constructed, making the focal point of the songs both clear and succinct. It's his story and he sticks to it. My favorite example of well-crafted lyrics comes about on "Boomerang Love" (perhaps not coincidentally, it is also the only song Buffett wrote by himself). Simply put, this is an extremely well-written song. The lyrics are personal enough to mean something to Buffett, but vague enough for me to interpret them for myself. Because of this, I can trust the singer's sincerity while simultaneously seeing myself in a reflection of the words. That's no easy feat and what makes them even better is the way that Buffett layers his story over a well-constructed chord progression and melody arrangement. "Why the Things We Do" may not be as classic, but it also contains its share of quotable phrases ("Truth is stranger than fishing" and "Invisible means are the key to support" are my favorites).

Perhaps because of their literary association with the book, the lyrics remain consistently excellent, but it's the album's production that stands front and center. For many fans, this glossy prominence often distracts them from the quality of the songs themselves. Either together or separately, Keyboardist-programmer Jay Oliver and drummer Roger Guth are credited as cowriters throughout the album, and along with producer Elliot Scheiner, they can take the blame or credit for the richness of this album's sound. From the opening bars of the first song, "Carnival World," it becomes immediately apparent that this isn't your father's Oldsmobile. With a computer-generated mix and highly sequenced (synthesizer-based) arrangements, *Off to See the Lizard* can send more than its share of longtime fans running for cover, and that's a shame. Older fans might have paid for it in the traditional sense but stylistically speaking, they never bought it. Traditional prejudices notwithstanding, this is one heck of a well-made album. It's pleasant and radio-friendly (to no avail), and the production suits Buffett's revamped writing style.

If "Carnival World" cannot be a radio hit, then I suppose it's necessary to assume that today's playlists are much too tightfisted and close-minded, because this is a great song that deserved a chance to be heard. With its uplifting chorus and three-dimensional soundscape, the album's second song, "Take Another Road," is just as intriguing. Listen to this song on headphones and you might better appreciate the workmanship that is applied here. By becoming a microcosm of Mark Twain's "Following the Equator," "Take Another Road" is an atmospheric wonder and an ideal song to accompany virtually any voyage of discovery. "The Pascagoula Run" is another fine melody that only benefits from the thoughtful production. Like the corresponding story, the song's protagonists are "Jimmy Delaney" and "Uncle Billy," providing us with yet another biographical reference that can now be entered into the Buffett legend. Despite the numerous qualities of these cleverly arranged songs, the best song is also the simplest, and it is saved for last. Buffett and Mac McAnally teamed up to write "Changing Channels," and together they created an aurally simple but lyrically complex pastiche that also manages to update Buffett's image of Margaritaville: "There's an island in the ocean where people stay in motion, Somewhere on the old gulf stream. Do they live or did I dream?"

With all of my praise for *Off to See the Lizard,* this is not by any means a perfect record. "That's My Story and I'm Stickin' to It" is a finely produced song with well-conceived lyrics, but the central vocal riff of the chorus ("Believe me or not . . .") is more corny than it is catchy. Another fault lies in its self-conscious relation to the book *Tales From Margaritaville.* The title is a coolly conceived and clever allusion that on reflection is actually a well-disguised commercial for the book, but who says that a commercial can't be entertaining? More blatant is "Off to See the Lizard," which desperately tries to cram too much information into too small a space. The wordiness only gets in the way of the occasionally gratuitous autobiographical verses, and the hip-hop–like construction makes the song too giddy for its own good.

Similarly wrongheaded is "Gravity Storm." It consists of a Cuban-disco rhythm that is superficially fun but also slightly embarrassing—while listening to it I can imagine Buffett singing in a midriff with a basket of fruit balanced on his head. "Mermaid in the Night" is easily the low point, though. Here, Oliver and Guth collaborated without their boss and the result is one of the silliest songs that Buffett ever put his voice to. Others might object to the overt sweetness of "I Wish Lunch Could Last Forever" but from my own standpoint the unabashed romanticism of this song is an enviable romanticism, and I for one wouldn't mind changing places with the main character for a while.

Hard heads relent. You can't expect Buffett to stand frozen in time, and even if he did, then you would probably feel compelled to criticize him for stagnating. Perhaps *Off to See the Lizard* was ahead of its time

> in 1989, or too sudden a stylistic shift for traditionalists, but you've had plenty of time to get over the jolt. Give it a chance, and you might recognize the stark symbolism that relates both to Buffett's own life, and the lifestyle that he has come to represent. As an independently entertaining companion to his first book, *Off to See the Lizard* provides another means and another vantage point for telling a few compelling stories. The book may give him a chance to spread his wings, but it's the album that brings these colorful tales to life.

As the eighties drew to a close, Buffett could reflect on a decade that began as a threat and ended as a dream. While he started out facing potential obsolescence, he ended up being more successful than he could have imagined. His retail ventures were booming, virtually all of his records were selling, and his concert audiences continued to grow steadily. The income that was generated by all of this meant that he was able to indulge freely in expensive hobbies such as flying, while expanding his real estate holdings. With comedian Bill Murray, he even purchased a share of the Miami Miracles baseball team. To top it all off, he was now the critically accepted author of a bestselling book. It was a time when longtime dreams and ambitions came true for him, and the nineties held the promise of continuing success.

6

The Nineties

I don't know if Jimmy Buffett had his very own seven-year plan back in 1983, but the steps he took since to insure his longevity have worked like a charm. For people interested in learning how to survive in something as crazy as the music business, someone ought to develop a college business course called "Jimmy Buffett 101." The man had only one substantial hit record and a few minor ones yet by the nineties, fifteen years after his recording prime, Buffett was bigger than he ever had been. No, check that. He was bigger than almost anybody, period. His concert tours were consistently grossing in the annual Top Ten. He had reinvented the concept of the fan club, turning it into a self-sustaining business venture with its own magazine (at a subscription cost of $5 annually and eventually upped to $10), restaurant, and widely marketed line of clothing. His back catalog was as popular as it had ever been, his greatest hits record was a consistent bestseller, his (along with daughter Savannah Jane) children's book was doing well, and his collection of short stories was a *New York Times* bestseller. Oh, yeah, he still made music, too, though not as often as before.

At the onset of the decade, Buffett took some time to help promote his elderly friend, Tony Tarracino, in his run for mayor of Key West. Captain Tony had run for office a number of times before but never got elected. The election was close, but thanks in part to Buffett's assistance, Key West's favorite bartender was now also Key West's mayor.

On a musical note, Buffett was offered a spot on the upcoming soundtrack for the movie *Arachnaphobia,* and came up with a gem of a tune, written to spec, called "Don't Bug Me." Played in its entirety over the final credits, it features Fingers Taylor and consists of a fun and melodic play on words, relating the disgusting but entertaining story line of a town infested with deadly spiders. On a literary note, he contributed a short essay to Don Henley and Dave Marsh's *Heaven Is Under Our Feet,* a collection of stories meant to increase awareness and raise revenue for the preservation of Walden Woods.

To kick off the final decade of the millennium, Buffett decided to give his fans a new take on some old material. A whole new breed of Parrot Heads had been enlisted (or born!) since the last live record, so a gentler, kinder document was required for this newer generation of fans. Besides updating his family-ready image for the nineties, it would also be a nifty way to generate revenue without the hassle of writing a whole new album. It was the old stuff that people clamored for anyway, and being the clever entrepreneur that he is, Buffett knew enough to give the people what they wanted.

Jimmy Buffett Live! Feeding Frenzy (1990)

MCA Records MCAD-10022

Some may say that Jimmy Buffett's music sounds best when played on a boat. Others may say that it sounds best while relaxing in a hammock in your own backyard. Still others feel that the best place to hear Jimmy Buffett's music is in a tropical-style bar, but by and large, the majority of people think that Buffett's music works best when performed live in concert. When a basketball stadium in snow country can become magically transformed into a tropical outpost, or when an outdoor amphitheater can be made to resemble a sun-drenched island, these people may have a very valid point, and *Feeding Frenzy* exists for exactly that reason. Recorded during "Jimmy's Jump Up" tour in the heart of summer at the Lakewood and Riverbend Amphitheatres in Atlanta and Cincinnati, respectively, this disc updates some of Buffett's most dog-eared material, with no real surprises. Between songs, Jimmy talks about déjà vu, and listening to this got me to thinking the same thing: haven't I heard all of this before?

Predictability is the key to this collection and if you don't mind hearing yet another version of "Margaritaville" (or "Fins," or "Come Monday," or "Volcano") then your spirit is in the right place. In "Cheeseburger in Paradise," Buffett sings "They eat the same thing again and again" and if you were to judge from this disc, then this observation could apply very well to the listening habits of Parrot Heads. Much of this collection consists of little more than recycled versions of worn-out classics, but the problem with recycling is that you usually have to sanitize the material before you use it again. Like beer bottles and newspapers, the songs on this album have been boiled down to their basic elements, scrubbed clean, and then remolded into the same exact shape. Personally, I liked 'em better when they had a few dings in them. At least then they had some personality. At its worst, *Feeding Frenzy* sounds like halftime entertainment or perhaps like a Walt Disney extravaganza—it isn't hard to imagine hearing this album blaring out over the public address system while cheerleaders dance in unison in front of the Magic Castle.

In a million years, this is something that never could have been said about Buffett's first live collection (from 1978), *You Had to Be There.* Where that album was reckless, this collection is often contrived. As much as I know Buffett would hate the comparison, Michael Utley has learned to play Paul Schaffer to Jimmy's David Letterman. This is one of the major problems with Buffett's new material. Like a late-night band that regurgitates sanitized versions of popular riffs, its slickness begins to resemble a commercialized parody of itself.

Most songs are lively and handled well, but that isn't enough to replace the original versions. Only a few songs are improved by the live format—"Last Mango in Paris" and "Gypsies in the Palace" both benefit from the presence of an audience. Otherwise, "Come Monday," "One Particular Harbour," "Honey Do," and "A Pirate Looks at Forty," along with the live staples "Fins," "Cheeseburger in Paradise," "Volcano," and of course "Margaritaville," are little more than pleasantly rendered versions of the original recordings. The only thing these songs have to offer over their counterparts is the energy of the crowd, but otherwise it's the studio version that wins out every time.

The most disruptive part of *Feeding Frenzy* is its opening. Instead of simply announcing the band, a short scenario takes place where a pair of stereotyped Jewish businessmen argue over the stage equipment. Is this entertainment? The whole thing is so bad that I'm embarrassed to admit even listening to it. From here, he launches into "You'll Never Work in Dis Bidness Again," with a cartoonish urgency that can only mean trouble. Then, in midsong, to my disbelief the band breaks into a parody of Jimi Hendrix's "Foxy Lady" while the Reeferettes sing "Foxy Bubba!" *Foxy Bubba???*

Maybe you should start this disc with track two, a Mac McAnally composition called "In the City." Then again, I'm not too sure about that, either. Although the melody is pleasant, the myopic lyrics capture none of the majesty but all of the menace of large population centers. All in all, it's not exactly an endorsement for the city way of life. Oddly, Buffett usually augments his performance of this tune by displaying slides of the town he's performing in. The hometown crowd always cheers when they recognize their own landmarks, but I can only wonder if anybody ever felt the quizzical sense of a benign insult being thrust at them.

OK, then, start at track three. From here at least, the performance remains consistent and free of disruptive surprises. The only real disappointment might be when you first discover that two seemingly new tracks aren't new at all. "Today's Message" is a "sermon" from Reverend Jimmy whereby he prepares his "choir" (meaning you, the audience), and "A Love Song (From a Different Point of View)" is . . . you guessed it. No Buffett concert is complete without this ragged sing-along, but Buffett orchestrates the lunacy of "Why Don't We Get Drunk and Screw" quite nicely for the more passive home audience. The only other new song is a reggae-fied reworking of Harry Belafonte's 1956 hit "Jamaica Farewell."

Live albums often force material to function at its lowest common denominator. That can explain why Buffett's concerts are often so good; his material works best when simplified. Live and in person, it's great, but on plastic, the juvenile tendencies of these tracks tend to become exaggerated. Hey kids! Wanna hear a song about a volcano? How about a shark? A cheeseburger? Hey, there's a song about the Jolly Mon on here! My own kids like this album more than I do, and I can understand why. While playing this CD, they dance around the house with underwear on their heads, and all I can think is, "How appropriate."

I'll be the first to admit that the best way to truly appreciate the Buffett (read *Parrot Head*) phenomenon is to hear it live, but the atmosphere doesn't readily translate onto plastic. You can't see the giant shark come out over the audience here. You can't see the volcano blow at the end of the show, either. Most important, you can't see Buffett and the band. You might want to consider this live album as an alternative, but take my advice. Seeing is believing. If you would rather hear Buffett's music in a live environment, leave *Feeding Frenzy* in the kids' playroom, hire a baby-sitter, and go to a show.

Feeding Frenzy filled a demand that the new Parrot Heads had been clamoring for. Debuting in November 1990 and rising to number 68, Buffett's second live album proved to be just about as successful as *You Had to Be There* (1978; number 72). To promote the album, autographed coconuts (yes, real coconuts) were sent to various promotion-related personnel. The Parrot Head spirit was alive and well, rejuvenated and reinvigorated for whatever else was in store. Buffett's perennial happiness continued to astound his faithful audience, and for good reason. How could anybody be this satisfied all of the time? In an age when frustration, heartbreak, and aggravation were common topics on the music charts, Buffett still offered his fans a chance to escape.

In 1991 Buffett had another soundtrack opportunity, but this time with a twist. Randa (*Children of a Lesser God*) Haines's latest project was called *The Doctor,* starring William Hurt in the title role as a deliberately aloof and glib surgeon who gets sick and thus gets a taste of his own medicine. To portray the surgeon's callous objectivity (and his need to stay calm and relaxed), the script has Hurt and his assistants singing along with a tape of Buffett's "Why Don't We Get Drunk and Screw" while performing emergency cardiac surgery. Later, when Hurt finds himself about to go under the knife, his staff, led by a shy assistant, sings the song to him as a form of solace. In either circumstance, Buffett's tune is a poignant choice for a plot that presents a solid case for compassionate, as opposed to clinical, medicine. More important to

Buffett's fans, though, it marked the very first time that one of his songs played a vital role to the story that used it.

With so much going right in his professional life, Buffett still needed to address the one thing that was most neglected during his tenure as pop music's single greatest entrepreneur; he needed to fix his family. During most of the past decade, Jimmy and Jane had lived separate lives. Seven years of long-distance love forced them to come to terms with the future. Their circumstances caused them to grow far enough apart to consider divorce. Before this had become a reality, they decided to step back and reconsider. Their separation had taken its toll, but neither of them really wanted to split, so at Jane's suggestion, the couple underwent counseling and began to pick up the pieces. Time apart was so much water under the bridge so they decided to concentrate on reconciliation. With the family reunited, Jimmy and daughter Savannah Jane began work on a sequel to their first collaboration. Since *The Jolly Mon,* Savannah Jane had entered adolescence, so the topicality of their next project reflected her impending maturity. Called *Trouble Dolls,* the book touched on the value of childlike faith, especially when faced with a potentially disastrous situation. In April 1991, the family bought a home in Nashville and began renovations. As a sign of their renewed commitment to each other, Jane became pregnant and on April 1, 1992, their second daughter, Sarah Delaney (lovingly referred to as "the Pud"), would be born.

Buffett's previous studio album, *Off to See the Lizard,* never broke the Top Fifty, stalling at number 57. Considering all of the marketing avenues that were available to MCA, that album probably could have charted better, giving Buffett further cause to doubt his record company's commitment to him. One solution to this problem would be for Buffett himself to take a greater interest in the business side of record company responsibilities. With so many other promotion-related ventures, it only made sense for him to try his hand at running his own record label. Of course, he would still need to rely on the long arm of MCA for distribution, but with his own label, he could maintain absolute control over the final release and perhaps have a greater say regarding marketing techniques and release dates (*Off to See the Lizard* missed its intended joint release with *Tales From Margaritaville* by a full three months).

After a few extended discussions with friend Robert Mercer, Buffett decided to take his Margaritaville organization one step further, incorporating his own record company, called (what else?) Margaritaville Records. Buffett would be the chief of staff, so to speak, and Mercer would handle day-to-day operations. Based in Nashville, the informal charter for the label, besides hosting Buffett's new releases, was to do its own artist and repertoire development, and then provide the finished product to MCA for distribution. MCA maintained no ownership in Margaritaville Records.

Mercer had quite a background in A&R, previously working for England's EMI Records, for which he signed and promoted such well-known and diverse acts as Queen, the Sex Pistols, and Pink Floyd. He was a key player in arranging for Roger Waters's historically significant performance of *The Wall* in Berlin. For a while, he was also responsible for managing Paul McCartney's career. Still, major A&R decisions were the responsibility of Buffett himself, and the first act that he brought to the fledgling label was a five-woman Cajun-style group called Evangeline. While Mercer went to work on developing promotional tactics and production methods for their new venture, they also went about preparing a long-overdue retrospective of Buffett's career for the new label's first release.

Boats, Beaches, Bars, and Ballads (1992)

Margaritaville Records 10613

I've learned a heck of a lot about numerous artists by familiarizing myself with their box sets. In the past decade or so, an awful lot of talented people have been honored with career retrospectives, and if you wanted to appreciate someone's body of work but never knew where to begin, a well-constructed box set usually solved the problem quite handily. By presenting an entire career in an organized fashion, these collections have the potential to bring new life to aging catalogs and spark the interest of an entirely new generation of fans. With a career that was over twenty years old and with just about as many albums under his belt, Jimmy Buffett was a perfect candidate for the boxed-set treatment.

Some boxed sets aim their sights at the already established audience, focusing on rare, unreleased, and alternate versions of songs, because this would appeal to the fan who already has everything. Others aim for a more broadened scope by leaning on familiar versions of well-known songs, hoping that a new audience will breathe new life into the tired chestnuts that otherwise would have outlasted their shelf life. Though it tries to please all comers, Buffett's box sits squarely in the latter camp, and it works like a charm. By the time I had heard *Boats, Beaches, Bars, and Ballads,* I was already familiar with Buffett's entire catalog, yet hearing these songs again in this format was a revelation, and not because of the handful of rare and unreleased tracks. First, this collection marked my first opportunity to hear most of these songs in the digital format, and the difference can sometimes be astounding. Thanks to technology and occasional remastering, once-flat mixes are vividly brought to life with a three-dimensional sense of depth that can rarely be obtained from recordings that pre-date 1980. Until now, I never took notice of the crickets on "The Captain and the Kid."

Second, the track sequencing wisely ignores a chronological arrangement for four theme-based discs (boats, beaches, bars, and ballads, of course), allowing for the older material to cross-talk with his newer work. Despite the changes that have taken place in Buffett's songwriting methodology over the years, there is an impressive amount of cohesiveness here and the song's styles often complement each other in ways that I might not have otherwise recognized. Heard back to back, "Cuban Crime of Passion" and "First Look" never sounded better. Even the clunkers sound all right. For instance, "Slow Boat to China" once struck me as a boneheaded mess but here, with the crisply humorous clarinet section standing front and center, I wonder what my problem was. Because it would be painfully redundant to readdress each of the songs on this collection, I'll briefly encapsulate each of the discs, emphasizing material that makes its first appearance.

Boats

The leadoff disc of this collection relies heavily on Buffett's first decade (eleven of the seventeen tracks date before 1979) and it has to be the most consistently reliable of the four. As for track selection and sequencing, this disc can't be beat. The first four selections are nothing less than majestic and from there, the disc only seems to get better and better. The two new and rare tracks, "Take It Back" and "Love and Luck," merit attention. "Take It Back" is both entertaining and clever in its depiction of America's no-holds-barred attempt to reclaim the America's Cup, and "Love and Luck" is simply too good to have been squandered until now. With its potent combination of New Orleans, Caribe, and Latin influences, this bouillabaisse of rhythm is finally taken off the back burner and served up fresh and hot. Following this are six of Buffett's most deservedly well loved recordings, rounding out what is probably the closest Buffett has ever come to compiling a perfect collection of music.

Beaches

Although this too is a wonderfully representative disc, it lacks the crisp sparkle and consistency of "Boats." Most problematic in this regard is the presence of a Christmas tune that is dropped smack-dab into the middle of things, making it an awkward choice to play all the way through at poolside. "Money Back Guarantee" is better, but still a mostly silly song equating love with a late-night television offer. Considering the scope of this collection, it would be remiss to not include the "songs we know by heart," but hearing the all-too-obvious "Margaritaville," "Volcano," and "Cheeseburger in Paradise" (for some reason, this song is overlooked on the album's liner notes) diminishes the element of surprise that is so invigorating on the first disc. In inverse proportion, eleven tracks here are post-1980. The energy level dips dangerously low in the middle, but is salvaged by the pure beauty of songs such as "Tin Cup Chalice" and "Distantly in Love."

Bars

Easily the least consistent disc of the set, "Bars" starts out strong and tapers off until it practically disappears. "Elvis Imitators" is a pretty damn funny idea and Buffett deserves a lot of credit for recording a song that should be required fodder for each and every duck-tailed ninny who thinks he's the King, but the disc never seems to recover from this aberration. It's a useless proposition to argue about track selection because each and every person would compile tracks differently, but methinks there are more representative bar-type selections in Buffett's catalog than "When Salome Plays the Drum," "Carmen," and "Sending the Old Man Home." Moreover, "Kick It in Second Wind" still sounds as musically half-baked as it did back in the seventies, only now it also sounds ideologically unsound as well. For its final selection, the previously unreleased "Domino College" kicks the disc back into its second wind with a little bit of humor and a healthy dose of attitude, but unfortunately it's too little too late to keep this disc on par with its brethren.

Ballads

Aaah, Buffett's strong point. Some of his best ballads appear elsewhere on this collection ("Nautical Wheelers," "Tin Cup Chalice," "Biloxi"), but there's still plenty more to choose from. Any disc that can combine songs as widely diverse as "Twelve Volt Man," "He Went to Paris," and "Coast of Marseilles" is bound to impress, and this makes the best argument for proving that Buffett is by no means a rock and roller. With the exception of "Pre-You" (how on earth did that find its way onto this collection?), the song selection here is superb, displaying the thoughtful side of Buffett's output. It also makes a fairly convincing case for proving that he has maintained a surprisingly consistent level of quality over the years. From "He Went to Paris" to "Changing Channels," with numerous stops in between, this disc ought to put a sock in the mouth of every naysayer who insists that Buffett can't write 'em like he used to.

Even more recent is the unreleased live recording of "Everlasting Moon," a lyrically intriguing song that was taken from the *Feeding Frenzy* tapes; "Middle of the Night," with its hopelessly mundane melody, is much less captivating. It's the classics that stand out here, and rediscovered masterpieces such as "Defying Gravity," "Ballad of Spider John" (neither written by Buffett), and "If the Phone Doesn't Ring, It's Me" convince me that nobody has a handle on the quality of Buffett's output more than the man responsible for creating it.

Well, there you have it. Basically, this is what a box set ought to be for an artist who has experienced Buffett's longevity—a classy, well-thought-out retrospective based on classic recordings. It is the consistency of his output that is most well represented, and *Boats, Beaches, Bars, and Ballads* does a better than admirable job of bringing this to light. Longtime fans need to hear this if for no other reason than to realize that Buffett is a multifaceted musician whose artistic changes have been natural progressions; new fans will wonder how songs this consistently good could have been overlooked by the media for so very long. Besides, all self-respecting fans will need to familiarize themselves with the *Parrot Head Handbook,* which contains Buffett's impressions on each song and various aspects of his professional life.

I know that I started this project being far removed from the world of Parrot Head–ism, but I'll happily confess that *Boats, Beaches, Bars, and Ballads* is one of the best box sets I have heard. As for not being a Parrot Head, my own wife is beginning to question my veracity on this point. Now that I'm done with my obligatory listens, I still continue to play this collection so loud and so often that she swears she sees little green feathers sprouting from my cheekbones. I continue to deny it, but deep down, I wonder if it could be true.

SQU-AWWWK!

For a record label's debut, *Boats, Beaches, Bars, and Ballads* did one heck of a job in providing some much-needed revenue. On its debut in June 1992, fans old and new jumped on it, causing it to sell in quantities that surpassed most of Buffett's single CD releases. Although it was a relatively expensive four-disc set, it rose to position number 68 and lasted for a nineteen-week run. Even after it completed its chart run, sales continued at a steady pace, causing Buffett's career retrospective to be one of the few box sets ever to achieve certified platinum status.

As the Margaritaville momentum continued to build, even the Disney organization would become interested. The corporation's offer, a deal to place Buffett-based restaurants in Disney theme parks, while flattering, would have meant a significant loss of control. After a great deal of consideration, Buffett decided against it. By 1992 he decided that he would hold on to the reins of his company and expand it to New Orleans. Kevin Boucher, the man responsible for the Key West nightclub, relocated to the Crescent City to oversee the expansion. He needn't have worried, as the business hit the ground running and never looked back. Margaritaville may once have been a state of mind, but now it was a thriving enterprise. In comparison, I wonder what would be the result if other rock stars followed Buffett's lead. Neil Young's "Rustic Sleepover Camp"? Bruce Springsteen's "New Jersey/Dust Bowl Theme Parks"? Madonna lingerie outlets? Meatloaf diners? Peter Gabriel's Third World Tours? Elton John's . . . can you just imagine what would be sold at an Elton John outlet? Wow.

To add to his already full plate, Buffett continued working steadily on the follow-up to *Tales From Margaritaville.* He formulated a character-rich outline and spent a great deal of effort interweaving the various subplots that had formulated in his head. Initially, he had envisioned a relatively small project, but as usually happens with these things, the work took on a life of its own and grew well beyond his original conception. This time, instead of a collection of occasionally semirelated short stories, Buffett arranged his disparate thoughts into a full-blown novel. Owing to the rollicking success of his first book, he was offered a significant advance for the work and because completing the deal was pretty much a no-brainer, he decided to act as his own agent, foregoing the 15 percent fee that is usually deducted from the author's share. Called *Where Is Joe Merchant?*, the book was completed in 1992 and shipped at well over 100,000 units. It would go on to top the *New York Times* bestseller list, eventually topping the 400,000-copy mark, and that was before it was released in paperback form.

Coinciding closely with his book release was a Buffett-penned article that appeared in the autumn 1992 issue of *Esquire Sportsman,* entitled "Everything in the Woods Wants to Eat a Quail (Including Me)." The article shows a different side of Buffett, not as a musician, sailor, writer, or aviator but as a sportsman. A telling quote arises in the text when Buffett admits to sensing a shift in his perspective, stating that in past years he "usually went back to the flats of Key West to fish. Then something changed. I could feel myself throttling back." With a thriving business that was expanding to a new location, a record company that was just getting off the ground, and a novel under his belt, not to mention his touring commitments, I don't know if most people would agree that he was "throttling back," unless you took into consideration his recording career. For two decades, Buffett had managed practically without fail to release new product on an annual basis but now, with so many alternate projects to distract him, it had been four years since *Off to See the Lizard* (1989). He was gathering material and trying to organize it for his next release, but it would be yet another year before the tentatively titled *Quietly Making Noise* would see the light of day as *Fruitcakes* (1994).

Meanwhile, fans had to make do with the odds, ends, and tidbits that came their way. Parrot Heads who went to the movies for a night out would have been pleased to hear Buffett's "Stars on the Water" appear incidentally in Sydney Pollack's film *The Firm,* starring Tom Cruise and Gene Hackman. Based on a book by John Grisham, the story line moves back and forth between Memphis, Tennessee, and the Cayman Islands, making it almost obligatory that the soundtrack contain a Buffett song.

If it was something new that fans were looking for, a taste could be found on the Margaritaville Records compilation entitled *Margaritaville Cafe Late Night Menu.* Compiling the recordings of a few acts who have appeared at Jimmy's Key West establishment, Buffett fattened out the package by adding three of his own recordings (none of which he wrote), interspersed with a number of solo recordings by the various Coral Reefers. For the most part, the disc was a coconut-scented (no, not literally) collection of better-than-generic bar songs, touching on salsa, southern-fried boogie, pop, bluesy soul, and country-funk. Most of the acts are entertaining if not independently commercial, making this an excellent forum for them to gain exposure and recognition beyond their region. Of the Coral Reefer solo ventures, Peter Mayer's (as "PM") "India" is most promising, casting Buffett's new guitarist as an able vocalist, songwriter, and performer in his own right. Also of note was Buffett's own contributions, including a fun version of Sam Cooke's classic "Another Saturday Night" (improbably released as a single) and a playfully goofy reggae number called "Reggae Accident," about a car accident with a carload of uninsured Rastas. Buffett's feigned Jamaican accent can be somewhat taxing, but his Bob Marley mannerisms are uncannily accurate. The best song, however, is the album's last, Buffett's cover of a Danny O'Keefe–Vince Melamed composition called "Souvenirs." While Buffett fans hungrily picked up this CD, Margaritaville Records simultaneously tried to promote interest in its most recent signing, another New Orleans–based act (as is Evangeline) called the Iguanas.

Margaritaville Cafe Late Night Menu was welcome but it was just a tease for fans who had been so patiently waiting for an album of new material. Just as distracting but even more compelling was Margaritaville's compilation of Buffett's first two pre-ABC/MCA albums that he recorded for Barnaby. *Before the Beach* was released in conjunction with *Late Night Menu* and contained Buffett's second "lost" album in its entirety, and the lion's share of his debut disc (editing the album's single

"The Christian?") Until now, this material was rarer than rare, so it marked the first opportunity for Parrot Heads to hear Buffett readily at a stage before his image was solidified, when the thought of a huge following couldn't have been anything more than a pipe dream. This time around, enough fans were enamored with Buffett to ignite a natural curiosity for his early work, sending the *Before the Beach* collection to register on *Billboard's* charts for two weeks, topping out at number 169 in June 1993. Somewhat surprisingly, the *Late Night Menu* collection would not chart at all.

In the early part of the year, one of Jimmy Buffett's most unusual live performances took place when he and the Coral Reefer Band dressed formally and took the stage at the Tennessee Ball, one of many parties that were held on the night of Bill Clinton's inauguration. Seeing Buffett on stage in a tuxedo was surprising enough, but the ultimate kicker took place when the newly elected president arrived and greeted Buffett onstage, saying "Yes, Jimmy Buffett is a friend of mine." Then, the First Family was introduced to Buffett's own family. After these formalities, President Clinton grabbed a saxophone and proceeded to jam along with the Coral Reefers on a very democratic version of "Changes in Latitudes, Changes in Attitudes."

The Chameleon Caravan Tour of 1993 had a number of other highlights, though none that were quite as politically connected. Income from a show in Miami was used to aid victims of Hurricane Andrew, and other shows also took on quite a unique flavor. Inspired by the New Orleans Jazz Fest, an annual event put together by Buffett's friend Quint Davis that features hundreds of musical acts performing on multiple stages, with plenty of food booths and cultural exhibits, Buffett attempted to put together his own microcosm of this sprawling event. Similar in scope to Perry Farrell's ongoing Lollapalooza events, Buffett's version was organized around the Margaritaville artists, with his own band headlining the show. Because New Orleans provided the inspiration, Buffett's first "Primo Parrot Head Party" took place on a 100-degree day in June at New Orleans' Tad Gormley Stadium. Besides Evangeline and the Iguanas, the eight-hour program also included sets by Michael McDonald and New Orleans' own prodigal son, Little Richard. Like Lollapalooza, Buffett wanted to make the event portable and hoped that this type of minifestival would replace his typical touring grind. Similar events would take place in Georgia and Ohio, but the logistics of organizing such a broad-reaching event soon caused the idea to be waylaid. The rest of the Chameleon Caravan tour would be (somewhat) more traditional. Consisting of forty-three shows, Buffett and crew toured through the summer and managed gross ticket receipts in excess of $16 million.

Recording for his next studio album finally took place in January 1994. With all distractions either set aside or completed, new music became the focal point. Because the Coral Reefers had become a relatively stable touring unit over the past few years, Buffett enlisted the entire cast and crew to join him at Compass Point Studios in Nassau in the Bahamas. By May, the package was completed and released to a nearly ravenous audience of Parrot Heads.

Fruitcakes (1994)

Margaritaville Records MCAD-11043

Before I played even a single note of *Fruitcakes,* I had a premonition that I wasn't going to like this disc. Due to the five-year hiatus since his last collection of new material, expectations were heightened but the goofy and elaborate CD package provided a few hints that made me suspicious that the music would be flimsy and without substance.

After a few listenings, though, I began to see a method creep through all of the madness. At its worst, *Fruitcakes* takes some of Buffett's most cloying musical characteristics and blares them at you. There are times when you will want to cover your ears and run screaming for cover. Then again, there are moments of profound insight and intelligence along with astounding musicianship that are woven throughout the entire collection. His voice, for example, is stronger and clearer than it has ever been. What is so unnerving is that these two opposing characteristics are homogenized to the point that they become inseparable. Although even the worst songs have moments of brilliance, the best songs find themselves compromised by a whole boatload of unnecessary complexities. Buffett's wordplay, though self-consciously clever, has rarely been better, it's just that he often takes his ideas too far.

Let's test this theory by applying it to the album's various and sundry tracks. The album's starting point (and its focal point) are the first two recordings, "Everybody's Got a Cousin in Miami" and "Fruitcakes." After a short recording of a carnival parade, the first track lurches into gear with a calypso-based rhythm that is absolutely brilliant in its execution. Buffett's lyrics were inspired by an incident whereby two Cuban refugee couples happened to come ashore on his Key West property. Buffett greeted them and made them comfortable while he notified the Coast Guard of his surprise guests. When the INS people arrived, a member of the party tried to impress the authorities by stating that he had a cousin in Miami. This real-life event set off a torrent of inspiration, and that's the problem, because Buffett simply doesn't know when to stop. By song's end, he completely abandons the song's original topic and instead launches into a fantasy about his band demanding a pay raise. Now, where did *that* come from? "Fruitcakes" is an equally interesting composition, only this time Buffett starts things off by ranting uncontrollably, screaming some nonsense about Junior Mints and borrowing his summation from the film *Network*. During this tirade, I found myself thinking "Is he kidding me?" Well, yes, he is. In concert, these comedic aberrations would have been fine but in the studio, they're too contrived to remain funny and become a time-consuming distraction that causes each of these songs to stretch beyond seven minutes. In the process, a pair of ingenious and superbly limber arrangements get stepped on by an overly loquacious frontman. Yes, it's Buffett's show but at the very least, his ideas would have benefited from some prudent pruning.

This is why the simplest songs fair best on this collection. "Lone Palm" is a pretty reflection on the need to keep things in perspective during the unpredictable shifts that take place in our lives. "Six String Music" does the same, proving that Buffett still has a knack for writing good, simple songs by writing a song (with G. E. Smith) about writing good, simple songs. "Love in the Library" proves the point further by remaining musically simple, though the consciously clever lyrics seem to prevent the listener from becoming emotionally involved in the tale ("read all you want into this rendezvous"). Therein lies another core problem with this disc. Buffett's talents are on display throughout, but most of the time he is too self-assured for his own good. Unlike his most effective work, which functions instinctively, here he is too focused on the effort exerted, forcing a glib perspective on listeners that has them observing instead of participating.

In "Vampires, Mummies and the Holy Ghost," Buffett's confidence goes beyond entertainment and becomes tiresome. At song's end, over a cartoonish vamp of horror music, Buffett rhetorically asks his audience, "Scared ya, didn't I?" Absolutely, Jimmy, absolutely. Even more frightening, though, are the album's cover songs. "Uncle John's Band" is a classic beyond measure and the Coral Reefers handle it well enough, but any attempt to meld the Grateful Dead's signature tune (one of them, anyway) into a tropical arrangement strikes me as pointless if not downright scary. I'm not saying that Buffett should disown Robert Greenidge (his pan player), only that he should be more frugal in the way that he employs the steel drum to his material.

His samba-drenched rendition of Ray Davies's "Sunny Afternoon" is another case entirely. On the Kinks' hit version, Davies sang the song with displaced irony, making it a comic and droll observation of wealth and ego. Buffett instead sings the song with mock sincerity (he even avoids the line "drunkenness and cruelty" by changing it to the more first-person palatable "Parrot Heads and parties"), thus ignoring the best aspect of the original version and coming within a heartbeat of exposing himself as the very character that Davies was parodying. "She's Got You" is a Hank Cochran masterpiece that Patsy Cline perfected over thirty years ago and if you are familiar with her version, then you will probably break into hives when you hear this bizarre gender-bending abomination.

Buffett's French-inspired tunes ("Quietly Making Noise" and "Frenchman for the Night") both fare much better. Here, Buffett's choice of phrases are as artful as anything he has ever written, and the music provides a sense of place that is more Martinique than Champs Elysées. Gimme an album of songs like these and I'll happily lay back with the CD player locked on autorepeat. More greatness can be found at album's end, with a wonderful ode to his second daughter called "Delaney Talks to Statues" and the almost as winning "Apocalypso." Given Buffett's taste for wordplay and his penchant for Caribbean rhythms, it's a play on words that I suppose was as unavoidable as it was inevitable. Written by Matt Betton, "Apocalypso" is a pleasant reflection on the end of the world (huh?). Ultimately, this well-concocted contradiction is a perfect ending to an album that is full of them. Combining elements of genius and mundanity, *Fruitcakes* is a contradiction that can be as annoying as it is clever, as disappointing as it is amusing, and ultimately, as frustrating as it is entertaining.

Fruitcakes was released in June 1994 and, almost beyond belief, *debuted* on the *Billboard* charts at position number 5. It would continue to chart for another nineteen weeks. That made *Fruitcakes* the highest-charting album of Buffett's entire career (his previous best was *Son of a Son of a Sailor*'s number 10 slot)! Well, that goes to show you how much I know about these things, but Buffett gave up long ago on heeding artistic advice and suffering the opinions of critics. When a level of success such as this could be obtained simply by following his own instincts, why should he subject himself to unsolicited points of view? *Fruitcakes'* debut position drove that point home quite profoundly.

If you were looking to rationalize the remarkable sales performance of this record, it could be done by combining two factors. First of all, the faithful Parrot Heads were awaiting this album for *five years,* an absurdly long time for a guy whose annual releases were once as predictable as clockwork. The second factor was the revamping of *Billboard*'s charting methods that took place in the interim. Where they once relied on retail outlets to report sales, they now implemented something called "Soundscan," a device that accurately measured sales as they took place at the register. Combine these circumstances and a number-5 debut starts to make sense, because an awful lot of people would be sprinting to their local record store, buying this disc faster than the retailers could open the containers they were shipped in. Any record that can sell out of the box is going to debut high on the Soundscan system, and that is more or less exactly what happened in the case of *Fruitcakes.*

Just as rumors regarding a *Margaritaville* movie began to dissipate entirely, a new series of rumors began to circulate, claiming that a screen adaptation of "Where Is Joe Merchant?" was to be optioned by Paramount Studios and might go into production. Another rumor (that turned out to be true) was Buffett's involvement in the theater. A longtime admirer of Herman Wouk's "Don't Stop the Carnival," he wondered if he might be able to adapt the story into the form of a musical. Published in 1965, "Don't Stop the Carnival" is based on Wouk's own experiences during his seven-year stay in the Virgin Islands. For years, Buffett had considered the novel to be a manual of sorts for expatriate life in the Caribbean. He even claimed that it played a large role in his own decision to buy a hotel on the island of Saint Barts called Autor du Rocher, only to watch life imitate art when the establishment experienced its own nighmarish chain of events. Eventually, it burned to the ground.

Best known nowadays as the author of *The Caine Mutiny* and two of television's most watched miniseries, *The Winds of War* and *War and Remembrance,* Wouk actually began his career as a writer of comedy. Unsure whether the famous author was still among the living, Buffett set out to get clearance for his project. He discovered that Wouk was very much alive, but was nonplussed to learn that Wouk hadn't heard of him. "Thanks for your interest, but who are you?" came the response. Buffett sent along a few recordings and a copy of his book, explaining who he was. Wouk was confused by Buffett's enthusiasm and asked, "Why would you want to do this?" Buffett responded, "Because I think it would be fun." In a short while, Wouk contacted Buffett, saying "I checked you out. You're good at what you do," and a meeting was arranged. Buffett traveled to Palm Springs, California, and in Wouk's backyard, underneath what they referred to as the "lucky tree," a deal was struck whereby Wouk would be the show's librettist and Buffett would write the music.

While Buffett's career experienced yet another commercial rebirth (or perhaps *escalation* would be a better word), he set out on his 1994 summer tour, only this time he decided to avoid long stretches, breaking the touring into smaller segments so he could maintain his energy level, but also so he could preserve some time for private matters. Jimmy got word that his father had been diagnosed with Alzheimer's disease, and so with his schedule abbreviated, he vowed to spend as much time with him as was possible. In this spirit, the pair took a midsummer trip to Nova Scotia, the land of their forefathers.

With thoughts of mortality occupying much of his time, Buffett himself came within coughing distance of meeting his maker on August 25,

1994, when his Grumman Widgeon (which he purchased just two years earlier) seaplane hit a wave on takeoff and flipped onto its back. Always one to fly by the book, Buffett followed appropriate emergency procedures and managed to escape, swimming from the wreckage when he was picked up by a passing boat. Though he doesn't like to talk about the accident other than to say that he feels he's a better person because of it, he told the *Coconut Telegraph,* "That's one ride we will not have at the Margaritaville theme park." Of course, this comment then set off speculation that the Head Parrot was in the process of developing his own theme park for Parrot Heads. What with his involvement in practically every other form of entertainment, the idea didn't seem too far-fetched or unlikely, but as it turns out, Buffett was only practicing his metaphors.

Film continued to play a role in Buffett's career, only instead of supplying songs, he was now providing his profile. His first onscreen appearance of the nineties was for the film *Cobb* (1994), based on the legendary Ty Cobb and directed by Ron Shelton. Buffett appears as a crippled heckler who taunts the baseball star from the stands and gets pummeled for it. Featuring a brilliant performance by Tommy Lee Jones in the title role, Buffett's scene exists as a hallucinatory flashback, causing his speaking lines to occur before the visual scene comes into view. We get to see Buffett's face for only a few seconds, after Cobb attacks him and he lies dazed and reeling from the shock. As someone who has had his fair share of experience with hecklers during the early part of his career, Buffett was allowed to ad-lib his speaking lines. The following year, he had a short cameo appearance as a 727 pilot in the film version of Michael Crichton's book *Congo* (1995).

Busy as ever, Buffett broadened his exposure well beyond his traditional Parrot Head base by appearing on two very different music collaborations. *Kermit UnPigged* was a collection of recordings for kids, featuring Jim Henson's Muppets performing humorous versions of classic material, much of it as duets with taller counterparts. Guests included Vince Gill, who is credited for the "unfrogettable" (*sic*) title, Don Henley, Linda Ronstadt, Ozzy Osborne, George Benson, and of course, Jimmy Buffett. For his featured selection, Buffett is teamed up with the Great Gonzo and Rizzo the Rat for a genuinely funny version of the Byrds' (via Roger McGuinn) "Mr. Spaceman." Another project that involved Buffett was the animated film *Fern Gully: The Last Rain-*

forest (1992), which used a Buffett-Utley composition called "If I'm Gonna Eat Somebody (It Might as Well Be You)."

On a slightly more mature collection, Buffett shared vocal credits on an almost equally amusing recording with a somewhat less fuzzy duet partner. In 1993, a collection of classic Frank Sinatra tunes was recorded with a special twist. As a means of tribute to the then eighty-year-old crooner and touching on nearly every living vocalist's dream to duet with the living legend, Sinatra was paired off with a broad range of stylistic interpreters who had been given the chance of a lifetime to work with the world's most famous saloon singer. The collection was entitled *Duets*.

To portray the full range of respect that Sinatra's reputation warranted, stars as varied as Barbra Streisand and Bono (these days, I wonder if they're so far apart) teamed with the Chairman of the Board, and the collection sold like hotcakes. These "duets" were actually separate performances that were dubbed onto prerecorded tracks and mixed, so most collaborators never actually met with Sinatra but instead communicated through the mail service. This method of operation occasionally resulted in Sinatra and his collaborator taking completely different approaches to the same song, and sometimes the results would be accidentally funny; Hearing Bono moan "I've Got You Under My Skin" while Sinatra enunciates his lines has to be one of the most bizarre and surreal recorded moments ever concocted.

The weirdness of this procedure was apparently not lost on Buffett, who was invited to participate on a second collection, aptly named *Duets II.* For his selection, he and Frank "collaborated" on the Kurt Weill–Bertolt Brecht classic "Mack the Knife." With no intention of disrespect, it would only be honest to note that Sinatra's voice had lost some of its luster since his prime and Sinatra himself seems prepared to resign himself to the fact that this version was bound to fall on its face. Instead of trying to out-sing his competition, Sinatra launches into an ad-lib that acknowledges the brilliance of previous versions, including Bobby Darin, Louis Armstrong, and Ella Fitzgerald. Buffett goes along for the ride and his relaxed demeanor keeps the recording from derailing entirely. At one point, Sinatra lapses into his tough-guy penchant for using the name Jack and (keep in mind that they were not together at the time) with drop-dead timing, Buffett chimes in with "That's Jimmy, Frank," making this one genuinely funny, albeit strange, recording.

Margaritaville continued expanding its roster and its catalog, adding both Todd Snider and Marshall Chapman to the fold. Snider released his debut album, *Songs for the Daily Planet,* and Chapman's release was a live recording from a woman's prison wryly entitled . . . *It's About Time*. Chapman was no newcomer but an experienced songwriter who had released three albums for Epic Records, and another on her own Tall Girl label. Buffett had written a few songs with her and also covered some of her material on the *Last Mango in Paris* album. For further enhancement of Margaritaville's mainstream exposure, a deal was cut with Chris Blackwell's Island Records that called for Island to handle all marketing, promotion, and publicity for Margaritaville's releases. Considering their philosophical and image similarities, it was a match made in paradise. MCA would continue to shoulder responsibility for distribution. Buffett's family added to its roster as well, adopting an infant son named Cameron Marley Buffett.

Now it was time for Margaritaville's chief executive to release a new record of his own. At the suggestion of producer Russ Kunkel, Buffett and a few members of the latest incarnation of the Coral Reefer Band (Peter Mayer, Jim Mayer, Roger Guth, and Jay Oliver) retreated to Key West to write and arrange new material at a relaxed pace. For inspiration and to provide a consistent theme for the album, Buffett suggested that songs be based on some of their favorite published stories. When enough material was compiled, they headed to Buffett's own recently revamped Shrimpboat Sound to polish off the recording.

Barometer Soup (1995)

Margaritaville Records MCAD-11247

I should have seen it coming, but I didn't. One thing I have learned on reviewing Jimmy Buffett's career is that he must be one of the most consistently inconsistent artists of all time. With oddly persistent regularity, his albums tend to alternate between greatness and mediocrity. Following this logic, and because I was mostly disappointed in its pre-

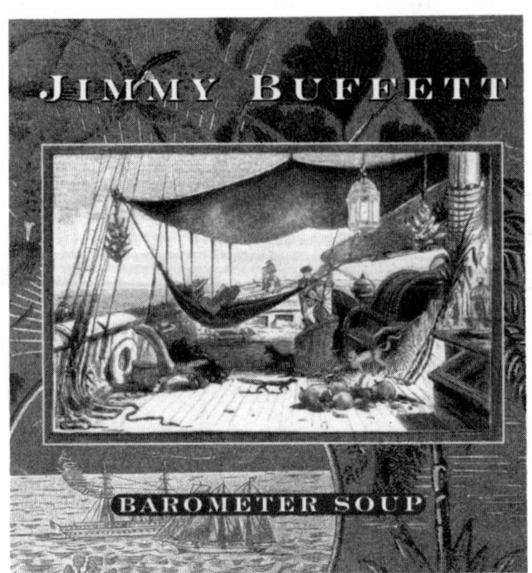

decessor (*Fruitcakes*), I more or less expected to like *Barometer Soup*. What surprises me is *how much* I like it. After numerous consecutive listens, it just gets better and better until I'm inclined to think of this as one of his best efforts. At times, I find myself thinking that it might even be his best. As enjoyable as cocktails at sunset on a midsummer weekend, Buffett's status as the kingpin of mellow self-confidence is furthered with an album that justifies every ounce of his acclaim.

Songwriting, production, and musicianship are rarely so uniformly and consistently excellent, no matter who the artist is. I'm not saying that *Barometer Soup* is perfect, but it's pretty damn close. As far as I'm concerned, every song on this album is played for its maximum potential, and Buffett and crew almost never fail in their intentions. Just as important, none of the songs overreach themselves, mostly because virtually nothing appears to be out of reach for this edition of the Coral Reefers. They tackle everything from simple folk songs to intensely syncopated soca, and each tune is independently brilliant in its own way.

Much of the credit must go to producer Russ Kunkel, who deserves a trophy for his work here. Plainly, I underestimated his talents on the last record, because *Barometer Soup* contains one of the most diverse and consistently thoughtful soundscapes that I have ever heard. For evidence, just listen to the blend of reverbed guitar and organ on "Barefoot Children in the Rain." Resting gently on a bed of acoustic guitar, bass, and drums played hard with brushes, I cannot imagine a more sympathetic arrangement, particularly for a gentle song about the beautiful simplicity of innocence. Equally astonishing is "Diamond as Big as the Ritz." While Buffett sings about the dangers of excessive greed, the production blends synthetic and natural sounds in perfect balance for a rock-steady rhythm that conveys an incredible sense of warmth.

Metro Parrot Head Club members with their bananas. The club held a "banana-dressing contest" in honor of the release of Buffett's *Banana Wind* album. (Photo courtesy of the Metro Parrot Head Club)

Lucky Parrots! Jimmy Buffett stops to chat with members of the Metro Parrot Head Club. (Photo courtesy of the Metro Parrot Head Club)

(*Left*) Kathy Shedd, the president of the Music Key Parrot Head Club, pictured here at a party in Nashville, Tennessee, was the first to fully immerse the author in the world of the Parrot Head. (Photo © 1997 Leigh Anglin)

(*Opposite*) These are the pictures that Kathy Shedd took of Jimmy Buffett and his daughter Savannah Jane in the early eighties, and that she had framed to present to Jimmy Buffett the night of his show on March 2, 1997, in Nashville, Tennessee. (Photos courtesy of Kathy Shedd)

These happy Phlockers won the award for "Best Decorated Hotel Room" in March 1997 at a hotel in Minneapolis, Minnesota. (Photo © 1997 Leigh Anglin)

(*Left*) A Carmen Miranda–looking Parrot Head shakes her thing at a March 1997 pre-show party in Knoxville, Tennessee. (Photo © 1997 Leigh Anglin)

(*Below*) Parrot Heads setting up a pre-show crosswalk for Fruitcakes to "strut naked through" in October 1997 in Irvine, California. (Photo © 1997 Leigh Anglin)

Indeed, warmth is the most telling characteristic throughout the record. Whether it is owing to the instincts of the production team, the playing abilities of the Coral Reefers, or focused arranging by the songwriting team, the album conveys a sense of closeness that never lets up. Most of this feeling stems directly from the songwriting. For source material, inspiration comes from the work of six authors (Mark Twain, Herman Wouk, F. Scott Fitzgerald, Jim Harrison, Carl Hiaasen, and Buffett himself), three kids, a friend or two, and one restaurant. With only two exceptions (Buffett's "Jimmy Dreams" and a cover of James Taylor's "Mexico") all songs are credited to the team of Buffett, Mayer, Guth, and Oliver, and they stay close to the emotional core of each topic. The album's leadoff song and title cut is a perfect example of this, because it immediately invites you into Buffett's relaxed world vision while simultaneously triggering a sense of nostalgia for the simple pleasures of his early work.

Acknowledging his appointed role as leader, it also provides a few clues to longtime fans who have become suspicious of his intentions of late. If you can accept the fact that his philosophies have been augmented since the midseventies, you will realize that Buffett is offering you heartfelt advice when he sings "Moderation seems to be the key." It took the man years to come to terms with this realization and for those fans who are willing to allow their hero to age gracefully, this is a profoundly simple and honest suggestion for finding happiness and satisfaction in the face of aging. "Bank of Bad Habits" says much the same thing, only in a more playful manner ("The wrong thing is the right thing until you lose control"). If it wasn't for the pointlessly silly "seven deadly sins" rap, this song would be letter A perfect.

The entire album conveys this sense of childlike honesty and revelation, but three tracks stand out in particular. "Jimmy Dreams" is a wonderful children's bedtime song that begs to reach the child within all of us. Playing with heartfelt simplicity, Buffett conveys his sense of satisfaction without lapsing into a messianic complex or condescension, as he is sometimes prone to do. I love it when Buffett reaches deep for his inspiration, because his songs are more likely to touch my soul when he is willing to reveal a piece of his own, and it is sometimes surprising to hear so much emotion penetrate Buffett's veneer. The sad portrait of "Remittance Man" is an astonishing change of pace for Buffett, suggesting that something much bleaker than restless curiosity could be the driving force of wanderlust. Sad, lonely, and genuinely moving, it focuses on the flip side of adventure and draws us in. The album's most gorgeous track, however, is "The Night I Painted the Sky," which by anyone's standards must qualify as one of the most heart-rending compositions he has ever written. Superficially, it is about setting off fireworks but emotionally, it conveys much, much more. Have you ever been touched by something simple and yet profound, something that caused your heart to ache with a lonely sense of nostalgia and a childlike sense of awareness so deep that it made you want to cry? That specifically is what this song manages to project and I am in awe of Buffett's ability to render it so beautifully.

Even the dumb songs are good. "Blue Heaven Rendezvous" is only an ode to an eatery, but if the restaurant is half as charming as this arrangement, then please make me a reservation for two. "The Ballad of Skip Wiley" is another jazz-blues aberration, but it's no cornier than a song ought to be that contains lyrics about kidnapping a beauty contestant in the name of environmentalism. Okay, maybe they aren't works of genius, but if you would relax a bit, you might realize that they're also fun and well executed.

Nothing is as well executed, though, as "Lage Nom Ai," a burning zouk-soca with syncopations that are absolutely faultless. For proof of the Coral Reefer Band's multifaceted talents, you need look no further. When I suggested earlier on that "Volcano" was a childishly simple example of Caribbean rhythms, I was thinking of something as authentically impressive as this. Speaking of which, "Don't Chu-Know" is another rhythmically clever composition (though lyrically trite) that suggests "Volcano" during the fade-out, although Buffett's free-form rap here is distracting if not outright embarrassing. Another example of unnecessary verbal jabberwocky arises at the album's fade, when Buffett feels compelled to rush through a silly recap of the album's songs and characters over a rocking version of James Taylor's "Mexico." More of an unfortunate embellishment than a disaster, the album survives this late-inning error in judgment.

Details are what make or break a record and it is the details that make *Barometer Soup* such a fine recipe. GOPs might complain that this isn't the old Buffett, but give them time and I bet that they'll come around. After *Fruitcakes,* was anybody expecting him to release his most subdued, thoughtful, and reflective album since *Floridays*? It might take some time to develop a taste for this record, but I believe that *Barometer Soup* is destined to be as legendary as Buffett's most classic work.

Much like its predecessor, *Barometer Soup* jumped to the top of the charts, appearing the week of August 19, 1995, and charting at number 6. It lasted on the album charts for seventeen weeks, thus proving that the inertia of his previous release was no fluke. Because adult-contemporary radio tends to fear anything that is new, Buffett's reworking of James Taylor's "Mexico" fit its format perfectly and it reached number 25 on its charts. It was the only song from *Barometer Soup* to be given any individual attention by radio.

Later the same year, Margaritaville decided to make Buffett's appearance on the Internet official and established its own Web site (called, appropriately enough, "Jimmy Buffett's Margaritaville"), adding to the plethora of Buffett-related Web sites that already existed. Though there are no accurate listings of each and every Web site that contains information on Buffett, it would probably be a safe bet to say that he is the most represented musical artist in cyberspace. America Online recently acknowledged this by giving Buffett the Most Active Online award. Dozens of dedicated sites exist and hundreds of others reference him. Though there are far too many to list them all, a few of the best include Chris Wilson's F(requently) A(sked) Q(uestions), Bill "Big Dog" Lack's Listserv, Dave April's Parrot(t)head Page (I believe the parenthetical *t* is a play on many a journalist's tendency to forget the last *t* in Buffett's family name), KC Angel's Gazetteer, Mike Hall's Church of Buffett—Orthodox, and Toby Gibson's Parrot Central. With access to so much information, Parrot Heads with a computer addiction can investigate biographical info, discographies, song lyrics, album reviews, magazine articles, tour dates, even song chords and Buffett-related recipes. In addition, there are numerous forums and chat rooms to express opinions and organize activities.

With the lines of communication so open, the Parrot Head organization expanded rapidly. In the late eighties, a Buffett fan named Scott Nickerson organized the first Parrot Head Club in Atlanta. Envisioning an organization that could be both fun and socially oriented, he contacted Margaritaville with his ideas. More than just a fan or social club, the Atlanta Parrot Head Club drew up a charter that called for its involvement in all sorts of charitable activities, particularly those that are community or environmentally oriented. One of their events, "Underwater Monopoly," not only raised more than seventy thousand dollars for Muscular Dystrophy but also set a Guinness World Record (for the longest underwater board game)! It wasn't long before other towns wanted to follow suit. In the interest of maintaining some continuity between the various clubs, Margaritaville asked Nickerson to act as an overseer of the various and sundry groups. A national organization, officially known as Parrot Heads in Paradise, became the official designation for the various clubs, who otherwise exist independently. For official recognition, each club branch must show evidence of involvement in at least four separate charitable or environmental concerns.

Each year, members of the Parrot Head clubs gather from all over the country to discuss business and have some Buffett-style fun. These annual get togethers are known as the "Meeting of the Minds" and take place each November in New Orleans. Another annual "phlocking" is the Listserv List's RACA (Rum and Cooked Animals, taken from the lyrics of "Bank of Bad Habits") Fest, which occurs every Fourth of July weekend in Ohio. Today, there are nearly one hundred geographical branches of Parrot Heads in Paradise, with an estimated membership exceeding 20,000.

Most Parrot Heads are opinionated people, and heated discussions can arise over even the most minuscule topics (don't even *think* of misspelling Buffett's name, for example), but the bonds among members are usually tight and go well beyond Jimmy Buffett's music (a topic on which they disagree vehemently), making them not only an independent community but a socially conscious one as well. Regarding charity, Parrot Heads have adopted many of Buffett's causes as their own, with funds being donated to his Save the Manatee organization, Greenpeace, Walden Woods, Artists Against Hunger and Homelessness, and dozens of others. If Jimmy Buffett suddenly stopped in his tracks, it's my guess that these organizations would continue to exist. With so many social events and charitable causes to bind them, Parrot Heads have transcended the simple perception of them as Buffett fans, and instead are a wholly functional social organization much like the Kiwanis Club or the American Legion may have been to a previous generation.

At present, this point is academic because Buffett continues to record and tour with regularity. The 1995 expedition was called the Domino College Tour, named for a Caribbean roadside social club that once inspired the song of the same name. A few Buffett-related recordings were released by Margaritaville Records in 1995. In July, another collection of Margaritaville Cafe acts was captured and collected on disc, only this time the focus was on the New Orleans location. Called *Margaritaville Cafe New Orleans,* it featured a wide variety of local talent scattered around a pair of Buffett recordings. Buffett's selections included Frankie Ford's "Sea Cruise" and, somewhat strangely, the suicidally depressing public domain folk tune "Good Night Irene." More fetching was *The Parakeet Album,* a collection of songs performed by a Nashville-based group of children known as the W. O. Smith Music School Singers. Released in November, it is intended for "Parakeets" (the children of Parrot Heads) and consists of the children's renditions of Buffett's more innocent compositions, backed by members of the Coral Reefer Band. Even so, a fair amount of revisionism was in order to maintain a sense of appropriateness: "Where I go I hope there's rum" (from "Volcano") becomes "Count my fingers, count my thumbs," and "cold draft beer, good God almighty" ("Cheeseburger in Paradise") becomes "cold root beer, good gosh almighty." Even some of his children's songs were toned down: in "Jolly Mon Sing," the line " 'cause their hearts were made in Hell" is whitewashed to "as she weaved a witchy spell."

At the start of 1996, Buffett's navigational exploits were once again in the news. Along with Bono from the Irish rock band U2, he flew into Jamaica for a meeting with Chris Blackwell. As they were disembarking from the plane, someone tipped off the Jamaican police force that a suspicious craft had landed in the waters near the Negril lighthouse. Without justifiable cause, the trigger-happy policemen emptied round after round into the floating plane as the pilot took off to refuel. An estimated one hundred and thirty seven rounds were fired, only two of which actually hit their mark—sharpshooters these guys most definitely weren't. Smarting from the gross negligence of the Jamaican police force, Buffett took mental note of the incident and decided to record it for posterity, incorporating it into the lyrics of a song for his next album.

For his next release, Buffett considered the idea of recording a mostly acoustic album. Old fans who heard the news were ecstatic in their anticipation, expecting a sharp reversion to the Key West style he had popularized in the seventies. On June 4, 1996, the album was released and instantly snatched up by an ever-increasing sea of Parrot Heads.

Banana Wind (1996)

Margaritaville Records MCAD-11451

Are there two Jimmy Buffetts? I can understand when an artist desires a change of direction or through maturation wants to refine his sound, but the variation of Buffett's output has me entirely puzzled. On one hand, there is the pensive, thoughtful artist who reflectively shares his impressions, accompanied by very well thought out and imaginative musical arrangements. On the other hand, there's the egotistical narcissist who insists on drumming superficiality at his audience over monotonous, unimaginative accompaniment. One sings his songs to us, the other sings at us. Like Jekyll and Hyde, it seems as if the more humane half of the duo has no control over the monster. When the monster wants to sing, there's no stopping him and on *Banana Wind,* it sounds as if the monster locks the real Jimmy Buffett in the closet while he runs amok.

The disappointment I felt on first hearing *Banana Wind* was almost tangible. Buffett's last album, *Barometer Soup,* was full of inspiration and vigor, especially for a guy who has been making artistically viable music for three decades. Not only did it prove that this veteran still had plenty of steam, it indicated that his artistic integrity was as focused as it had ever been. Then *Banana Wind* comes along and makes its predecessor look like an aberration. The tone of this album combines childish simplicity with judgmental anger, making Buffett sound like Mister Rogers after he realizes that his car was stolen. I can recall a television blooper when an unnamed host of a children's show thought he was off the air and muttered "That ought to keep the little f%*#ers happy." Buffett sounds a lot like that guy, following the on-air childishness and travel brochure commercialism of "Holiday" with the "Is-this-thing-still-on?" judgmental anger of "Overkill." He even tries to rap on this one, and the anger in his voice makes me want to hide from this guy more than tune in to what he is trying to say. Since when does Buffett's musical palette include angry rap? If this is Jimmy Buffett, then I'm Snoop Doggy Dogg.

Considering his wealth of accomplishments, Buffett must be granted a wide berth for his expression, but when he becomes smug about his success, I become disinterested. Who wants to listen to music that makes you feel inferior? Why should I subject myself to someone's pompous, self-congratulatory attitude, especially when it is laced with potshots? Granted, in the case of "Jamaica Mistaica," it was Buffett who was literally on the receiving end of these potshots, but as he himself once said, "If we couldn't laugh, we would all go insane." Nowadays, he seems to have experienced a change of heart. In his lyrics, he refers to these dangerously inept bunglers as "assholes." Elsewhere, he refers to a "Euro-trash accent," and "mean old backed-up farts." Regarding business types, he hypothesizes "It ain't about the talent, it ain't about the skill. It's about the silly stupid horseshit deal." This, coming from a man who charges ten bucks for a newsletter that advertises kitsch. Besides, are these adjectives really necessary?

When he's not insulting others, he's patting himself on the back. "I got a novelist eye . . . a license to fly" is his way of sharing his pride with us, and "some thought me crazy for being way too nice" is his way of summing up the Jamaica incident. Maybe so, but now that you've publicized the incident in a popular song, do you think that the Jamaican tourist board will agree with your self-assessment? I got my first inkling of this megalomania from the liner notes of *The Parakeet Album.* There, Buffett has the chutzpah to compare "Cheeseburger in Paradise" and "Volcano" to Huckleberry Finn and Br'er Fox as examples of classic story characters, then goes on to proclaim that he hopes "they will inspire the *next* great storyteller." Can you believe this guy?

Technically, the album remains true to Buffett's original intentions of keeping things acoustic, because it is free of electric guitars and synthesizers, but you wouldn't mistake these antiseptic recordings for any Unplugged session. Nor would you mistake them for Buffett's folk-acoustic work of previous decades. Because scrupulous production techniques compensate for any "analog" shortcomings, the acoustic instruments sound electric anyway, making the whole procedure a technical exercise in futility instead of an artistic breakthrough.

As for the balance of the tracks, I find myself blown away by the winds of mediocrity. "Banana Wind" is a half a song disguised as an instrumental. "Schoolboy Heart" is pleasant enough but I am too distracted by Buffett's bald attempt to play up his own legend among the Parrot Heads to take this at face value. "Only Time Will Tell" is about as interesting as watching a dog chase his own tail, and "Bob Roberts' Society Band" is little more than kitsch. "Desdemona's Building a Rocket Ship" is too dopey (and too long) to take seriously, and "Mental Floss" makes me think that the songwriter might have suffered brain damage from his own hygienic advice. Even "Cultural Infidel" suffers from a blatantly cartoonish portrayal.

Now, in the midst of this terribly negative review, how can I convey the fact that Buffett achieves greatness on this album? After "Cultural Infidel," the mood changes swiftly. Buffett abandons the ominous cartoon tone of the album with "Happily Ever After," a simple reflection on avoiding life's pitfalls and the problems inherent in trying to maintain a state of self-satisfaction. From there, he launches into one of the most self-indulgent but undeniably moving songs of his entire career. "False Echoes" handles the subject of his father's Alzheimer's disease with grace and dignity. Using Celtic stylings, Buffett sings slowly and deliberately to convey his emotional vulnerability, giving voice to the confused child who also happens to be a father to the son of yet another generation (the recently adopted Cameron Marley). With absolute ignorance of commerciality, Buffett intuitively fulfills music's ultimate purpose of expressing personal emotion in a universal language.

After a surprise comical interlude during which Buffett searches for the hidden track (screaming at his production coordinator and special assistant Mike Ramos), a rendition of Stephen Stills's "Treetop Flyer" appears unannounced at album's end. If you have trouble digesting the emotional honesty of "False Echoes," then this tale of a low-flying smuggler is the next best thing that *Banana Wind* has to offer. One fact is undeniable—most of Buffett's fans are ordinary people. The same can be said of his critics. Buffett, on the other hand, is extraordinary. I suffer no illusions on this point. It's just a shame that he sometimes feels compelled to remind us of this, and it is quizzical that he would do so on his most ordinary album in years. Now, will the real Jimmy Buffett please stand up?

Like each of his previous two album releases, *Banana Wind* shot straight to the top of *Billboard*'s album chart, debuting at number 4 on June 22, 1996. This not only marked his highest debut position but his highest chart position ever—even "Margaritaville" only rose as high as number 8. From this lofty spot, *Banana Wind* began its slow but steady descent, disappearing eighteen weeks later. This sales pattern indicated that Buffett's fans were so dedicated that most of them would buy his product before hearing a single note. As far as typical Parrot Heads were concerned, they didn't need to hear it to know that they wanted to own it. The very same week that *Banana Wind* vanished from the charts (October 26), *Christmas Island* debuted. Being a Christmas album, it charted a course quite different from its predecessors, climbing steadily until it peaked at number 27 on Christmas week. By the last week of January it was gone, giving it a fourteen-week presence on *Billboard*'s charts, a phenomenal performance for a seasonal release. Don't be surprised if it experiences an annual resurgence.

Buffett's 1996 *Banana Wind* summer tour began in June and, with a few scheduled breaks, continued into October. By year's end, he would rank ninth among that year's top-grossing tours, breaking $18 million in ticket sales, with attendance figures in excess of 600,000. This tour was slightly different from his previous outings, because it eliminated much of the vaudeville-type of comedy and elaborate staging of previous tours. Less high jinks meant more music, and fans were treated to a show that emphasized songs over slapstick.

Before the tour began, I was in New Orleans for the Jazz Fest and witnessed two separate instances of a serious crowd control problem. The first was on Friday, April 26, when Phish played at the fairgrounds on the Ray-Ban stage. Never in all of my visits to this event have I seen such an uncontrolled sea of bodies amassed for one show (the city has since banned Phish from returning).

Coincidentally, Jimmy Buffett was on this very stage just moments before Phish began their set, appearing as a guest of the Iguanas. The other instance of rampant insanity was more directly related to Buffett. On Saturday night, he was scheduled to appear at the Margaritaville Cafe, and it seemed as though half of the city's half-million tourists were attempting to gain admission to a club that might be able to comfortably handle one thousand. Once I saw the advertisement for Buffett's appearance in the *Times-Picayune,* I sensed trouble. If Buffett can instantly sell out a twelve-thousand-seat arena, what is bound to happen when he makes a well-advertised appearance in a nightclub? A few lucky bodies were able to get inside, but I couldn't help but feel sorry for the thousands who got caught in the crush on the street. My party headed crosstown to Tipitina's for a double bill of Zachary Richard and Buckwheat Zydeco, and the next day we read in the papers about the police busts and mob scenes that we had managed to avoid. From what I heard, though, Buffett's set was inspired, kicking off with a number of Beatles tunes ("Come Together" and "She Came in Through the Bathroom Window"—something that I'd bet a few locked-out fans were considering) and featuring a guest appearance by John Kay of Steppenwolf, who assisted the Coral Reefers on rocking renditions of "Born to Be Wild" and "Magic Carpet Ride."

In the May 2, 1996, issue of *Rolling Stone,* a Buffett-penned article appeared entitled "Why We Are All Strangers in the Everglades." In the article, he states his case for the preservation of Florida's natural resources and lucidly points out that the Everglades are no place for mankind to be poking about. Later in the year, he would speak at a rally in support of a tax on Florida's sugar growers that would be used to help restore the Everglades. The amendment failed but voters did approve the formation of a trust fund that was intended for the same purpose.

Already part owners of the Miami–Fort Myers Miracles baseball team, Buffett and comedian Bill Murray added to their collection of ball clubs by becoming part owners of another minor-league team known as the Madison Black Wolf. In December, Buffett announced that Margaritaville was developing a Parrot Head beer. Parrot Head root beer was soon added to the list of potential new products. *Christmas Island* completed his contractual obligation with MCA Records. Distribution for his new discs will now be handled by Island/Polygram, while his catalog remains in the hands of MCA.

Christmas Island (1996)

Margaritaville Records MCAD-11489

Besides being a religious holiday, December 25, 1996, also signified the day that Jimmy Buffett would reach the half-century mark, and to celebrate the occasion, he decided to offer up a pleasant collection of holiday tunes. In the liner notes, Buffett states that he hopes this record is what you would expect, and it is. Christmas classics, rockin' Christmas tunes, and a few originals are combined for a very pleasant and lighthearted spirit of fun in the sun. Perhaps because he wanted to maintain a multidenominational feel to his disc, Jesus is only mentioned once, on "A Sailor's Christmas." Other than this one plug for the holiday's namesake, the ex–altar boy from Alabama portrays the holiday mostly as a time for family, partying, and presents. Christmas albums shouldn't be critiqued in the same manner as other collections, though, so I will keep my comments within the spirit that Buffett intended.

If I had to pick just one of the advantages that colder climes have over sunnier locales, it's the Christmas season. City sidewalks, snow, ice skating and sledding, bundling up to go caroling, sipping warm drinks by a cozy fireplace, and decorating an evergreen tree are all ingredients that make Christmas in a cold climate a special pleasure. The onset of winter is so much more bearable because of Christmas, and its religious aspect coincides neatly with the reflection that is brought on by the impending New Year. I *like* snow at Christmas time, so my only real complaint about *Christmas Island* is that it is so darned *hot*. "White Christmas" and "Silver Bells" wouldn't cut it on a Buffett Christmas album, so instead, we are offered a sense of what Christmas is like in the Caribbean (or perhaps the South Pacific).

Five tropical tunes are the album's focal point, and I was pleasantly surprised at how well they all managed to capture the Christmas spirit. "Christmas Island" and "Mele Kalikimaka" are two Pacific-based songs that may not be classics but are still fun to hear. The other three are all original compositions. "A Sailor's Christmas" (Buffett, Guth) admits that "Christmas is a season better suited for dry land" and "Ho Ho Ho and a Bottle of Rhum" (Buffett, Guth, Mayer, Kunkel) is a comical farce that has Santa taking off to the Caribbean for a much-needed break from his two-thousand-year routine. The best song on the entire collection, however, is "Merry Christmas, Alabama" (Buffett, Betton). Here, the sound is distinctly like Buffett of ages past, with a country-style veneer wreathed around one of the best new Christmas songs to come along in ages.

The "classics" are a bit shakier, with a reggae-fied version of "Jingle Bells" that adds a Caribbean verse and a bizarre rendition of "Up on the House Top," where, for reasons that are beyond me, Buffett imitates a surf dude and comes off sounding like Tom Petty on laughing gas. The band sounds great, though, particularly Peter Mayer, who does a mean imitation of surf-guitar god Dick Dale. Mayer also sounds brilliant on a faithful rendition of John Lennon's "Happy Christmas (War Is Over If You Want)," though it will never be able to replace Lennon's own version in my heart. I never thought I'd say this, but after hearing Buffett's cover, I even began to miss Yoko Ono's full-lunged yowl on harmony. Another rock-tinged classic that Buffett attempts to grasp is "Run Run Rudolph" but this song is better when kept in the hands of Chuck Berry (or perhaps Keith Richards). "I'll Be Home for Christmas" is handled with grace and subtlety, and is much better suited to Buffett's croon.

Because friends and family are the essence of Christmas spirit and most of my loved ones live up north, I don't think that I'll be heading south for Christmas anytime soon, but if I ever get the urge to experience Christmas from a sunnier perspective, I'll be grateful for this depiction. When I'm scraping ice off of my windshield and having second thoughts, I imagine it will be fun to come inside and warm my hands in front of a fire while Jimmy Buffett sings to me about *Christmas Island*. Oh, and happy birthday, Jimmy.

In 1997, Buffett's focus was squarely on his most recent romantic fantasy, the musical version of "Don't Stop the Carnival." Buffett threw himself headlong into preproduction. For a while, all other projects were put aside while he worked tirelessly with Herman Wouk to perfect the stage show. Even his upcoming book, tentatively titled *Daybreak at the Equator,* was put on the back burner. As a means of formulating the presentation, Wouk wrote an outline that was adapted from his own script. Then he would submit a portion of the outline to Buffett, whose job it was to create themes based on each character. Pressure was intense to come up with music that was memorable in its own right and yet also capable of conveying the story line. As songs were completed, they were recorded by the Coral Reefer Band. Then, tapes were submitted to the stage band, a collective of nine Florida musicians known as Iko Iko. Buffett and Iko Iko entered the studio to record a version of Sheb Wooley's "Purple People Eater" for the soundtrack of *Contact* (1997), starring Jodie Foster and James Woods.

Five years of intensive work went into the development of "Don't Stop the Carnival," and on April 8, 1997, the show opened at the Coconut Grove Playhouse. Advance ticket sales were the greatest in the history of the theater. Directed by David H. Bell and starring Tony Award winner Michael Rupert as Norman Paperman, it was scheduled to run for five weeks, until May 4. Overwhelming demand and a reasonably positive critical reaction allowed the run to be extended for another four weeks. Some time after its opening, the *Miami Herald* published a review, noting an engaging story with memorable melodies and good lyrics, but in serious need of some creative editing.

Plans exist to take the show to the Great White Way, but not until Buffett and other powers that be are convinced that it will draw a steady crowd, critics be damned. We're still waiting, and I can't help but think that Buffett might now have additional reason to pause, particularly after the disastrous critical drubbing and subsequent commercial failure of fellow pop star Paul Simon's Broadway effort *The Capeman*. Buffett, meanwhile, has referred to his theatrical adventure as the most creative part of his life.

A few days before the show opened, Buffett granted a very detailed and candid interview to the *Miami Herald*, hoping to elicit a pre-show buzz. In the course of conversation, he mentioned that he spends most of his time in Palm Beach, at least while school is in (during breaks he visits his other home in Sag Harbor, on Long Island). A most telling part of the interview revolved around his instinctive desire to satisfy his audience. Among other things, Buffett implied a certain distaste for "Cheeseburger in Paradise" (Aha!) and mentioned that if he did the show that he wanted to do, it would be nowhere near the show he does now. Instead, he would prefer to do a show of ballads. He doesn't play a show for his own sake, however, but for his audience, and he'll be happy to play " 'Margaritaville' for the four-hundred millionth time." Remembering the sentiments of his 1975 recording "Making Music for Money," I can't help but wonder when the initiative for his life's work switched to his audience instead of for himself, but that's show business.

It might sound disingenuous, but I can understand Buffett's desire to satisfy the crowd. Artistically speaking, this could help explain why his upbeat material can sometimes sound forced and less heartfelt than his ballads. Furthermore, this strikes me as incongruous, since in every other aspect of his professional life, Buffett makes an art form out of doing what he pleases. As a lifestyle artist who from all outward appearances seems to have perfected the art of living, it only makes sense for him to do what makes him happy. His fans love it when he is happy, too, so I'd bet that most every Parrot Head would absolutely love to see a Buffett show that consists mostly of ballads.

Meanwhile, Buffett remains the busiest professional loafer on the face of the earth. Besides yet another recording with the Muppets (on *Elmopalooza*), he has a new CD, and a collection of songs from *Don't Stop the Carnival*. He has written an article for *Rolling Stone* magazine's March 19, 1998, issue, ostensibly about the Pope's visit to Cuba, and he has completed yet another book, titled *A Pirate Looks at Fifty*. Even middle age cannot hold Buffett's ambitions at bay. For a guy portrayed as the laid-back king of somewhere hot, his burgeoning workload remains intact. Any which way you look at it, Jimmy Buffett remains one lucky, talented, and hard-working guy.

Don't Stop the Carnival (1998)

Margaritaville Records Island 314-524 485-2

This is the story of Norman Paperman, and boy, the process of relating the story sure is complicated. One thing that is instantly apparent upon hearing Jimmy Buffett's latest CD is that it is quite a piece of work. The storylines of a half-dozen major characters overlap and musical themes interweave throughout the project, while the arrangements twist and turn to suit the story, remaining comfortably predictable without sounding overly redundant. This is all done in an effort to capture the essence of Herman Wouk's novel of the same name, about a New York City expatriate named Norman Paperman who decides to follow his impulse to abandon his hectic lifestyle for the slower pace of the islands. Norman Paperman is following the same advice that Jimmy Buffett has been giving for years, only here, incompatibility is a factor: Northern Norman just wasn't cut out for island life. It's Buffett's and Wouk's job to get this point across as concisely as possible—and there's the rub. There's just too much going on in Wouk's novel for Norman's inappropriate island jaunt to be adequately represented in a three-hour musical.

Perhaps the problem is due to the fact that Wouk has been conditioned to expect too much. In the past, Wouk has seen two novels made into two of the most successful television miniseries of all time (*Winds of War* and *War and Remembrance*). This format allowed for compound storylines and complex character development, something that simply cannot take place in the limited time frame of a musical. I'm not at all privy to the working relationship that was shared by Mr. Buffett and Mr. Wouk, but Buffett's CD gives every indication that he went out of his way to appease Wouk, who undoubtedly retained a strong allegiance to his book. This circumstance demanded that the writers retain as much of the novel's original intent (not to mention content) as was possible. To be sure, I cannot blame Wouk for not allowing his novel to be reduced to a cartoonish portrayal, but within the format of a musical, some creative license and additional story reduction might have benefited the project.

Since the story is paramount, the libretto is extremely busy, focusing on plot devices more than emotional development. This results in only a few songs that can stand on their own two feet. "Island Fever" and "Who Are We Trying to Fool" come closest to meeting the criteria of independence, but practically every other song contains a direct reference to the storyline or a character that prevents the song from leaving its environment. Who could make sense of "A Thousand Steps to Nowhere" outside of this play? Or why would anybody even want to hear the misanthropic ennui of "Up on the Hill" anywhere else but here? The Christmas-song adaptation of "Domicile" is an annoying thirty-some-odd seconds, but it conveys virtually the exact same sentiment as "Up on the Hill" in only a fraction of the time. Time is of the essence, so why not dump "Up on the Hill" and let the greedy little Christmas ditty make the point instead?

The most unfortunate outcome of there being too much story is that there is a shortage of emotional investment. Buffett never really sounds like Norman Paperman at all; he sounds more like Jimmy Buffett. That's okay in itself, except that it causes the listener to become disinterested in the characterization, or worse, distracted by it. As a result, we end up with the feeling of observing this carnival instead of attending it. I think it is safe to say that most of Buffett's fans buy his records because they are endeared to his personable perspective, but *Don't Stop the Carnival* is more of a cranial exercise than a personal expression. The beauty of Buffett's musical work often lies in its natural cadence and relaxed wordplay. Here, the wordplay is much too convoluted. What survives aren't the words but the creative melodies coupled with the unique Caribbean-influenced instrumentation that now belong almost exclusively to Buffett. The musical arrangements are simultaneously sophisticated and childlike, with an emphasis on the steel drum that is no longer simply an accompanying instrument but the basis for virtually everything. Considering the subject matter, this is only fitting but it is still impressive to hear the steel drum adapt to Buffett's deliberate versatility, from tangos to cool jazz.

Both Buffett and Wouk are extremely talented men and they have made one glorious effort at adapting *Don't Stop the Carnival* for the stage, but by trying to retain a sense of purity, it appears as if a new dilemma presents itself at every turn. I can only imagine how difficult it would be for Mr. Wouk to see his work boiled down and freeze dried to its lowest common denominator, but that has been the nature of more than a few successful musical adaptations. A good example can be drawn from a Broadway show that happens to be also based on a novel where the central character goes about chasing after windmills. I'll bet that Cervantes has been trying to pound his way out of the coffin ever since the liberal representation of his work became *Man of La Mancha,* but like it or not, there is hardly a soul who doesn't equate Don Quixote with "The Impossible Dream." For Norman Paperman, all that he has is "Public Relations." *Don't Stop the Carnival* might be very well-crafted, but the unfortunate result is an impressive collection of songs that sound more crafty than artful.

7

Light Literature, or Buffett's Books

The Jolly Mon

Jimmy and Savannah Jane Buffett
Illustrations by Lambert Davis
(Harcourt Brace Jovanovich, 1988)

Jimmy and his then eight-year-old daughter Savannah Jane wrote *The Jolly Mon* as a children's story, so I felt unqualified to review it as an adult. As immature as I am capable of being, that still doesn't make me part of their target audience so to keep the review relevant, I sought the impressions of a child or two. With their consent, I recruited my two boys (Kyle, age five, and Dare, age six) to assist me.

The plan was simple. I'd read from the book and when we were done, they would tell me what they thought. What could possibly be any easier than that? The first night, both boys rushed into their pajamas and brushed their teeth, eager to help their daddy with his Jimmy Buffett book. Since Kyle's bed is the larger of the two, the three of us gathered together in his room while I squeezed between the two boys and began to read the adventures of a traveling musician with a magical guitar who dedicates his life to making others happy.

When we were finished reading, I asked for their opinions. Dare spoke first.

"I liked it," he said.

"Me too," Kyle said.

"Okay, good. Now what do you like about it?"

"I just liked it," Dare said.

"Yeah, it was good," Kyle said.

"Don't you want to tell me anything else?" I asked.

"No," Dare said.

"Nope," Kyle said.

Sigh.

If this was going to work, we would need a new approach, so the following night I brought with me a cassette tape of Jimmy Buffett reading the story to musical accompaniment. I set up one tape deck on the left side of the bed to play the story and another tape deck on the other side to record our conversation. All I had to do was turn the pages. Still, though, extracting opinions from them was like pulling teeth. They just kept telling me that they liked the story, and that was that. All they wanted was to listen. Sometimes they would ask me a few questions or maybe make up some crazy stuff about the pictures, but that was the extent of their interest in this project.

Then it dawned on me. Because they were five and six, I realized that the concept of critical analysis was not particularly interesting to them. Duh, Dad. It wasn't their opinions that I sought, it was the questions they were asking and the comments that they made while the story went on. How did the book stimulate them to think about things? I could tell more about what they were getting out of the story by listening to their own thoughts and fielding their questions. A kid's mind can work in some very unique ways, so I decided to let their thought processes lead, and then I would follow.

Here, then, are a few questions and also an occasional insight or two, as provided by Dare and Kyle over the course of the next two readings.

First, Kyle's comments:

"I remember this story. He gets tied up by pirates, and he used his guitar and then he saw the dolphin. The dolphin was in the air, and the Jolly Mon too."

"Why is he called the Jolly Mon and not the Jolly Man?" We talked about Caribbean accents, and I told him that the people in Bananaland might talk like the people in Jamaica.

"That dolphin helps the Jolly Mon to breathe." We talked a bit about dolphins, how they are very intelligent and that they are not fish but mammals.

"You paint a picture of something that you like on a sail, right, Dad?" There's a picture of a dolphin on the Jolly Mon's mainsail.

"Can I paint a picture of a train on my sail?"

"Sailboats are boats that you don't have to row, right?"

Also, Kyle tends to narrate each picture for five minutes, nonstop. "Look, the Jolly Mon has three fish in his frying pan, or he almost does. Those two guys are trying to catch the same fish. That guy still has his shoes on! Jolly Mon sings good and gets more fish than those guys. When the fish come out of the water they dance around because the Jolly Mon sings so good . . ." (ad infinitum).

And now, Dare's comments:

During the Coconut Island segment, he said, "I like the music in the background."

"Is Orion really that balanced [meaning symmetrical]?" We looked up the constellation in a book about stars and also went outside to find Orion in the night sky. Both of us were surprised to learn that one of the brightest stars in this constellation is called Betelgeuse.)

"How do the stars tell you where to go?" We talked a bit about celestial navigation.

"Why can't you use a map?" We talked about sailing in open water where no land was visible, and using the stars and dead reckoning to figure out which way you are going.

"Why did she break a bottle of coconut milk?" I told him that it was a good luck tradition.

"Yeah, well, it's a pretty bad tradition. What if she's in bare feet?" I couldn't argue with that.

Pointing to a picture of Coconut Island with very tiny people below, Dare said, "Dad, look at that fat guy in the bathing suit. I'll bet that guy ate all the coconut cakes."

As we read the story together once more, both of my kids told me that they want to go back to the Caribbean. Kyle wants to see if fish really do jump into frying pans, but then figured that was what people used to do before they invented fishing. Dare said that he likes the illustrations and that they give him lots of nice ideas about traveling. All three of us broke out a map of the Caribbean Sea and talked about places that we would like to go visit. So, thanks to Jimmy and Savannah Jane, the three of us are planning our next vacation (with their mother, of course). Oh, and as for the story, I agree with my kids. I like it.

Tales From Margaritaville

(Harcourt Brace Jovanovich, 1989)

I wonder if the people who *read* Jimmy Buffett do so for the same reasons as the people who *listen* to him do, but one thing for certain is that the net results are the same. Tales of escapism and wanderlust fill the pages of his first collection of short stories, entitled *Tales From Margaritaville.* The only real difference between his stories and his songs is that the book allows J.B. more of a chance to stretch out and investigate the personalities of his characters while simultaneously fattening up his creative story lines—all without worrying about the inherent limitations of a rhyme scheme.

If you're already a fan of Jimmy Buffett's music, then it's a no-brainer why you enjoy his stories. However, this also depends largely on what your own priorities are. First, you must pay attention to the nuances of the words, and because reading is more of a personal experience than a shared one, it won't be much fun at parties. Second, it sometimes takes two hands to read the book, so you might have to worry about spilling your cocktail all over the nice, clean pages.

A good percentage of the stories in *Tales From Margaritaville* already exists in highly condensed form as songs (five songs from the album *Off to See the Lizard* share titles with short stories in the book), so chances are very good that if you liked the musical version, you'll also enjoy his expansive short stories.

Unfortunately one of the most telling characteristics of *Tales From Margaritaville* is repetition in the subject matter. The moral of every story here is virtually identical, namely, that we shouldn't fritter away our lives in pursuit of some intangible goal, especially by working at something that is unrewarding. Buffett is obsessed wih telling us how much better it would be to waste our lives chasing down dreams instead of wasting our dreams while plodding through life. The collection cites a plethora of examples where people escape from one situation to find another that is more fulfilling. Almost always, Buffett identifies himself with the lead character. Whether it's Tully Mars, the wisecracking cowboy with a corny sense of humor in "Take Another Road," or Romeo Fleming, the displaced author turned high school football coach in "Off to See the Lizard," it is not hard to see the reflection of Jimmy Buffett on these pages. Even the women are idealized, male fantasy manifestations of his own bad self. Imagine Jimmy Buffett as a svelte and sexy young female (yea-aggh) and you'll grasp the personalities of his lead female characters. From the independent-minded but ever-faithful Angel Beech ("Boomerang Love") to the ambitious dreamer from Martinique named Isabella who goes on to operate a successful restaurant in Paris ("I Wish Lunch Could Last Forever"), Jimmy Buffett's own frame of mind seeps through. This pervasive sense of self-identity gives the lead characters a motivation that instantly justifies their actions and compels the reader to concur, even when the consequences are potentially daunting.

Fear of change never enters into a Jimmy Buffett story. This isn't a Stephen King novel, where your best friend is suddenly going to turn into a flesh-eating zombie, or your dog is going to rabidly bite off your arm, so there is little reason for the reader to fear a plunge into the unknown. The worst thing that can happen in *Tales From Margaritaville* is a hurricane may strike, and even then they occur with such predictable regularity throughout the book that instead of provoking fear, they provide a reason for celebration, or a reason to make love, or a reason to find closure with your past. Jimmy Buffett doesn't want to frighten us. He wants us to relax. He wants us to trust him. He wants us to be comfortable, so he makes sure that there are no bogeymen in the shadows, and that the outcome will be just fine. Although his characters are constantly abandoning their present circumstances in search of something better, it is always presented as an exciting adventure, with little regret and even less anxiety. When it is time for the lead characters to get up, get out and move on, we know they'll survive the consequences. We don't doubt it for a minute. In fact, we know that there is really no other choice, because in the world of *Tales From Margaritaville,* chasing your dreams is the only intelligent and honorable thing to do.

This theme of dropping all of your self-induced obligations to seek fulfillment of a dream is a common one, but after a few stories I found myself getting a mite defensive about some of this. After all, there are a lot of people in this world who work at steel mills, or dirty coal mines, or dangerous precinct houses, or even toxic dump sites. They don't necessarily love their work (I'm willing to bet that they probably can't stand it), but they do welcome the paycheck that comes at the end of the week. I have a life, too, and part of it is unrewarding, tedious, and frustrating, but that doesn't mean I can just pack up and run, particularly because the mortgage, wife, job, and kids have become so indelibly ingrained into my character. Escaping is great, but *somebody* has to forge the metal, mine the coal, keep the peace, and process the garbage.

Then, it occurred to me. Day-to-day drudgery is frustrating for just about anybody, but it is this drudgery that inspires us to emulate those who avoided the hamster-on-a-wheel syndrome. It is why we sometimes live exclusively for the weekend, and especially for vacation time. When it comes, we'll head south, drink enough rum to make our livers quake in fear, dance our awkward asses off all night long to the exotically funky rhythms of the islands, and then sleep it off on the beach where we'll burn the skin off of our sorry, translucent bodies. We can do this because, in the end, we know that we're going to have to go back home. Perspective is everything.

As Buffett sings in the Mac McAnally song "It's My Job," instead of viewing employment as a willing form of enslavement, we should learn to like what we do, and then do it well. If you have problems with this, Jimmy Buffett is here to help.

Our misery causes us to love Jimmy Buffett, because he is the manifestation of an existence somewhere just beyond our grasp. There are days when all of us would love to just chuck it all in and head for open waters, but something always stops us. Why? It sure is a tempting thought and it certainly seems to suit Jimmy Buffett just fine, but how would we handle all of that freedom? What about our spouses and our kids? What about the mortgage payment? Not only that, but how are we going to afford new tires, or make the car payment, or repair the leaking roof? A microcosm of responsibility inundates us until we are hunched over from the weight of burdens that we unwittingly choose to carry. The funny thing is that we justify this by explaining how, if we were to spend all our time just traipsing around the Caribbean, our whole life will fall apart!

Actually, that's the point. Our life as we know it would fall apart, yes, but a whole new one would then open up. The problem is that most of us always choose the familiar. Better the demon you know than the demon you don't know, right? But, as Buffett insistently posits, why not take another road?

Generally speaking, Parrot Heads fall into one of two camps—those who faced the demon and those who won't (or can't). By far the largest camp of fans is made up those who will never make the transition to "fantasy island" life. These are the people who religiously attend Buffett's stateside shows, treating the event as a temporary and encapsulated form of escapism. The other camp, much smaller in comparison, is made up of those who have already been "transitioned," and consists of people you might see sailing by you on their private skiffs, or lounging on the beach at Jost Van Dyke or some other small, exotic, out-of-the-way place. These are the Caribbean "lifers" who see J.B. as the closest thing showbiz has to offer to their own reality. For the poor shlub who has mired himself into a pattern of thought that makes such behavior seem irresponsible if not impossible, Mr. Buffett's take on life is irresistible. According to Jimmy, nothing is as fulfilling as throwing off the shackles that bind you, for virtually every one of his stories is about virtually the same thing and ends virtually the same way—the happy ending. Ask any of the expatriated American Parrot Heads who now reside near (or on) the warmer side of the Gulf Stream, and they'll tell you. In the world of a Jimmy Buffett short story, "happily ever after" is about as easy to achieve as saying "Take this job and shove it. . . ."

To this Buffett might respond, "Now wait a minute. I never told anybody what to do with their lives. What someone else does is their own business and how they interpret my words and music is up to them, not me." If he did say this, he'd be right, too. We shouldn't copy the lifestyle as it is portrayed by Buffett so much as we should accept our own limitations and capabilities. Maybe the point isn't that we (myself included) are being misled by visions of grandeur and promises of utopia. Maybe the point is that we are being granted a reprieve that we can believe in. Escapism can be a powerful tool. If you're feeling trapped or limited, it is a wonderful thing that Buffett's fiction (and his music, of course) can provide a tonic for frustration and misery.

So, with every story, Jimmy Buffett prods us. In a not-so-subtle way, he reminds us that we should love what we do and if we don't then we should do something else. Life isn't about reaching your destination, it's about enjoying the journey because in this life, the only permanent destination is death. To quote a John Lennon lyric (from "Beautiful Boy"), "Life is what happens to you while you're busy making other plans." If time is so ephemeral, then why not have some fun while passing it away? Imagine, though, what might happen if Jimmy Buffett were successful in his mission to convince us to drop our plowshares and follow the sun. What then? I have this overriding image of tropical beaches being overrun by soot-covered factory workers with pale blue skin, all clamoring for their frozen margaritas while their condos by the sea swell to gargantuan proportions. Then the pensioners who finish out their obligations to their jobs will come down and charter all of the fishing boats, making it impossible for the *real* expatriates to do much more than reminisce about the good old days before Buffett convinced everybody to come south. This is exactly the scenario that Jimmy Buffett bemoans throughout the book, which strikes me as a contradiction of sorts. On the one hand, it's like he's telling us "Come on in, the water's fine" but once we jump in, he decides that the pool is too crowded or, as he put it himself, "Weather is here, wish you were beautiful." Ah well, maybe paradise just isn't for everybody.

Jimmy Buffett does not worry, either, about avoiding the tired cliché, even when it strains the reader's suspension of belief. In "Take Another Road," Buffett has no problem relating a tale where the character walks to the banks of the Mississippi River in Hannibal, Missouri (hometown of Mark Twain), and happens upon a frog floating downriver while perched on a log. Of course, this scenario inspires the character's own desire to move on, which, of course, he does. Later in the same story, the same character once again walks to the banks of the Mississippi, but this time in New Orleans, and when he looks down at the muddy water rushing by, what do you think he sees passing beneath him? Why, his old friend, Mr. Frog, of course.

Jimmy Buffett isn't concerned with whether or not you believe his stories, though. What does concern him is whether or not you are entertained and if you're a Parrot Head, then you'll certainly relate to his tall tales with a stimulating sense of adventure and familiarity.

Like the frog on a log in "Take Another Road," life is a cruise to an unknown destination, and if you can avoid making excuses or reacting defensively, then you just might realize that your lifestyle is long overdue for some not-so-serious changes. Again, to quote John Lennon, "Give up your mind, relax and float downstream. It is not dying."

Trouble Dolls

Jimmy and Savannah Jane Buffett
Illustrations by Lambert Davis
(Harcourt Brace Jovanovich, 1991)

After the experience of reviewing the Buffetts' previous children's book, *The Jolly Mon,* I knew exactly what to do for *Trouble Dolls.* Following the same format, I sat each of my kids down and read the story to them for a few nights. Taking the advice of Jimmy and Savannah Jane, who preface the book by saying, "Children, see what you can see," I planned on doing nothing but reading from the book and taking note of their various and sundry comments. This almost worked, but a few things prevented me from getting results similar to those I did with *The Jolly Mon.*

First, Savannah Jane had aged three years since that book. Instead of being a precocious child, she was now on the cusp of adolescence, so *Trouble Dolls* is significantly more mature in its subject matter. My own kids had only aged by a few weeks. Second, the book contains more text, so it took longer to read. The net result of this was that both of my kids would often end up fast asleep before story's end and I'd be lying there wondering whether they enjoyed what they heard.

The answer to this question came by the third reading. One night, I gave them a choice.

"Would you like to hear *Arthur's Chicken Pox* or *Trouble Dolls?*" I asked.

"*Trouble Dolls!*" they yelled in unison.

It turns out their silence was mostly the result of their being captivated by the story. An eleven-year-old named Lizzy Rhinehart must go on an adventure to find her father, who is missing in the Everglades. His plane crashed and it's up to Lizzy to rescue him before an approaching hurricane hits. While rummaging through her belongings, she comes across a family of Guatemalan "trouble dolls" which had been a gift from her father some time ago. Now that she was in need, the trouble dolls come to life and assist her in her quest. Because her mother is deceased a Seminole Indian named Mrs. Sweep is the child's primary caregiver and gives her permission to go on her adventure. Notwithstanding the fact that a woman who let a child head off unaccompanied into the Everglades would probably be arrested for gross negligence, my kids absolutely loved the story's premise, especially the excitement of sailing off on a solo adventure.

My kids' comments and questions were few. Regarding one of the book's illustrations, my oldest child was fascinated to see the framed pictures within the picture of Lizzy's home. "Dad, look! The Jolly Mon! Coconut Island!" (Lambert Davis's illustrations are consistently clever and stimulating). He also mistakenly took the manatee painting for a picture of dolphins. I explained the difference, telling them about the plight of the manatees and mentioned Jimmy Buffett's involvement in trying to save them. I told them how some people call them sea cows, and my youngest son cracked up at that. Since then, he has gone to the school library to take out books on the sea mammal. He also wanted to know why Lizzy and Mrs. Sweep were praying to two different gods, and my eldest jumped in with an answer, telling him "Because they're from two different lands." He had his own comments on the artwork, saying, "I wonder how artists get watercolors so bright. It looks like he put a lot of work into his pictures. Maybe he uses more than one coat." These guys were catching on quick.

One day when we were out shopping, the boys stumbled on a set of trouble dolls, and now they each keep a set in reserve, just in case I ever get lost in the Everglades.

Where Is Joe Merchant?

(Harcourt Brace Jovanovich, 1992)

It is often a surprising piece of information to those unfamiliar with Jimmy Buffett's myriad talents to learn that the laid-back singer of a nonchalant mid-seventies pop hit could have published a novel, and that it somehow managed to top the *New York Times* bestseller list. Even fans will be surprised by the cohesive writing that constitutes his first complete full-length story. As he sings in one of his compositions from 1983 entitled "Twelve Volt Man": "Just ask for some palm trees and tales from the South Seas, and I'll make sparks fly 'round your head."

The setting for *Where Is Joe Merchant?* isn't the South Seas but in the course of his adventurous Caribbean tale, Buffett certainly does make a few sparks fly. His first book, *Tales From Margaritaville,* was a mostly modest collection of stories loosely pieced together, but this time around, there's no denying the substance and prescience in Buffett's braggadocio. From the very first pages, *Where Is Joe Merchant?* exudes the confidence of an author who understands what he wants to say and knows exactly how to say it. With his first novel, Buffett has found his storytelling voice.

Buffett knows where he has been, so for geographical locations and characters, he sticks closely to the creed of his hero, Mark Twain, who once said, "Write what you know." Buffett learned a lot during his years as sailor, pilot, songwriter, and musician and crams as much of his personal experience into *Joe Merchant* as he could manage to fit. He draws from his own life to invent a parallel universe of renegade pilots, sailors, charter boat fishermen, rock stars, and fate crossed lovers who get mixed up in an unlikely scenario with ruthless crooks, island barons, and mercenaries. The novel's characters have well-tanned bodies and smell of coconut oil, like you'd expect, but the circumstances of their lives are not quite as simple or predictable. Wheras Buffett's music usually paints a picture of sunshine, relaxation, and fulfillment, this novel is something else entirely.

Throughout *Where Is Joe Merchant?* Buffett delves beneath the touristy facades of banana republics and shows us places that are often as frightening as they are beautiful, as dangerous as they are inviting. Superficial impressions are peeled away to reveal an underbelly of essentially lawless communities that can turn deadly at any moment. I expected beach parties, yachts, rock and roll, smuggling, and maybe some minor sexual intrigue, not severed arms, multiple murders, and impaling. I never expected to find so much trouble in paradise.

Frank Bama is the book's protagonist and the story mostly is told from his perspective. The narrative bounces between first and third person, depending on whether he is there to witness the action. Bama is a talented pilot who has been living his own life as if the rudder fell off. His wanderings cause him to go wherever circumstances send him and usually it isn't where he wants to be. Journalists, lawyers, bankers, murderers, and jet-skis are the impediments that contribute to his entanglements until a search for a presumed-dead rock star becomes a death-defying adventure.

Unlike Buffett's last adult work, the characters in *Where Is Joe Merchant?* aren't miniaturized composite reflections of himself but fully realized personalities with faults and attributes that are exclusively their own. Instead of using the author-as-god method, whereby everybody is created in the author's image, Buffett fattens his characters with some very non-Buffett-esque traits. He avoids neutral and ephemeral characters, making every person and event essential to the story at hand. In the world of Frank Bama, people are either lifelong friends who are willing to do almost anything for him, or they are obstacles that he must overcome. Each and every event has some significance as well, which sometimes can make even the most improbable events become predictable, if not believable.

Buffett honed his fictional personalities into thoroughly believable characters, but they often find themselves embroiled in unbelievable circumstances. In the course of 382 pages, the plot goes though more twists and turns than a mountain road, traversing some of the most unlikely events that I have ever come across in a work of fiction. At times, it even surpasses the work of John Irving and Kurt Vonnegut Jr. for its tendency to expect the reader to suspend all disbelief. For the book to work, you must accept the axiom "kismet happens." At times, I found myself staring at the page and thinking, *Okay, how in the world is he going to get out of this one?* only to have the most unbelievable solution occur.

When Frank Bama is knocked unconscious and taped to the seat of his aircraft, which is then hijacked and launched toward the stratosphere until it runs out of gas, a stowaway crawls from the forward hold to take control of the airplane, even though he has never been off of the ground before. When his girlfriend, Trevor Kane, is thrown overboard in the middle of the Caribbean Sea to certain death by drowning, she immediately finds a floating garbage bag to keep her buoyant. If that wasn't enough, Bama soon flies overhead and spots her drifting in the middle of the sea. These events would cause virtually any reader to grimace and raise an eyebrow, but the liveliness of Buffett's characterizations keep the reader on track without becoming distracted by these all-bets-off events.

Buffett himself often acknowledges this, through the thoughts of his characters. When Bama relates the events of the previous few days to his friend Blanton Meyercord, he pauses to say, "In telling the story, I couldn't believe it had happened." Well, to be honest, in reading it, neither could I. Meyercord then responds, "That sounds like somethin' out of a book," thus breaking the sensitive barrier that suspends us in this fictional state. Just a few pages later, Bama is once again prompted to say, "Although I couldn't believe it. . . ." The plot also has a tendency to veer toward B-movie or television-land idiosyncrasies. Within ten pages, three separate incidents occur where the bad guy is rendered unconscious by being popped in the head. Only the implement changes, from a bottle to the butt of a gun to a piece of driftwood. As the third body collapsed wobbling to the ground, I started thinking of *Three Stooges* episodes, with stars floating around the victim's heads to the sound of a cuckoo clock. It is instances like this when Buffett's tale becomes a bit too rudimentary and admittedly about as believable as a *Batman* movie, but even when it defies credibility, *Where Is Joe Merchant?* never loses its sense of humor or ceases to entertain.

What is apparent throughout the book is the author's professional manipulation of various plot devices to hold the story line intact. Because there are numerous characters operating independently of one another, Buffett needs to find ways to bring events to a head in a manner that is succinct and not too convoluted. This is laudable, because it allows him to keep the story moving at a fast pace, but occasionally, character motivation strikes me as a bit too sketchy, and maybe even a bit suspect. Why, for instance, would Root Boy crawl into the forward compartment of the airplane, except as a plot device to save Frank Bama from certain death? Here, Buffett at least provides the flimsy explanation that he didn't want to be around when the police show up, but at other times, he simply avoids explanations altogether. If Monty Potter was an experienced mercenary who (according to the story) changed his name so often that he sometimes forgot who he was, why was he still going by the name of Monty Potter, except to make it that much easier for his sworn enemy to find him?

People who are familiar with Buffett's body of music will notice a huge number of references to his song catalog. There is something almost eerie in the way that the characters of *Where Is Joe Merchant?* keep referring to Buffett's music without ever acknowledging the existence of somebody named Jimmy Buffett. In an early scene, for instance, the old fliers unite to sing a stanza from "Sending the Old Man Home" as if it were part of the public domain. Wherever the plot takes you, you can be sure that a song accompanies the story line. Buffett often makes direct reference to the song on the jukebox or the radio, but self-absorption with his own work can often be distracting. There are so many (too many, if truth be told) references to his songs that anybody unfamiliar with Buffett's catalog will miss a good deal of the author's intentions. After 100 pages, I decided to stop counting the self-referential quips that crop up in the dialog ("These days, everybody's on the run," "changing channels," the cousin in Miami, Freddie and the Fishsticks, Albion the talking dolphin, "Fruitcakes," "Don't try to describe the ocean if you've never seen it," and so on) and let Buffett apply his musical inventions to wherever he pleased, while once again trying to ignore the distraction caused by their real-life relevance.

I was impressed by Buffett's tenacious ability to achieve the ambitious goals that he had set for himself. How many pop stars have been able to make the transition from lyricist to novelist with any degree of success? There are many who shared Buffett's ambition and a few who have even realized their goal, but very few, if any, have been capable of achieving his level of success, both financially and artistically. Despite a few faults, *Where Is Joe Merchant?* is one heck of a piece of work, particularly since it comes from someone whose primary occupation is as a songwriter. The book surpassed all of my expectations and left me in awe, not only of the book itself but also of Buffett's creative diversity.

During his career as a recording artist, Buffett has eked out territory that is exclusively his. As a "lifestyles artist" who has now successfully crossed the seemingly incompatible genres of recording and writing, he has the undeniable appeal of a hardworking man who still makes life look like a beach. It is no wonder that his following is so large. He has spent most of his career providing examples for a happy and successful life, and when viewed in that light, *Where Is Joe Merchant?* becomes not only an entertaining source of escapism but also a source of inspiration.

You can get the gist of Buffett's own philosophy regarding this simply by checking the motivation of his characters. They don't hesitate, they just act. Is it better to wallow in existential angst, pounding your chest while pondering the big question Why?, or is it better to accept that shit happens and then get on with your life? If you are Frank Bama, the answer is self-evident.

Maybe the beauty of Buffett's existential philosophy (as he applies it to his artistry) is that it is really no philosophy at all. Just live your life, and do your best to make it enjoyable for yourself. Buffett's apparent sense of self-contentment lies in a simple acceptance of what life offers and satisfaction with his place in the scheme of things.

A lot can be learned from the examples set by Buffett's characters. If you compare the basic point of view that is inherent in the prose of *Where Is Joe Merchant?* with his earliest recordings, then you'll realize that Buffett's fundamental message has remained consistent. Fear of change can be a paralyzing thing. Set goals for yourself, but don't become a slave to your own ambitions. If you're lucky enough to find that your life is heading in the direction you desire, then learn to loosen up and enjoy it while you can. If you're not so lucky and find that you've been turned around by some unforeseen circumstance, then don't be afraid to escape. Life can be like that. Whether it's you eating the bear or the bear eating you, Buffett's philosophy can reach you from either perspective. If you listen closely enough, you'll realize that he really is saying something that is both comforting and beautiful.

A Pirate Looks at Fifty

Random House—1998

I have a theory about travel that, judging by the expressions of most people when I share it with them, must be rather strange. I figure that most of us have an innate sense of home, a place where we feel most relaxed and comfortable, but from which we have this unavoidable need to escape. Most human beings are curious types, so it is common for us to grow restless and develop a need to reach out for another place that could maybe also be called home. It's as if we are a type of reverse spring that is completely relaxed only when stretched from home base. Once we get pulled away, we find a purpose to our existence that just wasn't apparent while sitting at work or in front of our televisions. Paradoxically, it's this awareness that soon enough draws us back to where we started—the backward tension that pulled us away in the first place also creates the need for us to snap back to our home base. When we arrive back home, we are only too happy to be back in the place where we feel we belong, at least until the wanderlust has a chance to build up again. It's a weird theory, I know, but it's the only reason I can come up with that explains why we would ever want to leave some of the beautiful places that we visit, or worse, why so many of us are capable of returning to the suburbs. Buffett said pretty much the same thing many years ago when he sang "Wonder Why We Ever Go Home."

And so, in *A Pirate Looks at Fifty,* Jimmy Buffett stretches himself out in an entertaining attempt to discover the extent to which he is able to call a new destination home. Half travelogue, half reminiscence, Buffett's most recent work combines the two elements for which he is most revered by his fans: his ability to do freely what most of us can only dream of, and his legend. At first glance, the book appears to consist of little more than casually rambling tidbits and off-the-cuff observations. Buffett's prose can meander as much as Buffett himself does, but it's the unpredictable nature of his style that holds us to the page, wondering where he will go next. Depending on your willingness to follow along, this trait can be appealing, like a casual conversation between close friends at a bar, or annoying, like a glib socialite who doesn't particularly care whether or not you're interested in what they have to say.

It's always a pleasure to hear a good storyteller rip into a yarn, and Buffett is a walking compendium of stories. *A Pirate Looks at Fifty* collects many of them as short pieces, most under two pages in length, and cleverly assembles these bits in a manner that ties together aspects of Buffett's history with the travelogue that makes up the lion's share the book. His writing is almost always engaging, and I can only marvel at his ability to hold my attention while discussing even the most mundane topics. In one section, Buffett spends pages discussing his travails while searching for the perfect travel bag. Anyone who has ever listened bleary-eyed while their mate recounted a day spent shopping will know exactly what I mean when I say that Buffett is treading on dangerous ground here, but I remained alert throughout Buffett's discourse. Now, how does he do that? I could hardly care less about his traveling accouterments and yet I never yawned, which can only mean that Buffett's writing style employs a unique perspective that defies any tendency toward boredom.

Buffett's perspective has changed with age since his early songwriting days. Buffett was always relaxed while unraveling his melodic tales, but the ensuing years bring added weight to his words. Like a leather couch, Buffett's point of view now suggests the wear and tear that comes from years of experience: Despite the scars, it can be beautiful to grow older. Buffett has been one of the more fortunate. As he sees it, the trick is to avoid abuse and hope for a little bit of luck. The downside of this perspective is that he occasionally sounds a bit curmodgeonly. On his early records, it was entertaining and funny to hear a cocky kid in his twenties dismiss tourists and trailers with disdain. From the vantage point of a fifty-year-old, though, you'd expect more sympathy, or at least tolerance, for the ordinary. Now that he is older, not to mention incredibly successful, it is distracting to hear him become glib or pedantic. Every now and then, a certain haughtiness punctures the friendly mood that is difficult to overlook, as when Buffett labels virtually every white person whom he sees during his travels as a tourist (when falling from the lips of Buffett, "tourist" is not the simple descriptive phrase that most people take it to be but rather a judgmental and subtle insult). It's also self-incriminating, since he confesses that his wife, Jane, had done most of the logistical planning for this excursion, and that it consists mostly of short stays in four-star hotels, well isolated from the local populace. This perspective can often leave the rest of us feeling slighted, since Buffett presumes that his manner of adapting to an indigenous culture is superior to ours and yet somehow, Buffett survives this presumption. His prose is so natural and lacking in self-conscious deliberation that the contradictory nature inherent in his point of view must be taken in stride with his more insightful and revealing observations.

Speaking of Jane, where is she in this story? Although she is his wife and (for the sake of this story) his travel mate, Buffett appears to exert some effort to keep her out of the spotlight and refers to her only peripherally, like when her plans (and tastes) clash with his own (which, comically, is often). I suppose that Jane's perspective during the trip would be another book in itself, but her presence can be sensed throughout and it might have helped if she were more visible to the reader. This is perhaps one instance where Buffett felt compelled to retain a degree of privacy but it is the exception more than the rule, because the most striking characteristic about *A Pirate Looks at Fifty* is Buffett's candor. Sure, the autobiographical portions of the book promote aspects of his legend as much as anything he has ever done, but hearing Buffett's emotionally honest take on his plane crash, or on his father's Alzheimer's disease, drastically alters the emphasis from the myth to the man. Readers who are long-time fans of Buffett will be surprised to find so much personal revelation. These accounts allow the reader to identify with the up and down emotions of Jimmy Buffett, the flesh and blood human being, as opposed to "Jimmy Buffett," the stage persona. Considering Buffett's well-known penchant for privacy in his personal life, it's a pleasant surprise to find him sharing his emotional vulnerability and occasional screw-ups along with his glories. This is especially true when he discusses the emotional aftermath of the plane crash that took place off the coast of Nantucket. His willingness to share his moments of weakness obliterates the perceived fantasy aspect of his existence. All too often, Buffett's most obsessive fans (and believe me, Parrot Heads can be quite an obsessive lot) tend to pigeonhole their mentor, forcing him to smile and party down, even when it might not be appropriate. In these accounts, Buffett deliberately lets the mask slip, causing his well-constructed caricature to fade away. I wonder if the Parrot Heads are ready for this, or are so easily willing to let the myth go. It is very possible that the typical Parrot Head will be disappointed to discover so much reality in the life of this most talented fantasy salesman. Depression? Therapy? Self-doubt? Every reality check that Buffett conveys becomes a reality check for his most ardent fans as well.

Ultimately, though, Buffett's writing isn't intended to be any more serious than his music. His books are geared toward entertainment, not existentialism, and any over-analyzation defeats the essence of his work, which is escapism. What makes *A Pirate Looks at Fifty* different, though, is that it is Buffett himself who is escaping, while looking for the right perspective in approaching the onset of his next half-millennium. Maybe Thomas Wolfe was right (*You Can't Go Home Again*) but Buffett obviously likes the idea of tying up loose ends through foreign places. These "song lines," as he calls them, manage to bring things full circle when they enter your realm of existence to relate new experiences to the rest of your life. When all is said and done, only one place truly qualifies as home. It might be a cliche, but home really is where the heart is, not necessarily where you hang your hat. For the huge majority of us, home remains the place where we were raised. Even Buffett, the epitome of a global traverser, says as much in these pages about his own early days in Alabama. For a few others, home is a more portable case. As a concept, it is important that we come to terms with what constitutes our own idea of home. With this book, Buffett takes a giant leap toward resolving this very personal issue. For the sake of all of us who have grown to know Buffett through his life's work, I hope that he will continue in his search for the perfect home port and I also hope that when he ultimately (and inevitably) returns to the place that he calls home, he'll continue to share his insights with the rest of us.

Part Two

Three Days and Nights Spent Infiltrating the Parrot Heads

8

The Setup, or the Start of a Beautiful Relationship

When I started working seriously on my previous project, *The Jimmy Buffett Trivia Book,* an idea struck me that could be interpreted as either brilliant or crazy. I realized that I was writing and researching a book about Jimmy Buffett from the confines of my home, and that I was therefore quite limited in my perspective. You see, a confession is in order. I'm no Parrot Head. None of my friends are Parrot Heads, either. My agent suggested this project, but to do it right, I needed to find out what it was like to be a Parrot Head, and the implications frightened me a bit. Just how deep into foreign territory would I have to delve to get a fair and honest depiction of the truth? The answer would soon come, but the extent to which I would apply myself wasn't part of the equation when I started this book.

Keep in mind that I knew next to nothing about the subject at hand. I've been following popular music for my entire life, but Jimmy Buffett always existed on the periphery of my consciousness, as a nonessential player with little impact on the overall music scene. Buffett was an artist whom I didn't dislike enough to loathe, but I was sublimely indifferent to his catalog of work. Besides, how could I be expected to fill an entire book with information about nothing but Jimmy Buffett? It just didn't seem possible to me. "Don't worry," my agent assured me, "it'll be fun! The publisher wants a trivia book, so gather a few facts on the guy, then write a proposal. It'll be easy!" She's right, I figured. It is only a proposal, so give it a shot and see what happens. For a week, I scanned a few reference books and the album jackets of my minuscule Buffett collection. I gathered enough information, organized it, then submitted a somewhat wry and sardonic proposal based on their title. Within a week, my agent called to congratulate me, stating that I got the green light.

As anyone familiar with my obsessive tendencies could have predicted, it didn't take long before this simple project developed into an outline of gargantuan proportions. It became an overwhelming passion of mine. I dived headlong into the fray and soon enough, I knew more about Jimmy Buffett than I ever would have expected. With my background in musical analysis, I thought it would be interesting if I were to listen intently to every Jimmy Buffett record and then incorporate critical reviews of his work into the project. By doing so, I could avoid personal issues while focusing my energy on the qualities and details of the thing that made him famous in the first place; his fans and his music. If I did this right, I figured that Buffett himself might even find it interesting. To start things off on the right foot, I purchased Buffett's entire music catalog and started listening, compiling questions, and taking notes. Thankfully, I discovered that I enjoyed much of his work. Now it was time to get serious. One of the first things that I did was to try to contact Buffett himself—I figured that if I was going to write about someone, he really ought to know about it. I wrote a letter and mailed it along with a copy of my first book (a historical compendium of some of the greatest singles of all time called *American Hit Radio*) directly to Buffett, with a second copy going to Nina Avrimedes at HK Management (she represents Jimmy).

A few days after mailing the letter I was lurking about on the Internet, learning about some of the Parrot Head Web sites and searching for useful information, when I stumbled on Jimmy's letter to Steve Eng, the biographer who at the time was near completion of a very unauthorized biography on Buffett. The tone of the letter was harsh, to say the least, and as I read it my blood almost froze in my veins. My first reaction was to think that word traveled fast and this was somehow intended for *me.* That paranoia was quickly relieved, but the tone of the letter resonated, particularly Buffett's anger. This guy was not the laid-back happy camper I envisioned him to be. In no uncertain terms Buffett made it clear how he felt about somebody violating his privacy, and I wondered if his attitude would filter down to a project as innocuous as mine.

Buffett never responded, but Nina Avrimedes did call to discuss the letter and the project. She was quite gracious and pleasant, while letting me know that she didn't even have to ask to know that Jimmy was not interested in being involved. I had to admit, I couldn't have agreed with her more. Implicitly, though, it was suggested that I could continue without interference so long as I kept my word on avoiding personal issues. That being settled, I still had to evaluate the effect of Eng's book on mine. That shouldn't have been a problem, but my vision for the project had expanded well beyond the original idea of a simple trivia book. As I had revised it, it now contained biographical information, and a critical analysis of the artist's work, balanced by the requisite trivia questions. With so many ideas crammed together, I became less threatened by the impending biography and instead focused my efforts on ways to ensure my book's unique identity. The only problem was, my files were bulging with so much information that I was no longer concerned with being able to complete one Buffett book. Instead, I was concerned with whether the publisher would entertain a manuscript that was fully three times longer than it had bargained for. I didn't realize it yet, but the solution was self-evident; I was writing two separate works disguised as one trivia book.

9

Concocting a Plan

So how could something as simple and innocuous as a trivia book lead to all this? Getting back to what I was saying at the very beginning, I was well into *The Jimmy Buffett Trivia Book* when I had an idea that would cause the project to expand radically. Writing about Buffett while listening to his records and researching everything I could get my hands on was all well and good, but to do this right, I ought to get to a concert. I ought to meet the Parrot Heads and try to understand them. Sure, you need to take a few steps back to see something clearly—that is why I believe that Jimmy Buffett could never write a book like this, and why it would be supremely difficult for a Parrot Head to do, either—but I also should take a few steps in. Why not crawl inside and look back out? What does it feel like to be a Parrot Head? What is it that drives such fanatical dedication? I needed a plan and it didn't take long before I was enacting something that would at last put me in contact with Buffett's dedicated followers.

The first thing that I decided to do was to stop lurking about on the Buffett-based Web sites and "expose" myself as the person who was writing another book on the guy. I needed photos anyway, so I composed a letter, then posted it on a listserv, which means that it was automatically distributed to hundreds of serious Buffett fans. Once again, however, I found that for a guy who comes from New York City, I'm about as naive as anyone can be.

In practically no time at all, "replies" were posted and distributed to all listserv members, most of them making broad assumptions about my intentions. One respondent assumed that I was a spy working for Buffett's Margaritaville organization and that I was stealing not only the concept but the content of his Web page. Notwithstanding the fact that I was unaware of this Web site's existence, the rumor spread as only rumors can. People who had no clue as to what was going on were posting messages, calling me a thief, a bastard, or worse. Others suggested that I was only pretending to write this book so I could get some cool Jimmy photos for free. There was even a lawyer who was posting advice to some of the members about how they could go about protecting themselves from vultures like me. Ha! This was just too wacky to be believed. I began to get the impression that these people were like Moonies, only instead of going around in airports banging tambourines, they stared at their computer terminals, chanting Buffett lyrics. The whole situation had gotten so ridiculously off-base that I had to laugh about it. "If we couldn't laugh, we would all go insane," right? Everybody was absolutely clueless about what I was doing or what my intentions were, but I could tune in each day and watch as the flurry of weird accusations and infighting grew even further out of proportion. I mean, am I having fun yet or what?

I showed these messages to a few of my non–Parrot Head friends and they laughed with me, but they also laughed a bit at me. What the hell was I doing working so hard on a Jimmy Buffett book? Isn't the guy about chilling out? And who's going to care about it when it's done, anyway? Well, now I knew better. Parrot Heads are probably the most dedicated group of fans that has ever existed, and if I got it wrong or screwed it up, they'd probably hunt me down, or burn me in effigy. Now, it was not only my conscience that wouldn't allow me to write a bad book; my instinct for self-preservation began to play a role in all of this.

A handful of people responded to me off of the listserv via e-mail and it goes without saying that their responses were considerably friendlier. A few expressed concerns about my intentions (in light of the Eng book, I'm sure) and offered friendly advice, others graciously wished me luck, and a few more were kind enough to offer me rare photos that they had in their possession. One person was a previous employee of Jimmy's recently disassembled Margaritaville organization; another was president of a regional Parrot Head Club, who was hoping to ensure that this book would rectify some of the technical inadequacies of the previous efforts. I responded to everybody who wrote me. A few responded back, and e-mail relationships were established.

One of the most intriguing of these respondents was Kathy, a resident of Tennessee whose unabashed passion for Jimmy Buffett was unlike anything I had yet seen. She wrote that she had plenty of stuff to share and wanted to help me, provided she didn't get involved in the crazy politics that now surrounded me (and who could blame her for that?). Her passion was boundless, but some of her e-mail was so peppered with off-the-wall comments that I began to question her sanity. In one response, she told me that she had heard of a house outside of Nashville that used to (*used to*) belong to Buffett. Armed with this information, she then went on a pilgrimage to find it, bringing along a couple of cans and jars that she used to scoop sand and gravel from the driveway. She keeps it for her personal collection of Buffett-related paraphernalia. She calls it "Jimmy dirt." I'm not kidding.

Now, I didn't know Kathy yet, but I formed a mental picture (emphasis on the mental) of what I thought she'd be like. Coincidentally, I had rented the movie *King of Comedy* days before our correspondence. In this movie, Robert De Niro and Sandra Bernhard play off-kilter fans whose obsession with their idol (played by Jerry Lewis) turn into delusions. By the movie's end, they break into his home and kidnap him, and he is very nearly raped. With this imagery fresh in my mind, I feared Kathy might be something like these characters. Although it seemed crazy, wouldn't it be fascinating to watch someone like Kathy in action? What would happen if I were to spend some time in the company of the Parrot Heads? I might not ever be able to understand the extent of their passion, but at least I could get a firsthand account of their behavior.

My mind was made up. I figured that if Buffett fans were this maniacal, then I absolutely had to meet them, and if I wanted to do it right, then I had to do it on their turf. Maybe in the process, I could even get to meet the man himself and explain the gist of my project. By now, I was certain that he would not exactly welcome me, but I still had a compulsion to come clean and let him know that I intended no malice. Concerts were scheduled to take place in Tennessee, so I bought a plane ticket to Nashville. On Saturday, March 1, there was a concert in

Knoxville, two hundred miles from Nashville, with another show in Nashville the following night. Both shows had been sold out for weeks (Buffett shows always sell out within hours of ticket availability), but I expected to dig something up. For my agenda, I figured that I would hang out in the parking lot to observe the tailgate madness, attend the bars where the Parrot Heads gather, and go to the concerts.

Over the course of the next few days, I received regular e-mails from Kathy, updating me on plans as they were made. I wrote back, telling her plainly of my intentions to come down and witness Parrot Head–ism firsthand, as a not-so-passive observer. Because I had no idea about hotels or where to get tickets, she volunteered to help, and I was grateful for the assistance. She suggested that I travel with her group, and I told her I'd think about it. Meanwhile, her e-mails continued to astound and confuse me—she loved the idea of a trivia book and bombarded me with strange and obscure trivia info ("Can you name what big superstar artist Jimmy's partner discovered? What female artist? What is the name of the *Goldmine* article on Buffett?" and so on). She also told me that she had plans to break into Jimmy's soundcheck, and I figured that if she went through with it, I'd do it too. After all, I was traveling hundreds of miles to find out the extent of Parrot Head–ism. If they were gonna do something crazy, I'd be right there with them, getting arrested in the name of journalism.

Although I couldn't comprehend her dedication, I genuinely enjoyed our conversations and occasionally I would interrupt this bottomless fount of information just to tease her a bit, curious if she would react defensively. She did not, and was even a bit self-effacing about it all. She acknowledged that it was pretty crazy, and I began to get a better understanding of why she felt the way she did. I liked her. She mentioned that she bought a pair of tickets in the second row for Nashville's performance. With some coaxing, she also told me how much she paid (you don't want to know, or to be more precise, she doesn't want you to know). At one point she blurted out "I would *kill* to be able to work for him." I repeated this comment aloud, because she said it with enough enthusiasm to make me think that she really meant it! With raised eyebrows and a bemused smile I listened intently while Kathy continued with her free-form ramble.

The most surprising pieces of information came when Kathy began to tell me about herself. I originally figured that anybody as flat-out crazy as this would probably live in a crawl space underneath a laundromat, so when she invited me to stay with her, I wasn't too quick to accept. In the course of conversation, though, she unassumingly revealed that she lives in an upscale Nashville neighborhood. Some very well known entertainers are her neighbors. She's married, with two happy, healthy, and very intelligent kids. Hers is a normal, well-rounded life. These personal revelations gave me further cause to reevaluate my impressions of her. As my originally prejudiced images dissipated, they were replaced with images of a mostly rational person who suffered gladly from this one personal obsession, that being an unequivocal devotion to the man who invented "Margaritaville."

Most important to Kathy was something that she had made especially for Jimmy. In the early eighties, Kathy attended a Buffett show and had taken a few photographs. At one point, he was joined onstage by his daughter, Savannah Jane, who looks to have been about four years old at the time. She has three photos of Jimmy and Savannah. She thinks they are the most beautiful and touching photographs she has ever seen. She tells me that the resolution is so clear you can see what time it is on Jimmy's wristwatch. She had these three photos reproduced and enlarged, then framed, and she intended to deliver this gift sometime in Nashville. By now, I could tell that every fiber of Kathy's being was hell-bent on meeting Jimmy, and these photos represented an appropriate ticket to get her wish. Now, we both had substantially good reasons to meet the man; she would come bearing gifts, and I would bear offerings of peace. Together, we just might make it happen.

I confirmed that I was flying down Friday morning and would be returning on Monday. Kathy couldn't locate any tickets for Nashville yet, but she did find an extra ticket for the Knoxville show and said she'd meet me at the airport with her friend, Sue. Sue has a new convertible. I'll also be sharing a room with them when we're out of town. I hadn't realized this earlier, but because Kathy had recently formed a Nashville branch of the regional Parrot Head Clubs, it was her responsibility to set up meeting places and organize events for the Parrot Heads when they arrived. It was terribly important to her that things go well, and I could hear a trace of anxiety in her voice. She knew other clubs would be watching to see if the Nashville organization could hold its own. I was only one small part of this, but she never even suggested that I could have posed a threat to her credibility. At the time, it didn't occur to me, either, although it should have. After all, I'm writing a book about Buffett, and most if not all Parrot Heads know about Buffett's aversion to characters like me. If I were to do a hatchet job on the guy, or disparage the Parrot Heads, it could all be pinned on her. This would not have been true, because I was coming down with or without Kathy's consent, but that wouldn't have prevented a few disgruntled fans with ruffled feathers from resenting her hospitality. Still, she remained optimistic and at the very least I was confident that I wasn't going to be abandoned at the airport. After we hung up, I called a broker about ticket prices for the Nashville show—three hundred bucks for the tenth row, one hundred for a floor seat. I'll try my luck when I get there.

10

Day One

It's Friday morning and I'm flying to Nashville. Like Paul Simon going to Graceland, I'm seeking transcendence but expect the mundane. As a nonbeliever, I wonder how I'm going to handle all of this enthusiasm. I feel like an unconverted Roman soldier riding my horse into Jerusalem. Will there be a blinding light to make me change my mind? I doubt it. Because I haven't experienced my own epiphany, maybe one of the faithful will figure out a way to knock me off of my horse. During the flight, I play a tape of Buffett's *Riddles in the Sand* in my Walkman. It's the first time that I'm hearing this album. The tape includes the songs "Who's the Blonde Stranger?" and "Ragtop Day," the first of which concerns itself with an overnight fling and the next with cruising along in a convertible on a gorgeous summer day.

I look out of the plane window at the clouds below us while I drift away and my libidinous subconscious takes control . . . (fade to black). I find myself reclining in the backseat of a Mercedes Benz convertible with the top down. Two gorgeous blondes in sunglasses and skimpy halter tops are sitting side by side in front of me, laughing and driving down the highway with the wind in their hair. The sun beats down on us while we sip margaritas. They turn and smile at me enticingly and naturally, I smile back. For a second, I'm Neal Cassady and Hunter Thompson rolled into one. I'm Hugh Hefner and Tom Cruise. In the middle of this fantasy, the plane hits turbulence. I become conscious and notice a nauseous sensation in my stomach. I close my eyes again and try to pick up where I had left off but instead I have visions of a little red devil repeatedly stabbing a little white angel with a pitchfork.

When both the plane and my overactive imagination are back on solid ground, I stroll into the terminal to meet my hosts. Standing in the vestibule are Kathy and Sue holding a cardboard sign that reads "Writer Dude—this way to Knoxville." As a kind of welcoming gesture, they present me with a not-too-tasteless Tommy Hilfiger Hawaiian shirt, which I must promise that I will wear to the show. In seconds, we are out of the airport and in Sue's '96 Chrysler convertible, heading toward Knoxville.

On the way, Kathy unsheathes a large picture frame from a pillowcase to show me her gift. It's actually a very beautiful presentation. I am genuinely surprised and absolutely taken with the expense, care, and good taste she has shown in creating this. Kathy is at least as bubbly as she was on the phone and Sue strikes me as a bit more reserved. I figure that maybe she's only partially infected with the Parrot Head disease.

For the duration of the ride, we become acquainted and I interview them on a few details about being a Parrot Head. Knoxville will be Sue's third Jimmy Buffett show. It will be Kathy's thirty-third. That might explain Sue's relative sanity, I figure. Kathy hands over a stack of Buffett concert photos, the souvenirs of thirty-two attendances, and I rummage through them for a half hour or so. All the while, Jimmy Buffett is playing on the car stereo. My stomach is still bugging me, and now I attribute it to a case of nerves. Or maybe I'm overdosing on Buffett. It's three o'clock in the afternoon and I've been listening to Jimmy Buffett music since nine this morning. Maybe I need an antidote. I should have brought along some satanic death metal tapes, like Pantera or Marilyn Manson; not that I like music that simulates the sound of a car accident, but maybe it would offset this queasy feeling. Considering my physical state, I'm grateful for the apparent sobriety exhibited by my hosts. Before I got here, I half expected that part of the Parrot Head concert ritual would be to slurp tequila all day long. So far, it's been Diet Cokes and water. Only Kate gets a little crazy and adds to her already peaking energy level by downing a can of Jolt cola.

In transit, we have a lively conversation on the meaning of "Heinz 57," from "Cheeseburger in Paradise." Is he singing about a steak sauce or a ketchup? These things actually *matter* to Parrot Heads. Sue rips out her wallet to show me that she is a card-carrying "Member of the Royal Order of the Sleepless Knights—Richmond Parrot Head Club." To become a member, you need to do something called a pickle shot. My stomach nearly explodes, and I ask her to tell me what that might be at some other time. Can Kathy top this? Well, yes. From her wallet, she pulls out a "Bank of Bad Habits" ATM card. On the back it lists the seven deadly sins, all involving things that you shouldn't do with your neighbor's wife. An eighth deadly sin is pizza and at the moment I agree wholeheartedly.

Our first destination in Knoxville is the Mexican restaurant Garcia's. This is where the Smoky Mountain Parrot Head Club holds its monthly meetings and the gathering place for this weekend's festivities. As we pull into the parking lot, there's a news crew there preparing for some live coverage of the Parrot Head gathering that will take place. The show's host, Missy Kane, is wearing a jeans ensemble that is turquoise from head to toe. Within minutes, Kathy is on *Live at Five,* talking about the Parrot Heads while Sue and I hover in the background. Also in the background, the Buffett tribute band, St. Somewhere (their name is derived from the lyrics of a Buffett song called "Boat Drinks") plays Buffett songs. By now, to hell with my upset stomach, I need a drink. I order a tequila and grapefruit juice with salt.

Under normal circumstances, I would probably jump headlong into the fray and get involved with everybody here, but these aren't normal circumstances. Besides, I'm feeling worse by the minute. I stand by the bar, away from the thick of the action, and simply observe. Club members have a few extra tickets for the Knoxville show and are making them available to needy Parrot Heads, at face value; one absolute no-no among Parrot Heads is to sell a ticket to another Parrot Head at greater than face value. The restaurant also has a few tickets that they are auctioning off, the proceeds of which will go to a local charity. I still don't have a ticket for Sunday night's Nashville show, but this situation confirmed my hunch that I'd probably have little trouble in finding one. I'm impressed with the camaraderie of the room. The scene is calmer than I expected, but this is only the preparty party. Tomorrow is the real deal, when everybody will gather here before showtime for an entire day of preshow drinks and revelry. Now, though, we experience only a taste of what is to come.

There's plenty of drinking and the hint of sexual activity, but nothing that would cause anybody to get aroused. It's mostly bravado or exhibitionism, and it is almost always playful or silly. Occasionally, some guy might partially lift a girl's blouse, then she in turn might pull at the button on his jeans. Flashing and friendly gropes are considered to be perfectly normal behavior. Nobody gets angry or embarrassed by any of this. It's more goofy than it is sexy; within the Parrot Head community, it is all in good fun among willing participants.

All the while, St. Somewhere plays Buffett tunes, or tunes that fit his style (e.g., "Another Saturday Night," "Tequila"). One particularly flamboyant Parrot Head named Mark yells out "Macarena!" Predictably, the crowd boos. The band then launches into a few seconds of "Margaritaville," and the crowd boos again! Even Parrot Heads can OD on this stuff, I guess.

I meet a guy named John who strikes me as a mostly levelheaded sort who talks at length about the need to listen to more than the *Songs You Know by Heart* collection (Buffett's greatest hits) and that it is silly to listen to Buffett exclusively. I agree with him, but then he says that tomorrow night will be his fifty-fourth Buffett concert! Now, I can understand the need for diversity, but if you attend over fifty shows by the same guy, aren't you a little bit weighted toward the opposite trend? John denies the contradiction, claiming that Buffett is about more than his music. It's a party and an excuse for a gathering, he explains, but I suggest that with so many shows under his belt, he wouldn't have enough time on his hands to properly digest another artist. He responds by saying that he hears plenty of new music when he listens to the radio, and then it occurs to me that for almost two decades, Jimmy Buffett has almost never been played on popular radio. For diversity, all that a Parrot Head has to do is tune in to what is going on with the rest of the world. Once they've had their fill, they can simply turn it off, then return to their own special place.

After four or five hours of watching everybody slowly get drunk, it's time for a change of venue. It's late, so Kathy, Sue, and I decide to head for the hotel. About thirty or forty other Garcia's partyers have rooms there as well, and it is decided to continue the party there. By the time we arrive, collapsible tables have been set up outside the rooms, with beer, chips, and tequila in abundance. There is one boom box for every four or five people. Each boom box is playing Buffett music independently of one another, and the effect is like a drunken choir, with each member singing a completely different song. It's cacophony. Rooms 110 through 126 are all occupied by Parrot Heads (there was one exception, but we didn't find out about these poor folks until the next morning). There are other partyers upstairs and still more on the other side of the building. It was going to be a long night for anybody who checked in with the intention of sleeping. Two rooms have computers set up, and only one is portable. The other is an entire home system, including a video camera, which was used for sending digitized images of our party over the Internet. To escape the noise and get some food (don't these people ever eat?), I take Sue's car, grab a bite, and return with more beer, tequila, and a bottle of scotch (hey, old habits die hard).

Some Parrot Heads mingled and sipped their drinks, but the majority opted to hover around the computers. Judging from my own experience, most Parrot Heads' preferred method of communication is e-mail. Since I've been here, I have yet to meet a Parrot Head without an e-mail address (are you out there, lonely soul?). For the most part, this is a cyberspace community that was brought together by a concert. Now, here they all were, in the flesh, and all that anybody wanted to do was to get online and deliver live, "as it happens" messages. Many of this group hail from Atlanta, the home of the very first official Parrot Head Club, and they were anxious to relay our activities to the folks who couldn't make it here.

Most non–Parrot Heads would find the conversation to be agonizingly dull; rumors, trivia, previous shows, and set lists are typical topics that were regularly discussed. For example, one conversation revolved around the question of whether or not Buffett would be wearing socks onstage tomorrow night. I came down here expecting to find a benign group of overcompensating, latent partyers and tonight, that's pretty much what I got. I hung around for a while, but by midnight, I figured that I should check in. My upset stomach was turning into a full-blown sickness and I was getting concerned. With Jimmy Buffett songs blaring at me from five different directions, I said good night and headed off to bed, hoping that the rest would cure my ills. As I head for my room, five streakers, three men and two women, go flying past the crowd.

In my room, I mentally recapped the day's events and tried to make some sense of it. After fifteen hours of endlessly hearing Jimmy Buffett music, I felt like I went to a carnival and ate nothing but cotton candy all day. I still couldn't grasp what this was all about. What was the appeal that would cause so many people to dedicate such a large portion of their lives to this guy? It has everything to do with Jimmy Buffett, yet it has very little to do with him. So far, from what I've seen, the Parrot Heads are a self-sustaining culture that is unified under the guise of Buffett, but the community spirit transcends that. It's about beer (somewhat), tequila (somewhat), sex (somewhat), and computers (an awful lot), and Buffett's songs provide the endless soundtrack, but mostly, it's about a cultural identity. There's freedom to be found in this group, but actually, not *too* much. For example, etiquette, politesse, and reserve are just as common as ribaldry.

While I am lying in bed having these thoughts, some of the crowd enter my room with a life-size male blow-up doll and place it on the bed next to me. They call him "Richard." As I sit up to see what is going on, they snap a photo. Now, somewhere in this world there exists a photograph of me, half-naked, looking shocked at being caught with a male blow-up doll. Whoever has this photograph, name your price. And Mom, if you see it first, I swear, it's not what you think. I finally fell asleep at about one o'clock, only to wake up and spend the next few hours in the bathroom, forcing myself to feel better—I'll leave out the details. I crawled back to bed around four o'clock but was reawakened at 4:45 by Sue, who was totally wired and raring to go. "Let's get breakfast! C'mon y'all, wake up!! We're goin' to Cracker Barrel!"

For nearly an hour, she harangues us with pleas to get something to eat. I guess Sue's not as reserved as I had thought! At 5:30, she wins. We stumble into the blackness of the morning and head off to Cracker Barrel for breakfast. Guess who is playing on the car's CD player? I may not have a goddamn card and I didn't do a pickle shot either, but the way I figure it, I am now also a member of the Royal Order of Sleepless (K)nights.

11

Day Two

After a quick breakfast, it is decided that we have business to attend to. Before we head out, though, I notice that by some inexplicable miracle, my sickness has passed. I'm not even tired. I would have been happy to have merely survived the night, yet I feel pretty good and think that perhaps there is a magic associated with the Parrot Heads.

With little hesitation, the girls decide to head off to the college campus where tonight's show will be. We arrive at 7:30 and immediately spot the road crew's truck. Kate has her framed photographs with her, so she hauls the frame toward a roadie while Sue and I wait in the car. When she returns, she tells us that the band is scheduled to arrive at four o'clock. Guess where Kathy wants to be at four o'clock? Because the band isn't around, we head off in search of the hotel where they might be staying.

On the way to the Holiday Inn and the Hilton, they keep a sharp eye posted for "Jimmy sightings." Any human being who jogs past is met with a shout of "There's Jimmy!" The same holds true for any bicyclist, though they believe that Jimmy's bicycle must be red, because he sings about this in a song that dates from 1972. At the Hilton, Kathy goes to the front desk and asks if any band member's names are on the guest list. Predictably, they aren't.

Despondent, Kathy and Sue decide to head back to our hotel, but as we circle the building, we see two tour buses that match the roadie's bus at the auditorium. Aha! We've found 'em! Sue parks the car and we purposefully march into the lobby, Kathy carrying her framed photos and me hesitantly lugging a copy of my first book. Sue and Kathy are very excited they might meet Buffett, yet are worried because they aren't wearing makeup. We figure we'll get coffee in the restaurant and maybe the band will come down for breakfast. Kathy corners a few employees to show them her photos of Jimmy and Savannah Jane. The hostess kindly informs her that the band ate earlier, so we surrender and head back to our own hotel a half hour away.

During the ride, I wonder aloud if most Parrot Heads might deliberately keep themselves at a distance from Buffett and his crew. Nobody acknowledges this openly, but it appears as though most fans subliminally concede that they are very different from him and are satisfied to keep him at arm's length. We're all registered in a hotel that is miles away from the arena, but if their agenda included proximity to Buffett and the Coral Reefer Band, wouldn't they have registered somewhere here in the heart of town? They're all in the boondocks, when they could have been here at the Hilton. Was it poor logistics, or was it by design? I figure that part of being a Parrot Head is about partying endlessly in Buffett's honor, but that getting too close to the guy might be a breach of conduct. Maybe they don't *want* to meet him, for fear that it would destroy their impressions.

Everybody talks about Jimmy as if he's just a regular guy, yet virtually every Parrot Head back at the hotel showed no particular interest in meeting him. Many consider him to be unapproachable. This contradiction was wasted on Kathy and Sue, who desperately sought to break down that barrier. Kathy felt confident in the purity of her intentions, but still, she wondered if her behavior might border on stalking. I replied that she intends no malice and is clearheaded enough to avoid any delusional behavior, so she's probably safe from any such classification but still, this morning's events make me very aware of Buffett's vulnerability. What if we were to find him? Do they only hope for a few quick pleasantries, or might they expect more? Is there any disillusionment that they might actually become buddies with the guy? I keep my thoughts to myself but as we drive, I hope that they are clear-thinking enough to expect no more than to cherish the memory of coming face-to-face with the man who has somehow managed to become the focal point of their lives.

With the top down, we drive back to our room with "Last Mango in Paris" playing at ear-splitting levels. We only make one quick stop at a Kmart to resolve the "ketchup or steak sauce" issue. We find a bottle of Heinz ketchup ("57 Varieties") to study the label and decide that it is indeed what Jimmy was referring to. Well, that's a load off of my mind. It's barely 9:30 as we pull into our parking lot at the hotel and there's still no sign of life, so the car's stereo is pumped to an unbearable level—we'll blast 'em out! Slowly, over the course of the next three hours, Parrot Heads emerge from their rooms in various stages of morning-after bleariness. First comes Scott, then Charlotte, then Steve, who was awakened at five o'clock by some crazy girl screaming for breakfast next door (tell me about it). What at first appears to be a fairly normal group of people getting ready to face the day is slowly transformed into something else entirely. Today is the day that we will all "phlock" at Garcia's, then proceed to the event that has inspired all of us to be here in the first place, a concert featuring Jimmy Buffett and the Coral Reefer Band.

The weather today is gorgeous. Someone tells me that God protects babies and idiots, and we laugh as I wonder if that protection would extend itself to Parrot Heads and drunkards. While I recline in the back of the convertible, soaking up sun, men who only last night struck me as normal are now walking around in hula dresses. Another is dressed from head to toe as a parrot. A few have their faces painted. Crazy hats abound. One guy is wearing a shark on his nose. Many of the girls are wearing colorful buttons imprinted with their screen names—a great idea, because so many Parrot Heads only know each other via the Internet. There are enough Caribbean Soul (Margaritaville's clothing line) shirts here to fund a getaway cruise for two. Everybody is wearing a lei and a few approach me to reproach me on the inadequacy of my dress. Before long, I am shamed into going to my room to put on the Hawaiian shirt that was given to me. As I emerge, I am doused with a series of leis. Each time a girl does this, she tells me that I've been "lei-ed." As this happens I feel like the crew of the *Bounty* must have felt when they landed in Tahiti.

As crazy as we all look, it isn't deemed to be sufficient, especially my sorry-looking outfit, so we head off to a store called Party City. Steve invites me to take the ride with him and I gratefully accept. Last night,

Steve struck me as the most levelheaded guy in the pack and the person I'd be most likely to befriend. Today, he is wearing a hula skirt in public. He tells me that he's forty-five and a grandfather, and that he would like to take his granddaughter to a Buffett show, but his daughter won't allow it. His coworkers refer to Parrot Heads as "Peckerheads." As we walk into the costume store, I notice that dozens of Parrot Heads have taken over the place, trying on anything that they fancy. An incredulous girl behind the counter looks at us with obvious distaste, as if we're all escaped mental patients, and says, "You mean all of this is just for Jimmy Buffett?" Somebody ties a cardboard replica of a parrot to the back of my shirt. Now, with everybody satisfied that I look enough like an idiot to pass for normal, we head to Garcia's.

We walk in at 2:00 P.M., and already the party is in full swing. The restaurant consists of four subdivided rooms, and three are dedicated to the Parrot Head "phlocking," as is the outdoor patio. St. Somewhere plays away in the back room while people who are barely recognizable from the previous day prance about, drinking margaritas or beer, dancing, and generally cavorting. Dozens of people are walking around with cameras and video recorders, but I am the only one with a notepad, and it makes some people nervous—I'm constantly asked "What are you writing now?" as if I were making up some dreadful fantasy. Believe me, I don't have to make this up. From the restaurant, "normal" patrons occasionally wander in to stare at the wackos. Wearing their LaCoste sport shirts and brown slacks, they are instantly pinned as outsiders, and this makes me grateful for my Hawaiian shirt with the parrot pinned on back.

For five solid hours, we drink ourselves into oblivion. I mingle but eventually settle on the patio area, so I can enjoy the sunshine. Along with a couple dozen other sun-starved Parrot Heads, I spend most of the afternoon sitting on a high wall that surrounds the outdoor patio.

The I Tappa Corona girls are here (a sorority dedicated to partying in the name of Jimmy Buffett), and I'm told that an initiation is scheduled to take place. The explanation that I'm given is vague, but apparently it involves downing a drink that is wedged in the crotch of a male participant (no hands allowed!), then finishing it off with a lime wedge that he holds in his teeth. Usually, this all takes place while the participants are onstage. People are reclining on the restaurant's outer wall and pouring tequila into their belly-buttons while members of the opposite sex suck out the contents. I drink my Tecate out of the can, but thanks for asking. At one point Steve loses his balance and tumbles backwards, falling head over heels six feet to the ground, hitting bottom with a horrific thud. God has mercy on Parrot Heads and drunkards, though, and considering what could have happened, Steve is fine, except for a few painful bruises. By six o'clock, the restaurant is a heaving mass of goofy-looking, drunken bodies fighting their way to the bar, myself included. Spilled liquor, abandoned articles of clothing, and glass are everywhere. In the midst of this insanity, I have the ridiculous inspiration to call home. I fight my way to the phone and though I can't hear a thing, I dial. My six-year-old son answers.

Before I left, both of my kids kissed me goodbye, saying they hoped that I would have time to play with them when I got back. They both learned to resent Jimmy Buffett, and they blamed him personally for taking their daddy away for the weekend. My eldest, the six-year-old, said something about "stupid Jimmy Buffett." Now, while I was surrounded by hundreds of wasted Parrot Heads, this comment struck me as hysterically funny. I yelled into the phone, "It's funny to tell these people that you don't like Jimmy Buffett." No sooner did the words come out of my mouth before a nearby girl who overheard this grabbed the phone out of my hands. With no idea that I was talking to a child, she screamed "YOU DON'T LIKE JIMMY BUFFETT!? ARE YOU CRAZY?! JIMMY BUFFETT IS GREAT! WHAT ARE YOU TALKING ABOUT?!" She yelled for almost half a minute. I'm staring incredulously and laughing, wondering what my son is saying, when I see the girl's face turn ashen. "What did he say?" I ask. She looks at me meekly. "He said, 'Can I talk to my dad?' "

12

Show No. 1: Knoxville-Boling Arena, Knoxville, Tennessee (March 1, 1997)

An hour before showtime, buses arrive to take all of us to the concert. Considering everyone's condition, this is an idea that is more of a necessity than a convenience. The air exchange system is broken, however, and the windows are sealed. One hundred degrees of stagnant air surrounds us; we're going to the Knoxville-Boling Arena aboard the Knoxville-Boiling Bus. A few people were intelligent enough to sneak their drinks out of the bar, so various negotiations take place to share the wealth. Any girl willing to flash her breasts is rewarded with a sip of beer. I have no idea where Kathy and Sue are. Luckily, Kathy had the foresight to give me a concert ticket beforehand. Charlotte, a girl from Atlanta whom I met the night before, sits next to me and together, we kick out the emergency window and hang over the side like dogs out of a car window. For the first time in my life, I realize that I truly understand the expression "Are we having fun yet?"

None too soon, we arrive at the show. We proceed to our seats and brace ourselves for this long-awaited event. The venue is a typical sports arena, with folding chairs on the floor surrounded by steep cement inclines, laid out in a huge oval shape. My seats are just off of the floor, seven o'clock from the stage. With me are Michael and Kathy, whom I met earlier at the hotel, and a girl I just met named Lori. All three are confirmed Parrot Heads.

Before the show begins, a pair of characters affiliated with Buffett run through the audience with whistles and a foam coconut. The guy with the whistle has an extendable hoop strapped to his back. The other guy jettisons the coconut to various audience members. The idea is for the audience member to toss the coconut into the hoop. Call it either Coconut Basketball or Parrot Hoops. He works his way to the front of the stage and just before the show begins, he takes out a cannon-type device that is shaped like a banana. Powered by air cartridges, he aims the gun to the upper decks and fires Caribbean Soul T-shirts into the crowd. The lights dim and the Coral Reefer Band takes the stage. There is no warm-up band tonight. I settle in and prepare to find out what it is that I've been missing. Following, along with my obligatory comments, is the evening's set list.

- "Brazilia"—a mellow and mostly uninspiring instrumental. Buffett takes the stage. Of course, the appreciative crowd stands and applauds loudly. "This is the northernmost stop on our little winter tour, so we brought you the weather." The acoustics here are bad and I can barely understand him. Michael points out that Buffett is wearing socks, apparently a rarity and something he thinks is worth noting.
- "One Particular Harbour"—a great choice for an opener. Everybody remains standing and sings along, especially on the Tahitian chorus.
- "Don't Chu Know"—the sound hasn't gotten any better. It's like listening to a boom box in a tunnel. I can barely discern chord changes, let alone whatever subtle instrumentation may be going on. This venue is not conducive to a musical performance.
- "Holiday"—I'm not yet familiar with his latest work, but this is not too impressive. I think Barry Manilow could do an admirable cover version. All the while, Buffett is running around like a game-show host gone amok.
- "Grapefruit–Juicy Fruit"—I liked this song since I first heard it, but it strikes me as a song better suited to a small nightclub, not a sports arena. Buffet teases the audience by playing the two opening notes. From this sparse clue, it is instantly recognized and the crowd applauds wildly.
- "Come Monday"

• "Why Don't We Get Drunk and Screw"—why does he still do this? I've heard him complain numerous times about how this song pigeonholed him, but apparently he couldn't have minded so much. Twenty-five years later, I think he could move on if he so desired. To remove himself from the proceedings, he turns a video recorder on the audience while two huge monitors display whomever he focuses the camera on. The crowd sings the entire song—Buffett never sings a word.

• "Jamaica Mistaica"—as far as I'm concerned, this song is one big mistaica.

• "Changes in Attitudes, Changes in Latitudes"—a very good rendition of one of his most well written tunes.

• "Barometer Soup"—Buffett tells the crowd that he wrote the song for Jerry Garcia. This performance is also admirable.

• "Fins"—considering the compromising circumstances of lousy acoustics, this still manages to sound *very* good.

• "Cheeseburger in Paradise"—I always hated this song, but I must admit that it is easier to appreciate in a live environment.

Intermission
Score at halftime:
Buffett 7, Skepticism 5

The second set opens with Buffett playing an acoustic guitar, accompanied by Fingers Taylor on harmonica, to the seats in back of the stage. As the show wears on, he is joined by other band members and works his way back toward the front of the stage.

• "Pencil Thin Mustache"—well done—maybe even more enjoyable than the album version.

• "Son of a Son of a Sailor"—also very well done—it impressed me as heartfelt.

• "It's My Job"—done with the band. Songwritwer Mac McAnally sings a verse. The sentimental sweetness of this song makes me feel as if someone poured soda on my head and then dipped me in caramel.

• "Desdemona's Building a Rocket Ship"—I think I missed the point of this one.

• "Stars on the Water"—this sounded great.

- "Schoolboy Heart"
- "A Pirate Looks at Forty"—Buffett's very own classic, done in the respectful manner that it deserves.
- "Southern Cross"—a Stephen Stills classic that has somehow become a Buffett classic as well. It's a very powerful version tonight.
- "Brown-Eyed Girl"—a Van Morrison classic that I am not ready to concede to Buffett, but the crowd loves it wholeheartedly.
- "Margaritaville"—of course, and I didn't mind it, either. Fingers played so hard I thought his head might explode. Back in the bar, somebody opined that "Margaritaville" is really a sad song about a ne'er-do-well. Tonight's celebratory version blew that theory away completely.

Encore

- "Volcano"
- "Another Saturday Night"
- "Brand New Tennessee Waltz"—a Jesse Winchester song that hasn't been formally recorded and released by Buffett. A tasty ending for the Knoxville crowd.

Final Score:
Buffett 16, Skepticism 9

I may not have been bowled over, but I had to admit that he was at least impressive enough to earn a positive review. Had the sound been better, I very well might have been. I still didn't see the whole picture, but at least some of the Buffett magnetism was beginning to come into view.

13

Profile of a Parrot Head

Leaving the show, we were two busloads of pure exhaustion. Barely anybody spoke during the ride back to Garcia's, which was closed when we returned (thank God). Like delirious zombies, we all straggled toward our rides and drove back to our hotel rooms. For a few hours, we mingled again much like last night, only now with a mellow sheen that was not unlike having a postorgasmic smoke. Most of these people were not moving on to Nashville and it would be my last chance to hang out with them, so I stayed up and talked until 3:00 A.M. With the concert fresh in our memories, we talked mostly of other things. For the first time since I arrived in Tennessee, Jimmy Buffett had become more of a subtext than a focal point. With the anticipation dissipated, we were simply a group of relaxed people with no agenda, myself being the possible exception. As we talked, I once again tried to comprehend the driving force that held these people together. Tonight's concert was good, but it certainly wasn't enough to explain so much devotion and unity. There are plenty of bands that put on a good show. It still didn't define what it meant to be a Parrot Head, and now I was wondering if it could be done at all.

After the show, we sat talking about our separate lives back home and slowly, the truth about the Parrot Heads began to dawn on me.

Jimmy Buffett may have been the catalyst that brought this disparate group together, but there was something much stronger that holds them in this bond. I have trouble trying to convey my feelings here, because

I got to know many of these people quite well in the past twenty-four hours. They were overwhelmingly kind to me, and fun to be with, and I knew that I would miss them when we moved on in the morning. Originally, I wanted to draw a composite of them, define a typical Parrot Head, but now that idea seemed simpleminded and crude. There was complexity here, and contradiction. As people, their diversity extended way beyond any simple synopsis or stereotype. They were no longer a caricature to me. They're real, whole people—a little nuts, maybe—but real, whole people.

There's Charlotte, a (once) straitlaced Atlanta native who realized late in life that she toed the line for too long and decided that the time had come to have some fun. There's Chris, who feels as though she had lived her life backwards—married as "a kid," then to graduate school and the responsibility that comes with it. Her marriage was stifling and fun was at a premium, so she set out on her own. Now she immerses herself in Buffett as if she were bathing in freedom itself. There's Michael, a private, soft-spoken All-American type of guy who chose Buffett as a more likable alternative to contemporary "alternative" music. There's also Manatee, a big, shy guy who struck me as someone who truly needed a guiding force like Jimmy Buffett in his life. Somehow, he felt grounded by the optimism in Buffett's music. Steve, my benevolent driver, got married straight out of high school but is long divorced. Now, with his daughter raising children of her own, he was heading back east in the morning to his business partners. Hert and Bonnie have been married for thirty-five years and share an obsession for the Parrot Head phenomenon. In the course of our discussion, Hert tells me that he and Bonnie are the couple immortalized by one of the spoken passages on the "You Had to Be There" album. Sometime around the Christmas holidays in the late sixties, they were on their way to see a country artist named Ray Whitley when they stopped in to an Atlanta club called the Bistro for a drink. A very young Jimmy Buffett was scheduled to perform that night but nobody was there, so he politely shuttled them to the door before the management could insist that he play.

At first glance, Key West Dan is probably the closest to what many people expect a Parrot Head to be. He's as mellow as anyone I've ever met, with a deep tan and a personality that is as comfortable and uncomplicated as soft leather. Through the course of our conversation, though, I learn that he lived up north as an accountant for many years before burning out and heading to the sun belt for a new start. Now, he's a mailman. Lori is from Columbus, a young girl who loves to smile and is enchanted by the good times that the Parrot Heads represent. Leigh is an advertising executive who came all the way from South Dakota so he could party with the people he met online.

They all have their own lives, but as we spoke, there did seem to be a number of recurrent threads. A large number of Parrot Heads are either divorced or have one foot squarely out the door. More often than not, their ex-mate didn't appreciate music, or at least not Jimmy Buffett's music. Many felt as if they were being stifled in their previous lives. It goes without saying that Parrot Head–ism just isn't conducive to marriage unless both members are thoroughly entrenched in the insanity. This is what I call my "Yee-Ha!" theory. Many Parrot Heads are late bloomers when it comes to partying. Maybe they were the good kid all of their lives, or the dedicated student, or the compliant and faithful spouse, until something snaps and they realize that their lives are passing them by. Through a type of osmosis that is spawned by loneliness or a simple desire to have fun, they find themselves drawn into the Parrot Head fold. Years of self-denial are now compensated (or overcompensated) for, and they develop a real sense of belonging with others who have the same desire.

Parrot Heads know that a huge segment of the population thinks they are crazy, but they don't care about that. Viewed from the outside, dignity is not part of the equation, yet I've determined that Parrot Heads are proud of their obsession and that is what leads them to an even greater level of dedication and more outrageous style of dress. One thing that all Parrot Heads are very serious about is the right to be silly; to them, partying is a serious business. The more that society views them as untouchables for being overly dedicated to Jimmy Buffett, the more cohesion they have as a group. The fact is that for many of them, their dedication is driven more by the spirit of what the Parrot Heads share than by Jimmy Buffett's music.

Outsiders often view people who harbor obsessions as a threat to their own well-being. Even a group as innocuous as the Deadheads has developed a negative stereotype. To an unsympathetic outsider, Deadheads are often perceived as long-haired, unwashed, granola-munching acid-heads who twirl about in peasant dresses and tie-dye and sleep in Volkswagen Microbuses. The positive side of their dedication is downplayed or ignored by outsiders until it suits their prejudiced expectations and is rendered invisible. I happen to know a lot of Deadheads and none of them are anything at all like this stereotype. Well, now I know a lot of Parrot Heads too, and I can tell you that they are as diverse a group of human beings as any other that I've encountered, other than their unequivocal bond to the image that Margaritaville represents and a shared fanaticism for that lifestyle. Since I've been working on this book, though, I've received all types of disparaging comments from people whose attitudes about Parrot Heads range from bemusement to malicious distaste. Misconceptions abound. Once you cross the line into fanaticism, you must accept that you're no longer seen as normal by nonparticipants, so part of your dedication stems from your willingness to forgo being seen as normal. For better or worse, crossing that line is a commitment. Fellow obsessors will welcome you with open arms, but outsiders will categorize you and turn you into a figure of fun. If you were to run around the parking lot before a Jimmy Buffett concert in your underwear and parrot slippers with a palm tree sprouting from your head, chances are you'd be applauded. You could try the same thing before a Metallica concert, but unless you're built like Mike Tyson, I wouldn't advise it.

14

Day Three

Once you start to hear the world through the ears of a Parrot Head, your perspective is radically altered. When Kathy, Sue, and I started our drive back to Nashville, I practically begged them to play something besides Buffett, and they graciously complied by turning on the radio. To my own horror, though, the radio sounded as though it was playing foreign music intended for someone other than me. I could barely understand the mix of styles, or the contemporary appeal of these strange songs. My God, what's happening to me? I can't relate to the radio anymore! Parrot Heads must feel this way all of the time. Most people in the music universe ignore Buffett; subliminally, or perhaps in subtle retribution, Buffett fans often ignore anything that isn't somehow Buffett related. Ask Parrot Heads who their favorite artists are (besides the obvious) and chances are excellent that you'll get a list of people who are somehow affiliated with the main man. They'll name Coral Reefers who have released solo albums (Fingers Taylor, Peter Mayer, Michael Utley, and Robert Greenidge), or they'll name someone from the Margaritaville stable of artists (Marshall Chapman, Todd Snider, the Iguanas). On a reach, they might stretch out far enough to include people whom Buffett himself often covers (Steve Goodman, Jesse Winchester) or people who make guest appearances on his albums (James Taylor, the Eagles). Those who are really stretching the boundaries of acceptability might include artists that were once affiliated somehow with Buffett's own history (Jerry Jeff Walker, John Prine, the

Neville Brothers). This mind-set can lead to a vacuum that ostracizes the radio, and now that I've heard nothing but Jimmy Buffett for two entire days, I can understand why it requires a type of detoxification before you plunge back in to normalcy. After what I've been through, the radio sounds just plain weird.

This was a very frightening revelation and never in a million years could I have imagined that I'd become susceptible to anything like this. Generally speaking, Buffett fans didn't impress me as a musically adept bunch, and I figured that was why they were able to hear "the same thing again and again." Even after meeting them, I concluded that their devotion stemmed more from the philosophy they derived from the music than from the music itself, but now I was suffering from a similar complex. Oh, hell. "Kathy? Sue? Would you mind popping the Buffett tape back in? Thanks."

As we rolled into Nashville, the weather was completely different than the day before; cold and damp, with occasional downpours. After a quick lunch, Kathy felt compelled to show me the home where she obtained her prized "Jimmy dirt" so we drove off to the outskirts of town. On the way, she told me that once I saw the property, I would have a completely different view of the man. I would be able to appreciate Jimmy's selfless desire to restore his home as a historic showplace for the entire community. In the pouring rain, we stopped in front of the house and stared. According to Kathy's bottomless wealth of information, the house now belongs to Kim Carnes. To be honest, I felt a bit embarrassed just staring at this structure, especially because somebody kept walking out to the driveway, but that didn't stop me from convincing the pair to drive around back and view it from another angle. To me, it was an old house. To them, it was a shrine. It sits next to an ancient Indian burial ground and for reasons that I couldn't fully comprehend, Kathy and Sue felt this made Buffett a selfless philanthropist who deserved the Nobel Peace Prize. I scratched my head while they ooh-ed and aaah-ed, then we moved on. It was time to prepare for today's Parrot Head party and the ensuing show.

Both women lived in town with their families, so at Kathy's insistence, I was spending the night as her houseguest. While I got ready for the evening, Kathy made a few frantic phone calls. During one conversation, I heard her say that she was giving her extra ticket to me. It was a school night, so her daughter could not attend. From this turn of events, I was going to sit with her in the second row. I was stunned. Earlier in the day, I had paid her face value for a floor seat in the twenty-fourth row and as far as Kathy was concerned, that meant that we were even. It was a flattering privilege and an honor that I knew I could not repay, especially in light of how much tonight's performance meant to her. For weeks now, she had been planning today's itinerary and dreaming of the possibilities. The sincerity of her purpose overwhelmed me and it was right then that I realized I wanted nothing more in the world than for Kathy's wish to come true. She was bringing her framed photos to the show and I knew that above all else, she was hoping that this just might present a chance for her to finally meet Jimmy Buffett in person. I vowed that I would do everything within my power to make it happen for her.

The Nashville Parrot Head bash took place at a club called The Key, a strip mall–bound bar and grill that was designed to resemble a beachfront cafe. By the time we arrived, the parking lot was full to overflowing. The bar was the same. We barely scraped our way in the door and I was surrounded by a whole new sea of faces dressed in tropical garb. Tonight, I had dressed "normally" (a black linen jacket with a button-down white shirt) and as I met this new group of Parrot Heads, I realized that I had made a judgmental error. So as not to stand out so badly, I started begging people to lei me. Sue gave me a Parrot Head cap, which I put on top of the cap I was already wearing. She looked at me for a few seconds and drawled, "You look like an idiot with those two hats on." Pause. Here I was surrounded by people with rubber sharks on their noses, parrot slippers on their feet, palm trees sprouting from their heads, running around in clothing that I wouldn't even want to wear as pajamas, and *I* look like an idiot? I took a quick look in the mirror, then decided to remove the second hat. Thank you, Sue. I could hardly believe it, but there was St. Somewhere playing away in the back of the bar again. Are these guys following me or what?

Preshow drinks abounded and judging from the quality of my handwriting, I must've had myself one hell of a time. I met Tom, a friendly guy who was one of my early (nonhostile) e-mail correspondents. We bought each other a few beers and I updated him on why I came to Nashville. I also met a number of other onliners, including Courtney, the accredited founder of the I Tappa Corona crowd. We talked and drank until I was grateful that it wasn't my responsibility to drive. When the bar ran out of Corona beer, Kathy took us to the concert.

15

Show No. 2: Nashville Auditorium, Nashville, Tennessee (March 2, 1997)

The building that held this evening's concert looks like a Gotham City fantasy, with twin spires rising toward the heavens and spotlights beaming upward through the rain. Kathy's beaming too, but she's also visibly nervous. This has been a long time coming. At the turnstiles, she told a friendly security guard about her gift. He let us in and directed us to the security chief, who in turn flagged down one of Buffett's roadies. He told her that he would deliver the gift immediately, took it, then disappeared. Before we knew it, the three photos were whisked away. I asked Kathy if she had written her name and address on the back of the frame and to my dismay, she said she had forgotten to personalize it. We'd just have to wait and see. We went to our seats before the lights dimmed, then watched Marshall Chapman's opening set. Compared with last night, tonight's sound was nearly perfect. This hall was fairly new and it was obvious that acoustics played a major role in the building's design. From the second row, Chapman impressed me enough to make a note that I should buy a few of her CDs.

Throughout the opening act's set, Kathy sat quietly to the end and tried to disguise her anxiety. In true opening-act tradition, I made a number of trips to the beer stand, enough that the security guard no longer felt compelled to check my ticket each time I returned. To relieve my selfishness, I found where Sue was sitting and told her that

I'd trade seats with her sometime after Buffett started. While the audience played "Coconut Basketball," Kathy told me that if she catches a beach ball at a Buffett concert, she deflates it and keeps it as a souvenir. For a second, I remember the Kathy I had imagined from our early phone calls. Surrounding us in the front rows are people who look like they don't recognize whether they are at a Jimmy Buffett concert, a theater event, or a basketball game. Most front-row types are connected "players" who take their seats for granted. In comparison, Kathy has paid a small fortune to be here and has brought a gift at considerable expense besides, yet views her spot as a privilege. As the lights dim again, I feel proud to be sitting next to her.

The Coral Reefers take the stage and following them, sitting on stage right and directly in front of us, is Buffett's entire family. Sarah Delaney, Savannah Jane, wife Jane, and their young son, Cameron, all settled in to watch the show. Kathy was immediately filled with an overwhelming desire to know if Jane or Savannah Jane had seen her framed photos, so she stands on her seat and starts signaling them with her hands. I feel foolish but immediately do the same. Jimmy's wife, Jane, notices us right away (God bless her) and though she kept her impressions well hidden, she must have thought that we were a pair of inbred morons. While we drew rectangles in the air with our hands and pointed wildly at Savannah Jane, yelling out gibberish, she looked at us with a (sym)pathetic and kindly expression, assuming that we wanted *her* to take *our* picture. I was mortified. Despite the fact that she was surrounded by her family, including an infant son, I honestly believe that if I tossed her my camera, she would have come to the front of the stage and taken our snapshot. Obviously, she hadn't seen the framed photos yet. Just when I thought that this couldn't get any more embarrassing, a huge security guard with six necks came charging over and demanded that we get off of our seats . . . *now*!!!

It was about then that Buffett came out onstage. As he launched into "One Particular Harbour," the redness in my face began to fade. Damn, this song sounded good to me. As a father who hadn't seen his wife or kids for a few days, I watched Buffett's family watch him with comforting pride, and I felt a chill come over me. For reasons that would otherwise be difficult to explain, I knew at that instant that I had become a fan of Jimmy Buffett.

The show continued with a superpolished version of "Cuban Crime of Passion," and I was hooked. Even "Holiday" didn't sway me. "Grapefruit–Juicy Fruit," "Come Monday," and "Why Don't We Get Drunk" followed in succession and each sounded better than I had expected. Maybe it was the proximity, or maybe it was all that beer, but I felt that I may have discovered the essential spirit that makes this music work. Before the band launched into "Jamaica Mistaica," I found Sue and we exchanged tickets. From the twentieth row, I listened while Buffett told his audience about the 137 rounds of ammunition that were fired at his plane—only two of which hit their mark—but his opening monologue impressed me much more than the song itself. From there, the set went to "Changes in Latitudes, Changes in Attitudes" and I began to think that the lyrics held some relevance to me. Had I not come to Nashville, I doubt that I would have been able to enjoy this as much as I was. The smell of marijuana wafted toward me from a distance and it triggered a very surprising realization that was contrary to my expectations. Until now, I hadn't encountered one single Parrot Head getting high in the entire time I had been here.

"Barometer Soup" and "Fins" followed, then "Cheeseburger in Paradise," and while it played, I walked back toward the second row and stood in the aisle. When the seven-necked security guard (he must have grown another in the preceding hour) asked me to take a seat, I wanted to oblige (believe me), but instead I told him that I had given my seat to someone else. For a second, he frowned and looked at me a bit funny, then pointed to an unoccupied seat in the front row. I took it. Within minutes, Sue, Kathy, and all the people who were sitting around them were waving me over to join them. It was like one big, happy family there in the second row. The songs went on: "Pencil Thin Mustache," "Son of a Son of a Sailor," "Love Is Made of This" (a song featuring backup singer Nadirah Shakoor), "It's My Job," "Desdemona's Building a Rocket Ship," "Don't Chu Know," "In the City," "Schoolboy Heart." In this mood, songs that I previously found offensive were enjoyable, and songs that were once only enjoyable now had me captivated. I was having a lot of fun, despite myself. It might not have been a heavy discovery, but as the band launched into "Southern Cross," I had another realization: either you get it or you don't, and I was beginning to get it. Maybe the fact that I've been a lifelong Stephen Stills fan helped to give me a push in the right direction, but this song just sounded right in Buffett's hands. If you want magic to work, you need to believe in it. Once I began to ignore the machinations, complications, and contradictions that drove the Buffett machine, the illusion hit me square in the head and I decided that, for the moment at least, the illusion was good enough.

"Southern Cross" was as inspirational as Stephen Stills intended it to be, and then Buffett paused to tell a story and introduce a special guest. He reminisced about his younger days when he worked as a music journalist reviewing concerts (I discreetly slipped my pad into my pocket as he spoke), and told us that the very first live show he covered took place at the old Nashville Auditorium, featuring the band Steppenwolf. With that, out came a trim and fit-looking John Kay, the lead singer of Steppenwolf, who in his younger days looked like the type of guy who took baths in motor oil. A depsychedelicized version of "Magic Carpet Ride" followed. "Margaritaville" was next (Does Jimmy really have a tattoo?) and that ended the set. "Volcano" was the first encore, followed by a cooking, reggae-fied version of "Jambalaya," with guest Todd Snider. The show then came to an end with a pensive rendition of "Changing Channels."

16

The Letdown, or a Bristly and Truncated Encounter With the Head Parrot

After the show, Sue, Kathy, and I sat there while the auditorium emptied. It went unspoken, but I knew that we were all privately hoping to get some word from Buffett's crew about the framed photos. When the auditorium was nearly empty, we knew that it was time to concede defeat. It wasn't the end of the world—Buffett probably would get it—but it was anticlimactic to just walk away without a word. With security politely prodding us toward the exit, it was time to leave. Now, sometimes in life, things happen that just can't be explained. If you were to read about one of these things in a work of fiction, you would probably say that it sounded too ridiculous to be true and dismiss the story's credibility. Well, one of those things was about to happen. While we walked toward the exit, Kathy noticed something shiny stuck to the ground and bent over to peel it off of the floor. It was a backstage pass. At first, none of us believed it, assuming that it was a lost souvenir from a previous tour. As we talked about whether it was real or not, I thought that we should find out. Kathy was reticent and ready to leave, but I convinced her to follow me to the elevator that leads backstage. I walked up as if I owned the building, but the guard stopped me. Then, she saw Kathy's pass and waved us in. The elevator took us to the stage area. At each checkpoint, Kathy showed her pass and pointed at me, saying she was escorting "the writer from New York." We walked directly into the backstage area. A few other Parrot Heads were milling about, wondering what to do with themselves. Convinced that he would want to meet the person who supplied the gorgeously framed photos, I set out to locate Jimmy Buffett and introduce him to Kathy.

I pushed aside a curtain and stumbled on the load-out, where the various trucks were being packed, then turned around and headed back toward the hall where people were standing, looking lost and confused. Todd Snider, an artist on Buffett's Margaritaville Records, appeared, so I took a photo of him and Kathy. Kathy met a Parrot Head whom she knew from previous events. He was wheelchair bound and she explained that he played an integral role in raising money for the numerous charitable causes that the Parrot Heads support. Kathy was too excited for words, so while she stood aside, I again wandered off hoping to find Jimmy Buffett. If I did find him, I wondered what I would say. I knew that I came to Nashville with the intent of meeting the Parrot Heads, and just maybe, if the chance arose, to come clean with him about this book, but now if I saw him, I mostly wanted to ask if he wouldn't mind simply saying hello to Kathy.

The backstage bathroom was empty and so was the locker area. An abandoned table of catered foods stood to the side of one room, so I figured that we must have arrived too late. I returned to relay the bad news to Kathy and walked between her and the people standing about her. I leaned against the wall, looked up, and realized that she was staring at Jimmy Buffett! There he was, standing right in front of her. I asked her if she spoke to him, and she said that she tried, but got all frozen up. She did manage to blurt out a question, but no, he didn't see the photographs. I waited for a moment or two to see if anybody else was going to approach him, but nobody did. He was with someone whom I assumed to be Mike Ramos, and they turned to walk toward the load-out. I looked at Kathy and said, "Should I?" and she shrugged as if to say "why not."

As he neared the curtain, I yelled after him, shouting "Excuse me, Jimmy?" He stopped and turned to greet me. With no good plan of what to say, I simply began to state the truth. Pompously, but not deliberately so, I assumed he had received my letter and book, so introduced myself and asked if he had heard of me.

"No, who are you?"

Well, that tack didn't work so well. Like a kamikaze pilot completing his mission despite the outcome, I told him that I was in contact with his management and that I had been contracted to write a book about him, and that I wanted to let him know that I didn't intend—

"Goddammit, Nooooooo! I'm going to write the next book!"

"Yeah, but . . ."

With that, he turned around, raised his hand, flipped the curtain aside, and walked off.

Sigh. At first, I was dumbfounded. Keep in mind this was before I knew Buffett was working on his travelogue-autobiography, *A Pirate Looks at Fifty*. His dismissive reaction was predictable and partially expected, but it still stung me momentarily. My brain raced to find a suitable response, but he was gone. Feeling numb and stupid, I rejoined Kathy and tried to mentally justify what had just happened. "Okay, then, fair enough," I found myself thinking, *If you want the next one, Jimmy, it's all yours, because I don't think I could go through all of this again, anyway. In the meantime, though, I'm finishing* this *one. After all that I've been through, neither hell nor high water could stop me. Besides, I'm still proud and stubborn enough to believe that you'll appreciate it once you see it.*

In retrospect, I can understand why Buffett reacted as he did. I was hoping that I'd have the chance to explain myself, to convey what I had set out to do, but he had no reason to grant me an audience. Considering my meek and accidentally self-aggrandizing method of approach, it could have been worse, a lot worse, but at least I did what I set out to do so many months ago when I first said yes to this project. I wanted Jimmy Buffett to know that I wouldn't work behind his back, and now I can say that I told him to his face. Or at least, I *tried* to tell him to his face. Maybe one day he'll read this and realize that I meant him no harm. I'd like that. Maybe he'll realize that I tried to work without prejudice and that I did everything I could to understand both his music and his fans. Most of all, though, I hope that he appreciates Kathy's framed photos.